DATE DUE

PRINTED IN U.S.A.

Puerto Ricans in the Empire

Tobacco Growers and U.S. Colonialism

TERESITA A. LEVY

RUTGERS UNIVERSITY PRESS

NEW BRUNSWICK, NEW JERSEY, AND LONDON

Library of Congress Cataloging-in-Publication Data

Levy, Teresita A.
   Puerto Ricans in the empire : tobacco growers and U.S. colonialism / Teresita A. Levy.
      pages   cm
   Includes bibliographical references and index.
   ISBN 978–0–8135–7133–1 (hardcover : alk. paper) — ISBN 978–0–8135–7132–4 (pbk. : alk. paper) — ISBN 978–0–8135–7134–8 (e-book)
   1. Tobacco industry—Puerto Rico—History.   2. Tobacco—Political aspects—Puerto Rico—History.   3. Puerto Rico—Foreign economic relations—United States.   4. United States—Foreign economic relations—Puerto Rico.   5. Puerto Rico—Politics and government—1898–1952.   6. Puerto Rico—History—1898–1952. I. Title.
   HD9144.P82L49   2015
   338.1′737109729509041—dc23   2014014278

A British Cataloging-in-Publication record for this book is available from the British Library.

Visit our website: http://rutgerspress.rutgers.edu

Manufactured in the United States of America

For my late father, Luis Levy Fiol,
who taught me about our past

For my sons, Ari Miguel and Ilán Andrés,
who imagine our future

Contents

Figures

Tables

Acknowledgments

It is a privilege to be part of a community of scholars, artists, friends, and family in New York and Puerto Rico, and a simple *gracias* is not enough to convey the profound sense of gratitude that overwhelms me as I sit to write this page. Nevertheless, gracias I must give to the people who provided support, wisdom, and laughter while I was working on this project.

The archival research that informs this book would not have been possible without the assistance of the staff at the Centro de Investigaciones Históricas at the University of Puerto Rico, the Archivo Histórico de Caguas, the Archivo Notarial de Caguas, and the Archivo General de Puerto Rico. I will never forget their hospitality and their patience. I was fortunate to spend many weeks at the library of the Estación Experimental Agrícola de Puerto Rico, immersed in agricultural research and enjoying in equal parts the generosity of the staff and the glorious Jardín Botánico in the complex. I also thank the Asociación de Agricultores Puertorriqueños, who allowed the use of their organization's materials for this work.

My students at Lehman College have been a source of inspiration and intellectual renewal for the last seven years, and I thank them for joining me in the classroom. I am grateful for the many hallway chats, *cafecitos*, and debates about teaching and learning that I have enjoyed with my colleagues in the department of Latin American, Latino, and Puerto Rican Studies. I have shared much hard work, and a little desk space, with my dear friends at the Center for Latin American, Caribbean, and Latino Studies at The Graduate Center of the City University of New York. I thank them for the stimulating intellectual debates, their endless curiosity, and their friendship.

My lifelong friends and my family in Puerto Rico, who I am so lucky to see regularly, were a constant reminder that I was not just writing about the

"Puerto Rican people"; I was writing about them, their history, and their legacy, as well as mine, and such an endeavor carried an enormous intellectual responsibility. They made sure I was current on the joys and difficulties of living on the island, and I thank them for keeping me so very connected to *mi tierra.*

Every day, I am enveloped in the love, confidence, and unconditional support of my husband, Benjamin Lapidus, and our sons, Ari Miguel and Ilán Andrés. I am grateful for their patience and their curiosity, but most of all, for joining me in the adventure that is our life.

Puerto Ricans in the Empire

Introduction

*Colonial power, like any other, was an object of struggle and depended
on the material, social, and cultural resources of those involved.*

—Frederick Cooper

In December 1925, the editors of *El Agricultor Puertorriqueño*, the magazine of
the one-year-old Asociación de Agricultores Puertorriqueños, announced:
"The time has come to proclaim that we have the undisputed right to inter-
vene, cooperate, and discuss our administrative problems, our economic
problems, our agricultural problems that greatly influence the general welfare
of the community."[1] With this declaration, the membership of the Asociación
publicly affirmed their commitment to advocate in the legislative halls of the
colonial empire on behalf of all Puerto Rican farmers. Farmers across the
island, especially tobacco growers, heeded the call to action and affiliated with
the Asociación and other agricultural groups. Subsequently, they lobbied for
legislation and funding, participated in government-sponsored agricultural
programs, solicited agricultural credit from governmental sources, and
sought scientific education in a variety of public programs, all to improve
their opportunities for successful participation in the tobacco leaf market of
the United States.

Using the tobacco sector in Puerto Rico as a focal point of research, this
book examines the complex and varied ways in which Puerto Ricans participated in and negotiated with the U.S. colonial structures established on the
island after 1898. The relationship between Puerto Rico and the United States
was undoubtedly colonial in nature, but paradoxically it also conferred a new
set of rights, privileges, and freedoms on the Puerto Rican population.[2] Puerto
Ricans were able to take advantage of these new freedoms and, as this study
illustrates through the prism of the tobacco sector, they were able to influence
legislation and actively promote their self-defined interests to improve their
lives. To be sure, there are political, economic, and social limitations on how

a colonized people may negotiate with the empire that rules them, and this was clearly the case in Puerto Rico. However, this does not mean that colonial structures necessarily limited the ability to negotiate constantly, passionately, and often successfully. Tobacco growers, through their affiliation with the Asociación de Agricultores Puertorriqueños, repeatedly demanded that U.S. officials in Washington and on the island protect the tobacco sector and the well-being of the people involved in its production. In response, U.S. administrators included Puerto Ricans in decision-making processes, altered and extended legislation to the island, and allocated funding to support scientific experimentation that would improve the quality of agricultural products. The interactions between tobacco growers and the colonial government demonstrate that the colonial relationship between the island and the mainland was not unilaterally defined or manifested. Instead, the colonial process was a dynamic, elastic, and ever-changing one, where local actors often affected colonial policies.

The inclusion of the island in the tariff structure of the United States guaranteed the duty-free entrance of many island products into the U.S. market, and this dramatically accelerated the existing production of agricultural commodities. Tobacco became a major industry in Puerto Rico in large part because tobacco leaf was included in this tariff exemption. Puerto Rican farmers in the highland regions of the island made the cultivation of tobacco for the U.S. market their most important economic activity after 1900.

This book begins, therefore, by systematically exploring tobacco leaf cultivation for the U.S. market in order to understand the intricacies of how the sector expanded and how tobacco farmers (and their families) adjusted to the changes in their lives. Although U.S. economic policies and the dominant role of the American Tobacco Company in cigar and cigarette production had a profound impact on the tobacco sector, the cultivation of the leaf remained almost entirely controlled by Puerto Rican farmers. Tobacco cultivation required a large number of agricultural workers, and together with industrial workers in tobacco shops, they made the tobacco sector one of the largest employers in rural Puerto Rico.

Tobacco was perfectly suited for cultivation in the mountainous terrain of the highlands of Puerto Rico, where farms were generally smaller than those found in coastal areas. Tobacco could be grown successfully on small parcels of land and, because of relatively low production costs, it was economically viable for farmers with limited capital resources. Puerto Rican tobacco was also well suited for the taste of U.S. consumers, who were accustomed to the mellow flavor and smooth aroma of Cuban tobacco. In fact, exceptional tobacco leaf was being cultivated in the eastern highlands of Puerto Rico by

1888, a decade before the American occupation of the island.[3] After 1898, U.S. manufacturers were able to purchase the tobacco leaf that they and their customers preferred from Puerto Rico at a lower cost than that of Cuban tobacco. The ecological suitability of tobacco cultivation to the geography of the highlands, the economic interests of U.S. tobacco manufacturers, and the advantage that Puerto Rican tobacco had in the U.S. market because of the inclusion of the island inside the tariff "wall" of the United States, led to the fairly rapid expansion of the tobacco sector of the island after 1900.

It is perhaps surprising, then, that historians of early twentieth-century Puerto Rico have largely ignored the cultivation of tobacco. Instead, studies have focused on the development of the sugar industry because of its dominant role in the island's economy, and the discussion of tobacco has ended after its ritual mention as the island's "second most important product." The impact of the new colonial order on the sugar sector has served, accordingly, as the analytical framework for most discussions of the island's agricultural development from 1898 to 1940.[4]

This "sugar narrative" is a story of victimization and imperial abuse, in which economic, social, and political decisions made by colonial administrators were designed to protect the interests of U.S. sugar companies. In this narrative, the unscrupulous accumulation of land by large sugar companies, supported by the colonial state, destroyed the independent land-owning class and displaced Puerto Rican *jíbaros* (peasants), transforming them into landless wage laborers. "Sugar was king, a sick king," and the ills of the coastal sugar economy as described by many scholars became the central characteristics not only of Puerto Rican agriculture, but of Puerto Rico as a whole.[5] The colonial political status of the island, manifested economically in the plantation system developed by U.S. capitalists in the sugar sector, was converted into the cause of every economic, social, and political problem in Puerto Rico.

These generalizations, however, do not hold up to examination in most sectors of the island's economy, and this is emphatically true in the tobacco sector.[6] Although tobacco corporations did purchase some large farms, the percentage of the tobacco acreage under American control was minor. The bulk of American investment in tobacco production was instead in the industrial and marketing phases of tobacco production: establishing stemming plants and factories for handmade and later machine-produced cigars and cigarettes, controlling packing and shipping facilities, and ultimately determining marketing strategies for the vast U.S. mainland consumer markets. It was more cost-effective to purchase tobacco leaf from Puerto Rican farmers than to become vertically integrated; it was more profitable to be the marketer of the finished product than a producer of the raw material.

As a result, small-scale, politically involved, independent landowners cultivated most of the tobacco leaf in Puerto Rico. Additionally, from a demographic point of view, the tobacco districts were the fastest-growing regions
of the island in the early twentieth century because of opportunities to secure
land and participate as independent producers in local economies.

This book adds the cultivation of tobacco leaf to the agricultural narrative of
the island by analyzing the expansion of the tobacco sector and the resulting
social and economic changes in the tobacco regions, as other scholars have
done for Cuba and the Dominican Republic.[7] Tobacco-focused research has
existed for at least a century in Puerto Rican scholarship, although this has been
limited mostly to investigations in agricultural technology and the analysis of
economic data. Agricultural scientists, for example, have examined particular
aspects of the cultivation process, and these have been published in agricultural
journals or as research bulletins of the Agricultural Experiment Station.[8] Other
scholars have studied the income and expenses of tobacco farms to determine
what, if any, economic benefit was derived from tobacco leaf cultivation.[9] These
studies provide important material for this book, but here the findings are discussed within the larger context of negotiation of scientific technology and
advantageous legislation.

Juan José Baldrich's volume titled *Sembraron la no siembra* is perhaps the
best-known study of the island's tobacco economy and is worth summarizing.[10]
Baldrich presents a socioeconomic analysis of a farmer-led tobacco-planting
stoppage during the 1931–1932 growing season, which had the objective of
increasing market prices for tobacco leaf. Baldrich argues that, although the
strike succeeded in organizing the growers against the local merchants who
controlled farm prices, it failed in its efforts to increase those prices.[11] It was
this failure that marked the beginning of the transition for the tobacco grower
from landowner to landless agricultural laborer. Baldrich's work provides a
foundation for a later chapter in this book that discusses Puerto Rican political participation. The *no siembra* was the culmination of long-standing efforts
of the Asociación de Agricultores Puertorriqueños to lobby on behalf of
tobacco farmers, and members were key participants in the campaign.

Most other studies that deal with Puerto Rican tobacco focus on the industrial side of the process and on the workers who transformed the tobacco leaf
into aromatic cigars and cigarettes.[12] The important struggles of the tobacco
factory workers have been well documented and comprehensively analyzed,
and this book does not offer a new interpretation of their struggles. Tobacco
workers were a well-organized, politically active labor sector. Although the
leaders of the Asociación de Agricultores were familiar with tobacco workers'
efforts and politics, especially their involvement with the Socialist Party and

the Federación Libre de Trabajadores, this was not always an amicable relationship. The particularities of the relationship between tobacco growers and tobacco workers deserve more research, but they are beyond the scope of this study, which intentionally focuses on the cultivation process. It is worth mentioning, however, that the militancy of tobacco shop workers may have contributed to the responsiveness of legislators and administrators to tobacco growers' demands.

The meteoric expansion of the tobacco sector was accompanied by the unprecedented involvement of Puerto Rican tobacco growers in the structures of the U.S. colonial state both at the insular and the federal levels to promote and protect their self-defined economic interests. This history of activism and participation in the empire has not been among the dominant themes in the scholarly literature of early twentieth-century Puerto Rico. Instead, many scholars have interpreted the annexation of the island through the Foraker Act of 1900 as the creation of a colonial state in which American economic, political, and social structures were omnipresent and subjugated the island to the interests of the new imperial power.[13] This is a long-standing historical interpretation that began when American and Puerto Rican researchers, provoked by the effects of the Great Depression on the island, began a systematic evaluation of whether social or economic progress had been achieved after thirty-plus years of U.S. colonial rule.

Among the many studies that argued that the U.S. occupation of the island caused destructive effects was *Porto Rico and Its Problems* by Victor S. Clark, a former commissioner of education in Puerto Rico. The 1930 study, published by the Brookings Institution in Washington, DC, was a comprehensive study of the economic and social conditions on the island from agricultural development to public health.[14] Clark argued for the existence of indicators that life for the rural inhabitant was indeed better in 1930 than during Spanish colonial times: there were more students in schools, better housing, improved transportation, and sewage and potable water systems. But ultimately, Clark emphasized the negative effects of U.S. control of the island, such as the alleged increase in commercial agriculture at the expense of subsistence production, poor living conditions among agricultural workers, and corporate investments in land, which, he argued, had displaced local farmers.

Just one year later, Justine and Bailey Diffie's *Porto Rico: A Broken Pledge* offered the most outspoken indictment of American policies on the island.[15] The Diffies argued that there had been no sign of social progress for most Puerto Ricans in the first three decades of the twentieth century. The sugar areas of the island, with their high concentration of land ownership and masses of unskilled laborers, were symbolic of the failures of the colonial economic system. The United States had broken their pledge to lift Puerto Ricans out of a life of poverty and cultural darkness and instead had put in place economic policies that perpetuated the dreadful living conditions of the jíbaro, sentencing the island to economic serfdom. Interestingly, several months before the publication of the Brookings Report, José Enamorado-Cuesta, a Puerto Rican scholar, published *Porto Rico, Past and Present*.[16] Although Enamorado-Cuesta made many of the same observations as Victor Clark and Justine and Bailey Diffie, it was these later studies that became the classic volumes for the study of early twentieth-century Puerto Rican history.

The themes of economic, social, and political subjugation continued into the 1960s, and Puerto Rican historiography followed two distinct but related paradigms, each focusing on the benefits or shortfalls of control by the United States. One was the transformation of Puerto Rico from a "stagnant backward economy" in the nineteenth century to one defined by the "dynamic and efficient capitalism" of the United States.[17] The other was the transformation of Puerto Rico from a romanticized "traditional" nineteenth-century economy, where paternalistic socioeconomic relationships protected even the poorest of the *jíbaros*, to a colonial economy defined by the separation of land and labor. In the first paradigm, it was asserted that the United States brought order and logic to a chaotic and primitive economy.[18] The second contended that the United States destroyed, intentionally or not, a particular way of life and replaced it with one that was alien and damaging to Puerto Ricans.[19] In both of these interpretations the colonial relationship between the island and the mainland was defined as monolithic and unilateral, and the ability of Puerto Ricans to negotiate on their own behalf was dismissed as ineffectual, or never considered. This emphasis on the absolute power of the United States has had the unintended effect of overlooking the activities of common Puerto Ricans in their efforts to effect or influence the dynamics of their daily lives. Puerto Ricans were transformed into passive victims of a capricious empire and were characterized as a people without recourse.

To discuss but one example, Manuel Maldonado-Denis, a well-published and often cited Puerto Rican scholar who wrote during the 1960s and 1970s, argued that the colonial status of the island was "more obvious" under the American flag than it ever had been during Spanish colonial times, and that only Puerto Rico remained in "colonial bondage" in the Americas.[20] Like scholars before him, Maldonado-Denis decried the disappearance of the independent farmer who lost his land to "a monoculture and a plantation economy" and was "thrown into the labor market in the large absentee sugar factories."[21]

Maldonado-Denis also borrowed from Antonio S. Pedreira's *Insularismo*, a book published in 1934 that took the economic arguments of the time and transformed them into a psychological indictment of sorts of the people of Puerto Rico.[22] Maldonado-Denis expanded Pedreira's argument and described the supposed inaction of Puerto Ricans in the face of colonial abuse as the result of the "colonial mentality," defined as "the attitude of submission and acquiescence characteristic of the Puerto Ricans."[23] Maldonado-Denis was critical of the insular administration and portrayed them as accomplices of the "American power elite" and the "repressive tolerance" practiced by colonial authorities, in which the Puerto Rican was allowed to voice his discontent with the colonial system "in so far as he does not endanger it."[24] Puerto Ricans, according to Maldonado-Denis, bought into the colonial mentality and accepted everything that "magnifies the power, wisdom, and achievements of the colonizer while minimizing the power, wisdom, and achievements of the colonized."[25] This and other scholarly works of the time made the "psychologically damaged" Puerto Rican an integral part of the narrative regarding the effects of American colonialism.[26]

During the 1970s and 1980s, the historical profession shifted its focus toward studies of the everyday life of people across the social class structure. Historians of Puerto Rico became interested in the social and economic struggles of "Puerto Ricans without history" and began writing *la nueva historia* (the new history). Using methodologies adapted from the social sciences, students of *la nueva historia* searched for materials in long-neglected archival collections or nontraditional sources in an attempt to document the story of laborers, peasants, women, or other sectors of the population previously ignored by historians.[27] However, the debate over the effects of the American occupation continued along the conceptual frameworks proposed by earlier studies. Topics such as land concentration, the disappearance of the independent farmer, and the damages to the psyche of the Puerto Rican were conceived of as "facts" despite the utilization of new sources and the emergence of new themes of study.

One of the best-known and still widely read works of the period was *We, the Puerto Rican People: A Story of Oppression and Resistance* by Juan Ángel Silén. Silén agreed with Maldonado-Denis's thesis that the colonial structure had fostered inappropriate responses from the Puerto Rican political and economic elite and simply stated that "the weakness of our bourgeoisie toward imperialism is a fact."[28] However, unlike Maldonado-Denis, Silén framed its inaction as "a phenomenon of a political, not psychological nature" that "arose from the class interests linking it with the North American power structure."[29] Although there is an attempt to explain the responses of Puerto Ricans to American colonialism, the portrayal of Puerto Ricans as incapable of effecting change resonates throughout this work. This kind of interpretation dismisses as meaningless, intentionally or not, the activities of every Puerto Rican who joined a workers' union, agricultural organization, or political party. In effect, the life experiences of Puerto Ricans who maneuvered within the colonial system to maintain an active role in the political, economic, and social processes that began in 1898 are made invisible.

An important study published during this time was James Dietz's *Economic History of Puerto Rico: Institutional Change and Capitalist Development.* His discussion of the agricultural sector was more inclusive than the discussions of previous scholars and, although he focused on the development of the sugar sector, he broadened his study to include a consideration of the tobacco and coffee economies.[30] Dietz argued that Puerto Rican activism had brought about changes in the political and economic colonial structure on the island. As an example, Dietz argued that the passage of the Jones Act of 1917 was the result of "demands for greater self-rule and independence for Puerto Rico [that] came from all sectors and classes." Puerto Ricans became involved in the new colonial structure in a "variety of forces and parties representing specific interests and classes [that] developed to articulate demands for a change in the colonial relationship."[31] Dietz interpreted the economic situation on the island found in the various periods of the twentieth century as both the responsibility of federal colonial administrators and insular politicians who did in fact have an impact on U.S. policies and decision making. This was a radical, if not greatly acknowledged, departure from prior interpretations of island political life.

There was great anticipation over the publication in 1984 of Raymond Carr's *Puerto Rico: A Colonial Experiment.* Proponents of the island's continued affiliation with the United States as well as those who advocated for an end to the colonial relationship between the United States and Puerto Rico hoped that Carr, because he was British rather than American, would deliver an objective appraisal of American colonialism. Carr satisfied and angered both groups. He argued that "American capitalism had converted Puerto Rico into a fief of the great absentee American sugar corporations" and that as a result, the island had become "the poorhouse of the Caribbean." Puerto Rico's sad economic situation was, therefore, "the creation of an outside agent, the foreign devil."[32] However, Carr also took pains to delineate achievements in education, health care, and infrastructure that he credited to U.S. involvement on the island. In some ways, Carr accepted earlier critiques of the impact of U.S. involvement, especially his adherence to the absentee sugar corporation paradigm as representing Puerto Rican rural society. In others, he was careful not to launch a wholesale indictment of the twentieth-century Puerto Rican experience under U.S. rule.

Carr was also interested in Puerto Rican responses to the American administrators and vacillated between accepting the colonial mentality thesis and demonstrating that Puerto Ricans were involved in colonial structures. Carr argued that "the United States was confronted by a self-confident, political elite that had already grasped the local levers of power."[33] The fundamental problem with the colonial relationship between the island and the mainland was that because there existed "a colonial elite convinced of its capacity to rule," such a relationship became "unsustainable."[34] Unfortunately, Carr also concluded that Puerto Ricans were "natural authoritarians, satisfied with a government that provides jobs and lulls the population into supine, soulless acquiescence," and that such conformity allowed "their civil rights to be grossly and systematically violated by successive governments."[35] Carr's study did not, as many expected, settle once and for all the argument about the social and economic condition of the island vis-à-vis its colonial relationship with the United States. Instead, he agreed that the conditions of the island were the responsibility of both harmful colonial policies and the inability of the Puerto Rican people to decide on any better course of action.

Studies of early twentieth-century Puerto Rico written since the 1990s have remained focused on the dramatic changes on the island due to the American occupation. There are several themes that have continued to resonate through the historiography of the period. First, the development of the sugar industry was the central focus of the American colonial government at the expense of every other economic sector on the island.[36] A related theme is that the insular government acted in effect as the agents of U.S. corporations, promoting policies that protected U.S. economic investments to the detriment of the Puerto Rican people.[37] Finally, the "damage" done by colonial policies to the self-esteem of the Puerto Ricans has continued to be a topic of interest for many scholars.[38]

Some recent studies have been successful in adding complexity to the debate over the effects of American colonialism by placing Puerto Rican economic development within the context of globalization and the forces of international markets. They have also stepped away from using 1898 as a demarcation point and have looked several decades back into the nineteenth century and several decades forward in the twentieth to determine the extent to which American colonial policies either accelerated already occurring trends or altered the island into an unrecognizable capitalist territory.[39] There is also an interest among scholars in the particular processes of belonging to an empire by analyzing U.S. constitutional law and how it applied (or did not) to Puerto Rico; the role of the island in American military strategy throughout the twentieth century; and the cultural particularities of a "nation" within an empire.[40] Additionally, scholars have continued to examine the participation of women, workers, and others in contesting the colonial state and altering colonial policy.[41]

César J. Ayala and Rafael Bernabe's book, *Puerto Rico in the American Century*, provides an intellectual foundation for this book.[42] Ayala and Bernabe agree that sugar was a crucially important product in the economic development of Puerto Rico, but discuss the impact of other agricultural products as well, including coffee and tobacco. They argue that Puerto Ricans were undoubtedly active in the empire, and meticulously document the political, intellectual, and cultural milieu on the island to demonstrate the complex ways that Puerto Ricans responded to the U.S. model of "progressive colonialism."

The theme of resistance to the colonial apparatus was also explored in Rosa Carrasquillo's recent study about the landless in the town of Caguas, a tobacco-growing municipality in the eastern highlands of Puerto Rico.[43] Carrasquillo argued that it was the Cagüeños' determination to protest land privatization legislation in the late nineteenth and early twentieth centuries that guaranteed the rural poor of the town a place in the development of local civil society. Landless Cagüeños argued that their use of land as a homestead or for commercial cultivation gave them a rightful civil claim to the parcel, and they refused to comply with colonial directives that would have forced them to abandon their land.[44] This book expands on this theme and demonstrates many other ways that Puerto Ricans in the tobacco regions of the island, Caguas included, resisted what they deemed to be unfair laws and demanded ones that they believed were beneficial.

The most recent book that comments on the agricultural development of Puerto Rico is Dionicio Nodín Valdés's *Organized Agriculture and the Labor Movement before the UFW: Puerto Rico, Hawaii, California*, a study of the efforts of agricultural laborers to organize in those three locations.[45] Nodín Valdés argues that agricultural workers in the American empire, which extended throughout the Pacific and included Puerto Rico, were not disengaged from the economic and social processes that affected them. Instead, they actively participated in a self-directed organizational campaign to secure their position as workers in the new colonial economy.

In recent years, the effects of U.S. colonialism in Puerto Rico have been of interest to scholars that specialize in American Empire Studies, a field of study that has moved from focusing on purely theoretical debates over American exceptionalism.[46] In particular, Julian Go's recent work *Patterns of Empire* challenged scholars across the disciplines to analyze the concrete economic, social, and political processes that gave rise to and maintained a continuously contested American empire.[47] In fact, the November 2012 meeting of the American Studies Association was titled "Dimensions of Empire and Resistance: Past, Present, and Future," placing empire studies at the fore-front of the agenda for scholars of the Americas. It is crucial, therefore, to understand what "empire" meant in the context of Puerto Rico's history and how Puerto Ricans responded to the new colonial structures put in place by the Foraker Act of 1900.

The colonial project in Puerto Rico was of a tutelary nature. That is, those characteristic processes of American-style democracy, such as participating in local elections, drafting legislation, and administrating the everyday affairs of the island would operate in Puerto Rico under the guidance of U.S. officials. Over time, and with practice, Puerto Ricans would be "granted more duties and functions . . . and in general American control would be slowly loosened."[48] This was the plan of colonial officials to deal with what they considered to be a naïve and politically inexperienced people, but in reality, Puerto Ricans were neither. Instead, when U.S. colonial officials arrived in Puerto Rico, they found an established, well-educated, and politically experienced elite, with a "Westernized intellectual orientation" that allowed them to demand participation using the "modern liberal discourses of self-rule, liberty, and individual rights."[49] The plans, goals, and strategies of colonial officials had to shift to respond to this reality, as Puerto Ricans were willing to go toe-to-toe with U.S. officials and argue convincingly for legislation that would benefit the island. In addition to the efforts of political and economic elites, and equally important in terms of the evolution of colonial structures, were the "acquiescence, struggle, and resistance of the various sectors of the people in the colonial territory."[50] A colonial empire would not be able to maintain power if it did not negotiate with these local, often well-articulated interests. This was the case in Puerto Rico, where the right to affiliate (ironically guaranteed under U.S. law) meant that groups throughout the island, farmers in particular, could organize to create political capital to effect change.

As colonial empires are established, they must also "formulate various *strategies* and deploy multiple *tactics, techniques,* or *modalities*—sometimes unstated or unofficial—to realize their policies and extend or sustain them-selves."[51] In the same fashion, we have to understand the tactics, techniques, or modalities used by Puerto Ricans—whether official or not, stated or assumed—that were used to respond to U.S.-imposed colonial structures. Examining the cultivation of tobacco leaf for the American market affords us the opportunity to do just this: to examine how a segment of the population pressured, lobbied, and campaigned to win the extension of colonial policies that improved their economic well-being. Puerto Ricans demanded inclusion in the empire, in terms that were defined not only by the colonial power but also by the colonized.

Go argues that "at the heart of the meaning of empire was political power," which can be manifested formally or informally, directly or indirectly.[52] In Puerto Rico, we find manifestations of imperial power that include all of these. It is for this reason that Puerto Rico is an extraordinary case study for understanding the political, economic, and social structures of the American empire in the early twentieth century. For example, the designation of Puerto Rico as an unincorporated territory of the United States by the Foraker Act of 1900 was a clear statement of formal and direct colonial power. The Foraker Act declared that the United States had "exclusive authority to legislate over Puerto Rican affairs, subject only to the restrictions imposed by fundamental individual rights as interpreted by the U.S. Supreme Court."[53] With this act, the imperial state maintained sovereign control of a subject place and its people.

However, "the U.S. did not have to have an empire based on territory: it could extend informal control instead."[54] The locally controlled civil government structures that were established on the island after 1900, the large-scale investment in all areas of Puerto Rico's economy, and the mandated transfer of federal tariff collections to the local treasury, were all informal or indirect manifestations of imperial power. The insular government may have appeared to be "nominally independent" in terms of local affairs, but it was obligated to answer to an ultimate authority for nearly everything.[55] Efrén Rivera Ramos, a respected lawyer and legal scholar of Puerto Rico, argues that it has been precisely these "subsidies, degree of self-government, and ability to reside in the States [that] have obscured the nonrepresentative quality of U.S. sovereignty."[56] In short, the United States used a "multiplicity of imperial power" to maintain viable colonial structures in Puerto Rico, and this was sometimes accomplished at the invitation of Puerto Ricans themselves.[57]

This was the case with the granting of U.S. citizenship to the people of Puerto Rico through the passage of the Organic Act of 1917.[58] Because Puerto Ricans had demanded citizenship from the earliest years of the American occupation, the granting of citizenship was "a watershed in American colonial history and quite probably the turning point in Puerto Rico's political development."[59] As with other manifestations of empire on the island, the granting of U.S. citizenship was fraught with complications. On the one hand, citizenship guaranteed access to individual rights and privileges enjoyed by citizens in the United States, protections that Puerto Ricans had not enjoyed during the Spanish colonial era. U.S. citizenship opened an entirely new avenue for political participation. It is not surprising that membership in agricultural societies increased after 1917, and lobbying efforts took on special significance when Puerto Ricans could affiliate and lobby as citizens of the empire. On the other hand, U.S. citizenship in Puerto Rico was limited because it did not include voting representation in the U.S. Congress. It also made Puerto Rican men eligible to serve in the U.S. armed forces while denying Puerto Ricans living on the island the power to vote in presidential elections. Nevertheless, U.S. citizenship, even in the limited way it was defined in Puerto Rico, carried a "virtually universal expectation of a permanent relationship" between the island and the mainland, once again complicating the characteristics of U.S. colonialism in Puerto Rico.[60]

Colonial empires, like other institutions, "are ultimately shaped by human beings, and power relationships reflect the dynamics of social, intellectual, and political movements organized by people themselves."[61] Puerto Rican participation in the colonial state and U.S. responses to Puerto Rican pressures demonstrate that imperial power was constantly negotiated, and that it varied depending on time, political entities involved, popular responses, or economic needs. The study of tobacco cultivation on the island allows an examination of all of these: how economic expansion triggered by new colonial policies resulted in increased political activity and demands for participation.

The first part of this book details the expansion of the tobacco sector in Puerto Rico after 1898 and the resulting socioeconomic transformations in the tobacco-growing regions. Chapter 1, titled "The Development of the Tobacco Economy in Puerto Rico," presents an analysis of the expansion and contraction cycles of the tobacco sector and discusses the value of the tobacco sector, both in terms of dollars and in terms of people dependent on its success. This chapter relies on data from sources such as the U.S. Census Bureau, Department of Agriculture and Governor of Puerto Rico annual reports, and tobacco industry analyses from the island and the mainland. The number of *cuerdas* under cultivation and the total production of tobacco leaf in pounds increased steadily from 1898 to 1930.[62] After 1930, the tobacco market contracted due to external pressures resulting from the Great Depression, and by 1940 it began a permanent downward spiral. Smoking preferences in the American tobacco market, international events, and natural disasters had both immediate and lasting effects on the cultivation of tobacco. Tobacco farmers responded to these changes and adjusted their production, showing great adaptability and current knowledge of the latest tobacco news from around the world. This chapter also identifies two main areas of tobacco cultivation on the island, the eastern highlands and the western highlands, and discusses the particularities of each region. More than a collection of economic data, this chapter demonstrates the capability of Puerto Rican tobacco farmers to deal with changes in a global market within the context of U.S.-imposed colonial structures.

Chapter 2, "Life in the Tobacco Regions of Puerto Rico," analyzes the demographic transformations and changes in land tenure patterns that accompanied the expansion of tobacco leaf cultivation. This chapter also relies heavily on data available in government reports, but differs from the previous one in that it concentrates on the people who lived in the tobacco regions to demonstrate that tobacco cultivation affected a significant segment of the Puerto Rican population. The number of farms and the population in the tobacco regions of Puerto Rico increased from 1898 to 1940, as people moved into the eastern and western highlands to take advantage of economic opportunities in the tobacco sector, even though the importance of tobacco as an export product declined during the last decade under study. The demographic analysis of the tobacco regions includes analysis of characteristics of the working-age population and family structure. The chapter also includes an analysis of the number of farms and the characteristics of those farms, including income earned, the costs of running the farms, and the number of agricultural laborers in the region. The presentation of such detailed analysis allows for comparisons between the families residing in tobacco regions and those in sugar regions. This chapter argues that, although tobacco families earned less cash than families in the sugar regions, they were more likely to own the land they were farming, thus ensuring that they derived more benefits from their chosen economic activity.

The second part of this book discusses how Puerto Ricans negotiated three areas in which imperial power can appear nonnegotiable: access to the political structure, changes in legislation that directly affected the colonial populace, and the transfer of technology. In the political arena, tobacco farmers joined local agricultural leagues as early as 1919, and the insular farmers' association, the Asociación de Agricultores Puertorriqueños (AAP), from its foundation in 1924. The AAP served as the advocate, in both Washington and San Juan, for all farmers on the island. With the support of tobacco farmers, the AAP challenged federal and insular policies that they deemed unfair and successfully lobbied for the extension of beneficial federal agricultural legislation to the island. Once that legislation was extended to the island, tobacco growers took all necessary steps to actively participate in available programs. To improve profitability, tobacco farmers organized cooperatives to take advantage of newly created credit structures, to purchase necessary cultivation supplies in bulk, and to sell their products for more favorable prices. Finally, tobacco growers, once again taking advantage of federal legislation they themselves demanded, supported scientific research to determine the most technologically sound cultivation methods, which they subsequently applied to their own farms. The evidence in the three chapters in this part of the book demonstrates that Puerto Ricans' relationship to the American empire was not "murky . . . uncomfortable . . . vulnerable"; instead, it was one of activism and participation.[63]

Chapter 3 is titled "Politics: Tobacco Growers and Agricultural Organizations," and it argues that tobacco growers became an effective political force
in the colonial structure through their affiliation with local agricultural societies and with the insular Asociación de Agricultores Puertorriqueños. The
right of free association, demanded by Puerto Ricans and guaranteed by the
new U.S. colonial state, meant that Puerto Rican farmers could form associations and create marketing and credit cooperatives to exert control over their
economic sector. They also participated in protests, strikes, political campaigns, and lobbying efforts in Washington and San Juan to demand fair
prices, economic incentives, and social programs. In return, insular and federal officials responded to such pressure by altering legislation, providing
economic relief, and including Puerto Ricans in their decision-making.
Tobacco growers' involvement in such organizations resulted in improvements in their social, economic, and political positions.

Chapter 4, titled "Law: The Extension of Federal Agricultural Credit
Legislation to Puerto Rico," argues that Puerto Rican farmers skillfully negotiated the legislative process and colonial bureaucracy both on the island and
the mainland to secure the extension of credit legislation to Puerto Rico, an
extension that was not guaranteed because of the island's territorial status.
The early part of the twentieth century was a time of dramatic changes in the
agricultural economy of the United States resulting in agricultural legislation
designed to protect the living standard of American farmers. Of particular
interest to Puerto Rican farmers were the government programs that created
an institutional credit infrastructure, one that offered long-term loans and
short-term production credit at lower interest rates than noninstitutional or
private lenders. Puerto Rican farmers deemed such legislation crucial to the
well-being of the agricultural sectors because they were often captive to high-
interest, predatory lending practices from noninstitutional sources. In addition, this chapter argues that tobacco farmers quickly took advantage of
newly available capital: they not only requested credit in greater numbers
than all other types of farmers on the island, but they also received the largest
share of available institutional production credit.

Scientific inquiry and experimentation had a profound impact on the
tobacco sector. Chapter 5, titled "Technology: Modern Agriculture, Home
Management, and Rural Progress," argues that the development of tobacco as
a profitable export product occurred because Puerto Rican tobacco farmers,
through their affiliation with agricultural organizations, lobbied for funding
allocations that would support scientific experimentation. U.S. and Puerto
Rican scientists affiliated with the Agricultural Experiment Station, a publicly
funded research institution, demonstrated that growing tobacco was more

profitable if farmers selected more productive varieties of tobacco; maintained better seedbeds; used appropriate fertilizers; and adopted control methods to check disease and control insect damage. Farmers attended lectures and demonstrations to learn these new technologies, and then applied them on their own farms. The direct result was a significant increase in the yield of tobacco leaf per cuerda, an increase that occurred only because of the widespread use of such sophisticated scientific knowledge. The women of tobacco country also participated in the transfer of technology by becoming home economists.

In a 2005 review of scholarly works on the effects of colonialism in Puerto Rico and on Puerto Ricans, Emilio Pantojas-García argued that scholars continue to treat the colonial relationship as the cause of most of the social, economic, and political problems of Puerto Rico.[64] The problem continues to be that Puerto Ricans are left out of the conversation. Where are the voices of the hundreds of agriculturalists who fought for the extension of agricultural legislation? Where are the writers, the editors, the farmers, and the scientists who contributed to the dissemination of knowledge, whether political, scientific, or cultural? Where are the families that dealt with the changing social and economic landscape? This book accepts the advice given by Efrén Rivera Ramos, who challenges us to remember that "explanations must not conceal the unequal balance of power between the U.S. and Puerto Rico as political communities. At the same time, they must take into account the capacity of Puerto Ricans for agency."[65] This book is a contribution to the scholarly debate of the effects of U.S. colonialism in Puerto Rico. It presents the history of Puerto Rico and Puerto Ricans in the empire as a history of activism and participation.

CHAPTER 1

The Development of the Tobacco Economy in Puerto Rico

From the time the grower delivers his crop until it is finally exported or manufactured the tobacco goes through from ten to twenty operations, one bundle or hand at a time—in some operations, one leaf at a time.

—Charles Gage, 1939

The efforts of tobacco growers to secure beneficial legislation, economic protection, and financial relief for their crop cannot be understood without first examining the particularities of the tobacco sector during the first decades of the twentieth century. Tobacco cultivation in Puerto Rico experienced cycles of expansion and contraction during this time in response to local conditions, global economic realities, and shifting consumer trends. This chapter presents a comprehensive analysis of these cycles. The tobacco sector expanded rapidly and consistently until 1929, increasing in importance as a source of commercial exports. From 1907 through 1917, tobacco was the third-most-important commercial crop produced on the island after sugar and coffee. In 1918, tobacco surpassed coffee as the second most important commercial crop after sugar. The export value of tobacco on the island peaked in 1920, when tobacco surpassed sugar and represented 38 percent of the total value of commercial crops (sugar accounted for 25 percent).[1] From 1921 to 1940, tobacco remained the second-most-important commercial crop after sugar. Tobacco cultivation was not only important commercially, but it was also crucial as a source of income for the rural population. In 1910, over 14 percent of all farms on the island reported the cultivation of tobacco leaf, and by 1940 that proportion had increased to 30 percent.[2] In addition, the sale of unprocessed tobacco leaf and the manufacturing of tobacco products became essential to the insular government as revenue providers, constituting up to 30 percent of the insular state's income per year during the 1930s.[3] In short, tobacco's importance as a commodity for the U.S. market, for the well-being of the rural population, and as an income producer for the insular state was marked and increased throughout this period.

This chapter also examines two distinct tobacco regions.[4] (See figure 1.1 and table 1.1.) The first includes the municipalities in the eastern highlands, where tobacco leaf cultivation first expanded after 1898. The darker, shade-grown tobacco leaf cultivated in this region was considered of high quality and admired for its taste; as such, it fetched higher prices per pound in the market. The second region includes those municipalities in the western high-lands, where the expansion of tobacco cultivation occurred later and relied heavily on chemical fertilizers. The brighter, coastal and semi-coastal tobacco cultivated in the western highlands was used as filler for cigarettes and cigars, and commanded much lower prices in the market than the darker tobacco of the eastern highlands.[5]

Although data analysis may seem an impersonal way of understanding human political and social processes, it provides a concrete framework through which these very processes can be examined. Puerto Rican tobacco growers were able to negotiate necessary benefits not only because the sector was important for the insular government as a revenue producer, but also because it provided employment for a significant sector of the rural popula-tion of Puerto Rico. For example, fluctuating prices paid for tobacco leaf may be indicative of how much tobacco is available to sell or how smokers' prefer-ences change over time; or it may determine how many farm laborers will be hired for a season. Therefore, by including precise economic data, a clearer, more complete picture of the tobacco sector of Puerto Rico emerges.

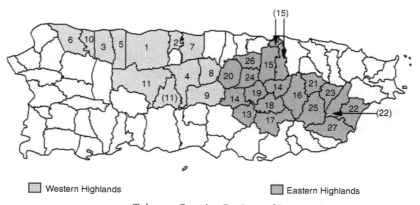

FIGURE 1.1 Tobacco-Growing Regions of Puerto Rico.

TABLE 1.1

TOBACCO-GROWING REGIONS IN PUERTO RICO, 1899–1940

Western Highlands	*Eastern Highlands*
1. Arecibo	12. Aguas Buenas
2. Barceloneta	13. Aibonito
3. Camuy	14. Barranquitas
4. Ciales	15. Bayamón (Cataño, Guaynabo, Río Piedras)[c]
5. Hatillo	16. Caguas
6. Isabela	17. Cayey
7. Manatí	18. Cidra
8. Morovis	19. Comerío
9. Orocovis[a]	20. Corozal
10. Quebradillas	21. Gurabo
11. Utuado (Jayuya)[b]	22. Humacao (Las Piedras)[d]
	23. Juncos
	24. Naranjito
	25. San Lorenzo
	26. Toa Alta
	27. Yabucoa

[a]Orocovis was called Barros in the 1899 and 1910 census.

[b]Part of Utuado was taken to form Jayuya between 1910 and 1920. All figures for Utuado cited in this book will include those for Jayuya from 1920 to 1940.

[c]Part of Bayamón was taken to form part of Guaynabo between 1910 and 1920. Part of Río Piedras was also taken to form part of Guaynabo between 1910 and 1920. Part of Bayamón was taken to form Cataño after 1920. All figures for Bayamón cited in this book will include those for Río Piedras for 1910 and those for Cataño, Guaynabo, and Río Piedras from 1920 to 1940.

[d]Part of Humacao was taken to form Las Piedras between 1910 and 1920. All figures for Humacao cited in this book will include those of Las Piedras from 1920 to 1940.

But tobacco leaf cultivation was not a post-1898 phenomenon, and so its history must begin during the time of the Taínos, Amerindians who lived in Puerto Rico and throughout the lands on the Caribbean Sea at the time of Spanish contact. Called *cogiba* or *cohiba*, Taínos would dry the leaves in the sun, grind them, and smoke the ground leaves in a Y-shaped wood pipe called *tabaco*.[6] Taínos also twisted the dried leaf, wrapped it with a smoother leaf called a *pura*, and smoked it much like cigars are smoked today. When the Spanish settled the conquered island after 1508, they quickly became users of the aromatic leaf, bringing it to Europe during their travels, and trading it for other goods, both legally and as contraband. A market soon developed for leaf tobacco, and tobacco cultivation expanded not only in Puerto Rico, but throughout the Caribbean. Theoretically, all exports were destined for Seville, where the Casa de Contratación, a Spanish government agency that monopolized the colonial trade, would be responsible for marketing the leaf. In reality, much of the tobacco grown was sold at local ports throughout the Caribbean, thereby circumventing the Spanish *quinto*, a 20 percent tax on traded goods. Because the Spanish Crown was unable to control such rampant trade, it prohibited the cultivation of tobacco for commercial purposes.

The prohibition was ineffective and did not stop the cultivation or the trading of tobacco leaf. By the early seventeenth century, the Crown shifted its policies in order to reap the benefits of the continued demand for tobacco. A *decreto real* of 1614 permitted tobacco cultivation for commercial purposes and Puerto Rican tobacco production expanded as a result. By the middle of the seventeenth century, a pound of tobacco leaf was valued at 2 *reales* in the export market, and it was estimated that the total value of exports was about 8,000 *reales* annually.[7] In 1784, the Crown opened a Real Factoría Mercantil in Puerto Rico charged with the exclusive right to export tobacco leaf and to secure the product from island farmers. This meant the establishment of a buyer's monopoly for tobacco, which controlled the prices paid to agriculturalists for their product.

Island tobacco farmers, dissatisfied with Spanish monopoly policies, responded with an increase in illegal commerce with foreign nations, principally the English and French. The Crown finally relented in 1815 and reduced export taxes, not only for tobacco, but also for other products making up the export sector such as sugar, ginger, hides, and indigo. By 1828, almost 2.5 million pounds of tobacco were produced on the island, and production increased yearly until it peaked in 1880, when it was estimated that Puerto Rico produced over 12 million pounds of leaf.[8]

The U.S. occupation in 1898 and the resulting economic policies accelerated the expansion of the active tobacco sector. The incorporation of Puerto Rico into the tariff structure of the United States also allowed the easy flow of U.S. capital into the island's economy for the establishment of tobacco manufacturing plants.[9] Unlike what would occur in the sugar sector, however,

U.S. investment in the tobacco sector remained largely in the manufacturing area, leaving the agricultural process largely in the hands of the Puerto Rican farmers.

CHARACTERISTICS OF PUERTO RICAN TOBACCO

Three types of tobacco were grown in Puerto Rico, classified according to their geographic characteristics: interior, coastal, and semicoastal.[10] Filler tobacco was cultivated in the interior highlands of the island, especially in the eastern highland region. Filler tobacco, which accounted for 95 percent of the total island tobacco crop, was of the Virginia No. 9 and Utuado X varieties of tobacco classified as Type 46.[11] The characteristics of Puerto Rican tobacco made it appropriate for blending with other types of filler tobacco from the United States for the manufacturing of cheaper cigars. Because of the smoothness, aroma, and distinctive taste of Puerto Rican tobacco, American manufacturers compared it to Cuban tobacco. For the manufacture of higher priced cigars, Puerto Rican tobacco would be used alone or blended with Cuban filler tobacco.[12] Unlike Cuban tobacco, however, Puerto Rican tobacco was not subjected to a tariff when it was imported into the United States, thereby making Puerto Rican tobacco economically advantageous to the manufacturing sector without any sacrifice in quality.

Coastal tobacco was grown on the northwestern and southeastern littorals of the island. It was not as carefully cultivated as interior tobacco, and was not considered to be of high quality. The leaf was short and heavy in taste, and coastal tobacco was mostly used to produce chewing blends, since the salt from the sea made its taste unpleasant for smokers but mellow for chewers. Coastal tobacco was also used as scrap for very cheap cigars and cigarettes.[13]

Semicoastal tobacco was cultivated in the island's lower altitude valleys located close to the coastline, and its quality fits somewhere between that of interior and coastal tobacco leaf. The slightly higher elevation of these tobacco fields, located on terrain that changed from coastal plain to mountains, protected the leaf from the searing heat of the coast. Their proximity to the saline coastal air, however, affected the taste of the leaf grown there. Semicoastal tobacco was mostly used as filler for cigars and cigarettes.[14]

Shade-grown wrapper tobacco, the most exquisite and valued of the island's tobacco leaf, was produced on the island between 1902 and 1927 on lands owned by a subsidiary of the Porto Rican–American Tobacco Company (PRATC) in the La Plata Valley in Aibonito, Cayey, and Comerío and in the lowlands around Caguas, Gurabo, and Juncos.[15] Wrapper tobacco was used as the outer leaf for high-priced cigars. Because it was the first leaf a smoker would taste, great care was taken in its cultivation. However, the shift in consumer taste to cheaper cigars and cigarettes during the 1920s, along with the labor-intensive nature of its cultivation, eventually made production of shade-grown wrapper tobacco unprofitable for the PRATC. In 1927, its production was ended and the land on which it was grown was sold to the insular government as well as to individual farmers.

The Cultivation of the Tobacco Plant

Tobacco cultivation can be separated into different and specific stages: planting and cultivation, harvesting, curing, and fermenting. The tobacco season usually began in June or July with a careful plowing of the fields. By early August, the land was plowed and cleaned of all weeds, rocks, or other debris, and farmers would use oxen to dig ditches about ten inches deep and three feet apart.[16] Farmers would then scatter tobacco seed by hand into the ditches and water them twice per day. Those who had more abundant financial resources would use cheesecloth to cover the seedbeds from pests and the weather for the first two weeks after the planting. The seeds would germinate and grow into seedlings in thirty-five to forty days, but were not considered ready to transplant until after sixty to sixty-five days. Seedlings were then planted every thirty-two to forty-eight inches in rows that were set fourteen to eighteen inches apart.[17] The transplanting would begin as early as the final weeks in September, although most farmers preferred to wait until the middle of October and early November, when the hurricane season was over. Once in the growing fields, the tobacco plants had to be fertilized regularly, sprayed for insects, and inspected for disease, and this meant the constant attention of the tobacco farmer. It would take forty-five days from the transplant date for the tobacco plants to be ready for picking, a painstaking process that would occur in stages beginning with the leaves closest to the ground. The harvest would continue for another thirty days, until the plant was bare of all leaves. Usually, the harvest began anytime between December and March, depending on weather conditions and the initial planting date.[18] From the soil preparation for the seedbeds to the final harvest, the tobacco cultivation cycle would last from six to seven months. Farmers who planted early in the growing season often had time to plant a second crop with purchased seedlings that were ready to transplant, but because the soil was depleted of minerals after the first planting, the quality of the second crop was not as high.

After the harvest, the curing of the tobacco leaf would begin. Green tobacco is between 80 and 90 percent water, and the leaf must be carefully dried to bring out the correct color and flavor. The curing process, if accomplished properly, would "facilitate those chemical changes which will produce leaf of the desired character."[19] Improper curing could ruin a good leaf; therefore, curing was one of the most important post-harvest operations in the productive process. Tobacco was cured in three distinct ways: flue-cured, fire-cured, and air-cured. In the flue-curing process, green tobacco was hung over metal flues or ducts and cured by heating up to 180°F. Fire-cured tobacco was hung to dry over a smoldering fire. Air-cured tobacco was cured in tobacco barns that had controlled ventilation, where the natural evaporation process cured the tobacco. Secondary heat usually played no role, although it may have been used on occasion to control humidity.[20] In Puerto Rico, most of the tobacco was air-cured, since this required the least amount of capital investment. Some farmers were financially able to cure their own tobacco, but most took their leaf to curing barns owned by local merchants, tobacco corporations, or cooperative associations. Curing barns were usually constructed of a simple wooden frame with walls made of palm thatch or cane leaves and a zinc roof, and were up to forty feet long.[21] The curing process took from thirty-three to forty days and was highly sensitive to weather changes, ventilation problems, and the overcrowding of leaf. If there was too much rain the leaf would not dry properly; too little and it would dry too quickly. If there was too much air circulation the complexities of the flavor would not fully develop; too little and the leaf could become moldy. If too much tobacco was hanging in the curing barn, it would make overcrowding and ventilation harder to control, which could lead to moldy leaf.

The high risk of damaging good tobacco leaf was a constant concern for tobacco farmers. Accordingly, the Agricultural Experimental Station in Caguas, an insular agricultural scientific institution affiliated with the University of Puerto Rico, had a tobacco specialist on staff who developed several flue-curing projects as alternatives to air-curing during the 1920s. Although experiments were successful, they required a larger capital investment that most tobacco farmers could not afford and therefore took over a decade to implement. During the decade of the 1930s, consumer preference shifted to cigarettes. Because most of the tobacco used for cigarettes was of the flue-cured variety, flue-curing as a processing method became more important.[22] Many tobacco farmers in Caguas, Cayey, Aibonito, and Comerío had adopted flue-curing and were able to meet the demand for this type of tobacco.[23]

Most Puerto Rican tobacco farmers did not have the financial means to build curing barns. On average, one barn was needed for every three acres of tobacco grown. As a result, farmers depended on arrangements with other farmers or with *refaccionistas* (local financiers), tobacco corporations, or cooperative associations who owned curing ranches, to prepare their crop for sale.[24] One of the common problems Puerto Rican tobacco farmers faced was that there were not enough curing ranches to accommodate all of the tobacco grown on the island in any given year. This meant that many planters were forced to let the harvested leaf lie in the field until a particular ranch had room for their crop. Delaying the curing and leaving the tobacco in the field where it was susceptible to weather conditions and insects could negatively impact the final quality of the leaf.[25] A related problem was overcrowding once the tobacco was hung for curing, which could result in damp and moldy tobacco. Both of these situations affected the price a farmer received for his product.

Once farmers finished the curing process, they would deliver the tobacco to a warehouse designated by a lender, or to a leaf dealer or a tobacco corporation, where the tobacco leaf would be fermented. It was then classified into grades, fermented, and once again graded and classified. Although there was no standard system for Puerto Rican tobacco, it was generally classified according to the type of tobacco leaf planted, the time when the leaf was cut off the tobacco plant, and its appearance after curing, including its color, weight, and whether the leaf was whole or in pieces. It was usually at this point in the processing of the tobacco leaf that the farmer was paid for his product by either lenders, dealers, or corporations, when most of the weight had been lost in the curing phase of processing.

Once the tobacco was classified by grades it was ready for fermentation. During this process, tobacco was packed into *estibas* (bundles) of 50 to 60 *quintales* (one quintal equals 100 pounds). A small card, much like an index card today, was attached to each estiba to record the daily temperature inside the bundle. Fermentation was the manipulation of the temperature of the tobacco leaves to eliminate the natural greenish tint and to produce leaf with a uniformly brown color. The core temperature of a newly formed estiba of tobacco would rise to 126°F in a period of four to five days. When that occurred, the estiba would be untied, torn down, and remade with the previous inside tobacco placed on the outside, and the top and bottom layers placed in the center. The estiba would be heated, unpacked, and repacked another four or five times until the core temperature became stable at 118–122°F.[26] After the tobacco leaf was fermented, it was again classified into grades. If the leaf was in a warehouse owned by a corporation, then they would own it outright and the industrial part of the process could begin.

If independent lenders or leaf dealers owned the warehouse, then it would be sold to local, U.S.-based, or international buyers using the price structure assigned to the particular grades. Thus the higher the grade of tobacco leaf, the higher the price paid for it.

Tobacco Leaf Production, 1910–1940

As stated earlier, tobacco cultivation in Puerto Rico went through a series of expansions and contractions from 1910 to 1940 as the global market for tobacco products changed. Tobacco growers in Puerto Rico adjusted their production to meet these changes, although they were not always successful. A closer look at the specific cycles of expansion and contraction will be useful at this point.

The number of total cuerdas under cultivation and the total production of tobacco leaf in pounds increased overall from 1910 until 1927, with yearly fluctuations. (See table 1.2.) After 1927, both began a series of highs and lows characterized by an overall downward trend until 1940.[27] Land under tobacco cultivation increased from over 22,000 cuerdas in 1910 to over 34,000 in 1917. A year later, an astounding 51,000 cuerdas were planted in tobacco throughout the island, an overall increase from 1910 of 132 percent. The largest number of cuerdas ever prepared for a growing season was 81,900, planted in 1927, and the lowest number was in 1932, when only a little over 10,000 cuerdas were planted. After the peak of 1927, the number of cuerdas under cultivation fluctuated yearly until 1940 with an overall downward trend.

Production of tobacco leaf in pounds followed a similar pattern. Production increased 35 percent from 1910 to 1917 with slight yearly fluctuations. The number of pounds produced from a harvest peaked in 1927 at 50 million, with the second-most-productive year occurring in 1938 when the island's tobacco harvest was slightly over 44 million pounds. The least productive year was 1932, with 6 million pounds of tobacco produced on the island. After the peak of 1938, tobacco production rapidly declined until 1940 to levels below those prevalent in 1917, and it never recuperated thereafter.

Although tobacco was cultivated in almost every municipality in Puerto Rico, the tobacco regions defined previously were responsible for the greatest portion of cultivation and production. From 1910 to 1940, over 61 percent of land planted in tobacco and 65 percent of the total production of the island was found in the eastern highlands region. The western highlands region accounted for 28 percent of tobacco cuerdas on the island and 26 percent of tobacco leaf. In total, the tobacco regions in the eastern and western highlands of the island cultivated 89 percent of all tobacco cuerdas and produced

TABLE 1.2

TOBACCO CULTIVATION IN CUERDAS AND PRODUCTION
IN POUNDS IN PUERTO RICO, 1910–1940

Year	Cuerdas	Production
1910	22,143	10,828,000
1912	18,000	12,800,000
1913	23,000	15,000,000
1914	18,000	13,000,000
1915	17,000	12,000,000
1917	34,540	25,410,000
1918	51,444	25,772,000
1919	39,067	19,363,000
1920	42,232	25,339,000
1921	40,000	25,000,000
1922	35,000	22,500,000
1923	41,500	26,000,000
1924	40,000	25,000,000
1925	34,023	23,000,000
1926	58,000	36,000,000
1927	81,900	50,000,000
1928	40,345	27,000,000
1929	39,075	28,000,000
1930	43,312	32,500,000
1931	50,000	37,300,000
1932	10,079	6,000,000
1933	25,300	16,783,000
1934	45,500	25,000,000
1935	38,000	22,500,000
1936	43,809	26,000,000
1937	50,000	34,983,000
1938	63,000	44,069,000
1939	18,688	13,825,000
1940	33,265	21,713,000

Sources: Data for 1910 from Bureau of the Census, *Thirteenth Census of the United States Taken in the Year 1910. Statistics for Porto Rico, Agriculture* (Washington, DC, 1913), 72–77 (hereafter cited as *Agriculture Census 1910*). Data for 1920 from Bureau of the Census, *Fourteenth Census of the United States Taken in the Year 1920.* Volume 6, Part 3. *Agriculture* (Washington, DC, 1922), 408–415 (hereafter cited as *Agriculture Census 1920*). Data for 1930 from Bureau of the Census, *Fifteenth Census of the United States: 1930. Outlying Territories and Possessions* (Washington, DC, 1932), 232–237 (hereafter cited as *Census 1930*). Data for 1940 from Bureau of the Census, *Sixteenth Census of the United States: 1940. Reports for Puerto Rico: Census of Agriculture* (Washington, DC, 1942), 60 (hereafter cited as *Agriculture Census 1940*).

TABLE 1.3

TOBACCO CULTIVATION BY REGION, 1910–1940

Year	Eastern Highlands		Western Highlands	
	CUERDAS	PRODUCTION (IN POUNDS)	CUERDAS	PRODUCTION (IN POUNDS)
1910	12,698	6,124,120	5,918	3,247,150
1920	24,229	13,612,444	9,549	3,586,263
1930	33,589	19,787,707	15,270	8,707,356
1940	16,855	12,598,524	8,609	5,581,590

Sources: Data for 1910 from *Agriculture Census 1910*, 72–77; for 1920 from *Agriculture Census 1920*, 408–415; for 1930 from *Census 1930*, 232–237; for 1940 from *Agriculture Census 1940*, 60.

91 percent of all tobacco leaf in Puerto Rico from 1910 to 1940. It is clear that the eastern highlands were much more important in terms of the area cultivated and volume produced. (See table 1.3.)

A closer look at the rate of growth in the two tobacco regions illustrates the rapid expansion of the tobacco sector from 1910 to 1920. Between 1910 and 1920, the number of cuerdas under tobacco cultivation increased by 90 percent in the eastern highlands, a yearly rate of increase of 6.7 percent. In the western highlands, cuerdas under cultivation increased 5 percent per year for a 61 percent increase over the decade. Total production also increased dramatically in the eastern highlands by 122 percent, a rate of 6 percent per year between 1910 and 1920. The western highlands reported an increase of only 10 percent in total production, and the yearly rate of growth for the region was just about 1 percent.[28]

Tobacco cultivation in the eastern highlands expanded at a higher rate than in the western highlands from 1910 to 1920 for several reasons. First, the eastern highlands remained the center of the island's tobacco cultivation during the early twentieth century because it had been the most important growing region during Spanish colonial times. Tobacco growers in the region had the knowledge and experience to handle immediate and increased demand for the U.S. market. Hence, it is logical that the rate of expansion would be higher in a place well equipped to handle it. Second, the eastern highlands enjoyed favorable soil and climatic conditions for the cultivation of Type 46 tobacco leaf, the type most in demand. A constant supply of Type 46 leaf, consistent in quality, was necessary, and tobacco growers in the region benefited from government programs that supported their growing efforts. These included better institutional and noninstitutional credit structures, as well as the extensive involvement of agricultural scientists and tobacco farmers in researching and testing the latest technologies in tobacco cultivation.[29]

Most of the leaf tobacco produced on the island was exported to the United States for manufacturing into cigars and cigarettes in American factories. The finished product would then be reexported around the world. Export figures from 1900 through 1902 indicate that tobacco leaf exports from Puerto Rico to the United States averaged 664,000 pounds. In 1903, exports increased by more than 300 percent to reach almost 2.4 million pounds. From that year until 1917, there was a slow and steady increase in the volume of leaf exported to the United States. It was the opening of markets in Europe after the end of World War I that resulted in a sharp rise in demand for tobacco from the Americas. From 1917 to 1918, there was an 85 percent increase in the quantity of tobacco leaf exported from Puerto Rico to the United States, and between 1917 and 1921, tobacco exports increased by 56 percent in volume and by over 126 percent in value. (See table 1.4.)

Rising demand resulted in increased prices, which fueled the expansion of the tobacco market after the First World War. From an average price of 31 cents per pound from 1900 to 1917, prices paid for Puerto Rican tobacco increased to 52 cents per pound in 1918 and 1919 and to 65 cents per pound in 1920.[30] A year later, in 1921, because of a reduced crop, tobacco sold for an average of 93 cents per pound, the highest export price ever paid for Puerto Rican tobacco. (See table 1.4.) Tobacco cultivation expanded to such a great extent by the early 1920s that 20 percent of the total Puerto Rican work force was involved in its cultivation.[31]

The tobacco market in Puerto Rico responded to economic, political, and natural forces that affected the number of cuerdas under cultivation, total production, and the prices paid for tobacco leaf. From 1920 to 1935, the tobacco market in Puerto Rico had to contend with major hurricanes that caused devastation in tobacco plantations, shifting consumer preferences, and a worldwide economic depression after 1929.

In July 1926, the west-central portion of Puerto Rico was devastated by Hurricane San Liborio. Damages were calculated at over \$2 million, and the greatest losses were reported among coffee and tobacco plantations. Many tobacco ranches, used for the drying and curing of tobacco leaf, were destroyed: 300 in Aibonito, half of all ranches in Orocovis, all ranches in Guayama, 50 in Jayuya, and 34 in Caguas.[32] Because the hurricane occurred in July, when the crop previously cultivated was in the barns for curing, farmers suffered terrible losses. Throughout the tobacco regions, 65 percent of all tobacco-curing barns

TABLE 1.4

EXPORTS OF LEAF TOBACCO FROM PUERTO RICO TO
THE UNITED STATES, 1900–1940

Year	Quantity (in pounds)	Value	Price per pound
1900–1901	557,000	$121,000	$0.22
1901–1902	666,000	112,000	0.17
1902–1903	770,000	135,000	0.18
1903–1904	2,386,000	261,000	0.11
1904–1905	2,196,000	422,000	0.19
1905–1906	1,397,000	477,000	0.34
1906–1907	3,681,000	1,157,000	0.31
1907–1908	4,979,000	1,678,000	0.34
1908–1909	3,868,000	1,202,000	0.31
1909–1910	4,120,000	1,255,000	0.30
1910–1911	4,362,000	1,547,000	0.35
1911–1912	5,457,000	2,320,000	0.43
1912–1913	8,150,000	3,148,000	0.39
1913–1914	7,534,000	3,104,000	0.41
1914–1915	9,052,000	3,187,000	0.35
1915–1916	8,021,000	3,026,000	0.38
1916–1917	9,256,000	3,829,000	0.41
1917–1918	17,114,000	8,968,000	0.52
1918–1919	15,664,000	8,111,000	0.52
1919–1920	20,173,000	13,318,000	0.66
1920–1921	14,564,000	13,552,000	0.93
1921–1922	22,370,000	8,994,000	0.40
1922–1923	19,574,000	9,459,000	0.48
1923–1924	23,298,000	13,170,000	0.57
1924–1925	22,721,000	9,838,000	0.43
1925–1926	24,521,000	13,945,000	0.57
1926–1927	30,730,000	20,580,000	0.67
1927–1928	29,807,000	17,062,000	0.57

(*continued*)

TABLE 1.4

EXPORTS OF LEAF TOBACCO FROM PUERTO RICO TO
THE UNITED STATES, 1900–1940 (*continued*)

Year	Quantity (in pounds)	Value	Price per pound
1928–1929	27,410,000	12,881,000	0.47
1929–1930	26,014,000	11,914,000	0.46
1930–1931	25,180,000	13,165,000	0.52
1931–1932	17,035,000	6,714,000	0.39
1932–1933	12,928,000	4,403,000	0.34
1933–1934	18,846,000	6,329,000	0.34
1934–1935	19,974,000	7,146,000	0.36
1935–1936	23,157,000	9,254,000	0.40
1936–1937	23,581,000	9,135,000	0.39
1937–1938	20,699,000	8,239,000	0.40
1938–1939	23,208,000	7,398,000	0.32
1939–1940	17,087,000	6,029,000	0.35

Source: United States Department of Labor, Age and Hour Division, Research and Statistics Branch, *Puerto Rico: The Leaf Tobacco Industry* (Washington, DC: Government Printing Office, 1941), 4.

were destroyed by San Liborio.[33] It was estimated that the tobacco crop for 1926 would be 30 percent lower than in the previous year. Reports made by tobacco farmers across the region are evidence of the severity of the situation. Feliz Jiménez, a tobacco grower from Aibonito, lost seven ranches and calculated that his available crop would be reduced by 40 percent. Nicolas Ortiz Lebrón expected a reduction in his crop of 35 percent, and Anastasio Noriega expected 50 percent less tobacco from his farm, although they both planned to rebuild some of their lost ranches immediately.[34]

In preparation for the 1926 harvest, farmers had increased the number of cuerdas they planted in tobacco, partly due to reports that tobacco supplies from other parts of the world would be limited and of inferior quality.[35] Because acreage had been expanded to 58,000 cuerdas for 1926 (from 34,023 for the 1925 crop year), the total crop, even after San Liborio, still amounted to over 36 million pounds. The ability of Puerto Rican tobacco farmers to adjust cultivation to forecasted market conditions is remarkable and demonstrates their constant access to information regarding the worldwide tobacco market.

To assist with these efforts, *El agricultor puertorriqueño* published a report on the state of the industry in each of their issues. For example, in the first issue of December 1925, the report mentioned the prices obtained by growers to date (40–90 cents per pound); stated that the crop was estimated to reach 1.264 millions pounds (compared to 1.241 in 1924); and made general comments on the industry, such as "export demand has greatly increased" and the "consumption of cigarettes in the United States continues to increase."[36]

A reduction in available tobacco on the island after the hurricane of 1926, together with correct predictions of a reduction in tobacco stock from around the world, resulted in a 34 percent increase in prices paid to farmers (38.17 cents per pound) over the previous year. For the 1927 crop year, therefore, farmers once again increased the acreage planted to further take advantage of the strong demand for Puerto Rican tobacco.

There were reports that the tobacco harvest in Santo Domingo would be "considerably reduced," from 50 million pounds in 1926 to an expected 15 to 20 million pounds in 1927, due to heavy rains followed by an extended drought.[37] Low prices and low demand were also projected for tobacco from the Philippines. Plantings in the United States were reportedly 4 percent lower than in the previous year, and the Cuban harvest suffered from both the fury of a tropical storm and a drought.[38] Farmers in Puerto Rico, therefore, increased their plantings with the assumption that they were fulfilling a need that other countries would not be able to meet. In fact, the tobacco sector was so optimistic in its outlook for the 1927 market that refaccionistas willingly increased the amount of money available for production credit.[39]

Tobacco farmers increased the total acreage under cultivation in 1927 to 81,900 cuerdas, a rise of 41 percent from the previous year. Production totaled in excess of 50 million pounds, an increase of 39 percent over 1926.[40] Tobacco reductions in other countries were not as low as had been expected, and the market could not absorb such an enormous increase in supply from Puerto Rico. Prices paid to tobacco farmers dropped dramatically to 19.84 cents per pound, a decrease of 48 percent, making the 1927 crop a disastrous one for tobacco farmers across the island.[41] As noted in a government report, tobacco farmers "have not recuperated from the recent disaster of 50 million pounds."[42]

The difficulties of 1927 were aggravated by Hurricane San Felipe II, which swept through the island in September 1928, resulting in calamitous financial losses.[43] Throughout the tobacco regions, the storm destroyed many newly planted seedbeds and curing ranches, to the detriment of not only the current crop that was being fermented in the ranches but also the future crop that was in the seedling stage. In total, 6,316 tobacco ranches were destroyed at a loss of over $1.4 million, and 25 percent of seedbeds throughout the island were completely lost. The storm also damaged manufacturing factories, paralyzing the industrial processing of the leaf for the season.

Damages to the tobacco crop due to San Felipe II once again resulted in an increase of 20 percent in the price paid to farmers for the 1928 harvest. This slight recovery was quickly annulled by the stock market crash in the United States in October 1929, which once again reduced the farm price of tobacco to 19.18 cents per pound. In September 1932, Puerto Rico would be hit by the most catastrophic hurricane of the century, San Ciprián. Over 3,000 people were injured by the storm across the island and more than 400,000 lost their homes. Property damages alone were calculated at over $40 million.[44] The tobacco sector was devastated. A government worker in Caguas sent to survey the damage done by San Ciprián commented: "All of the tobacco ranches that this agent has seen, and all others that he has received information about, have been completely destroyed."[45] Rafael Menéndez Ramos, the commissioner of agriculture and commerce at the time, acknowledged the effects of the storm: "Farmers are mentally depressed because of the losses. . . . Tobacco farmers lost one million dollars in ranches and equipment during the hurricane."[46]

Puerto Rican tobacco was affected by an enormous crop that caused a glut of product on the market, three catastrophic hurricanes in six years, and a worldwide economic depression. At the same time, smoking preferences had shifted considerably and permanently beginning in the 1920s from heavy, large, and expensive cigars to lighter, smaller, and cheaper cigars and cigarettes. (See table 1.5.) Consumption of more expensive cigars in the United States fell from 80 per person in 1920 to 42 per person in 1939, a decline of 48 percent. Demand for cigars priced over 5 cents, which accounted for 62 percent of the total of manufactured cigars in Puerto Rico between 1920 and 1925, fell to 11 percent of the total between 1935 and 1939.[47] (See figure 1.2.) Conversely, the sales of cheap cigars (5 cents or less) accounted for less than 25 percent of all sales from 1920 to 1925, but increased to more than 80 percent of all cigar sales by 1940.[48] The result was that the same well-regarded Puerto Rican tobacco that had been used for cigars priced between 8 and 15 cents each, began to be used in cheaper cigars priced at 5 cents or less.[49] The decline in sales of more expensive cigars is also reflected in the reduction of cigars exported to the United States from Puerto Rico, a 64 percent decrease from 1929 to 1935. For tobacco farmers, these changes resulted in a significant drop in the price received for their product. Farmers were paid an average of 25 cents per pound for their tobacco from 1920 to 1929 and only an average of 15 cents per pound from 1930 to 1939, a decrease of 43 percent.[50]

TABLE 1.5

NUMBER OF PUERTO RICAN CIGARS ACCORDING TO CLASS
FOR THE UNITED STATES, 1920–1935

Year	Class A no more than 5 cents each	Class B 5 to 8 cents each	Classes C, D, and E more than 8 cents each	Total
1920	58,134,000	7,410,000	81,243,000	146,787,000
1921	51,533,000	7,583,000	65,406,000	124,522,000
1922	100,904,000	15,020,000	52,655,000	168,579,000
1923	91,411,000	13,176,000	35,550,000	140,137,000
1924	122,560,000	15,681,000	48,310,000	186,551,000
1925	141,810,000	11,483,000	50,459,000	203,752,000
1926	109,508,000	8,826,000	30,136,000	148,470,000
1927	116,209,000	4,033,000	20,405,000	140,647,000
1928	119,967,000	7,020,000	20,267,000	147,254,000
1929	122,503,000	3,876,000	14,305,000	140,684,000
1930	148,243,000	3,022,000	8,985,000	160,250,000
1931	92,467,000	828,000	4,612,000	97,907,000
1932	58,709,000	1,046,000	1,036,000	60,791,000
1933	57,565,000	2,781,000	958,000	61,304,000
1934	56,504,000	2,006,000	665,000	59,175,000
1935	49,343,000	1,369,000	599,000	51,311,000

Source: Charles E. Gage, The Tobacco Industry in Puerto Rico, United States Department of Agriculture, Circular No. 519 (Washington, DC: Government Printing Office, 1939).

The shift in preference to cheaper cigars coincided with an overall shift in consumption from cigars to cigarettes.[51] Cigar consumption in Puerto Rico fell continuously after 1929, and by 1935 annual consumption had decreased 48 percent from 1929 levels. (See table 1.6.) Cigar imports from the United States to the island were minimal during this time, not reaching even 1 percent of the total number of cigars consumed. In other words, Puerto Ricans were smoking Puerto Rican cigars, which guaranteed a domestic market for the Puerto Rican product, regardless of what was produced for export.

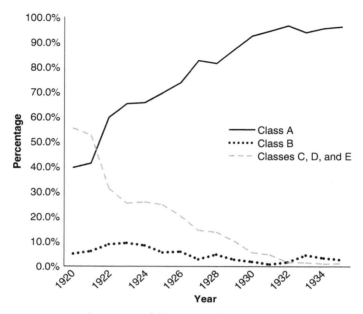

FIGURE 1.2 Percentage of Cigars According to Class, 1920–1935.

As preferences changed and economic necessity demanded a shift from cigars to cigarettes, the domestic market for Puerto Rican cigars was mostly lost.[52]

In contrast to cigar consumption, cigarette consumption increased 58 percent from 1929 to 1935. (See table 1.7.) What is interesting about this increase, however, is that the proportion of Puerto Rican cigarettes that were being consumed steadily decreased during that time period. In 1929, over one-third (36 percent) of all cigarettes smoked on the island were made on the island. By 1935, only 9 percent of all cigarettes consumed were of Puerto Rican origin. Instead, cigarettes imported from the United States took over the local market. Like cigar manufactures, and at the same time that consumer preferences were shifting from cigars to cigarettes, Puerto Rican cigarettes were being replaced in the local market by American cigarettes.

The impact of the shift in preference, reflected in the manufacturing statistics, cannot be overstated. Writing about the state of the tobacco industry in 1941, Jorge J. Serrallés and Martín Vélez of the Agricultural Experiment Station in Río Piedras stated: "It can very well be said that . . . the most important factor [affecting the situation in the tobacco sector] has been the enormous increase in the consumption of cigarettes, with the consequent decrease in that of cigars."[53]

A closer look at the statistical data for the tobacco regions illustrates these changes in the tobacco market between 1920 and 1930. For the decade as a whole, both regions experienced growth, but to a lesser extent than from 1910

TABLE 1.6

CIGAR CONSUMPTION IN PUERTO RICO, 1929–1935

Year	Puerto Rican cigars	Cigar imports from the US	Total cigar consumption in PR
1929	55,453,000	133,000	55,586,000
1930	48,494,000	58,000	48,552,000
1931	43,524,000	33,000	43,557,000
1932	36,547,000	185,000	36,732,000
1933	32,003,000	88,000	32,091,000
1934	28,530,000	167,000	28,697,000
1935	28,881,000	150,000	29,031,000

Source: Gage, *Tobacco Industry*, 44–45.

TABLE 1.7

CIGARETTE CONSUMPTION IN PUERTO RICO, 1929–1935

Year	Puerto Rican cigarettes	Cigarette imports from the US	Total cigarette consumption in PR
1929	239,324,000	421,353,000	660,677,000
1930	211,686,000	468,234,000	679,920,000
1931	166,510,000	445,600,000	612,110,000
1932	122,248,000	448,982,000	571,230,000
1933	91,339,000	549,113,000	640,452,000
1934	70,638,000	599,083,000	669,721,000
1935	69,526,000	666,818,000	736,344,000

Source: Gage, *Tobacco Industry*, 48–49.

to 1920. The number of cuerdas under cultivation increased in the eastern highland region by 38.6 percent and in the western highland regions by almost 60 percent. The yearly rate of growth was 3.3 percent for the eastern highlands and 4.5 percent for the western highlands. Production also increased by 45 percent in the eastern highlands, at a yearly rate of growth of 3.8 percent. The most significant expansion occurred in the production levels of the western highland tobacco districts, which increased 142 percent from 1920 to 1930, at a

9.3 percent yearly rate of growth. Although the eastern highlands were still planting more cuerdas and producing more tobacco, it was the western highlands that experienced phenomenal rates of growth. The difference in rates of growth in the two tobacco regions can be attributed to the shift in consumer preferences described above. The increase in consumption of cheaper cigars meant that tobacco leaf did not need to be as fine as for more expensive cigars, and thus the western highlands was well suited for the less exquisite type of tobacco demanded in this new market. The same was true for cigarettes, which were preferred to cigars after 1929. The expansion of the market for this particular leaf also meant that scientific efforts were shifted from the darker tobacco of the eastern highlands to the brighter one of the western highlands.

The decade of the 1930s was characterized by great changes, both positive and negative, in the number of cuerdas under cultivation and the total production of tobacco. The least productive year, measured in either total cuerdas under cultivation or quantity produced, was 1932, when a little over 10,000 cuerdas produced 6 million pounds, a decrease of approximately 80 percent in both from 1931. In 1932, tobacco farmers attempted to limit the acreage under cultivation to recuperate from the 50-million-pound crop of 1927 and reduce the stock of leaf on the market. However, there was an expansion in yearly production and cuerdas under cultivation from 1933 to 1937, largely because of Agricultural Adjustment Administration programs to aid farmers and improved credit facilities.[54] The most productive year of the decade was 1938, when 63,000 cuerdas were planted, producing more than 44 million pounds. From then on, tobacco cultivation in Puerto Rico plummeted and would never recuperate.

The tobacco regions experienced high contraction rates from 1930 to 1940 in both the number of cuerdas under cultivation and in production levels. In the eastern highland regions, there was a decrease of almost 50 percent in the number of cuerdas planted, a reduction of 6.7 percent yearly. The western highland regions did not fare much better, with a reduction in the number of cuerdas planted in tobacco of 44 percent, a yearly rate of decrease of 5.6 percent. Thirty-six percent less tobacco leaf was produced in both regions, a number perhaps less severe than the reduction in cuerdas, but a significant number nonetheless. Scientific cultivation technologies designed to increase the average yield per acre had spread through the island and become standard practice in both regions. Therefore, although the reduction in acreage was dramatic from 1930 to 1940, the yield of tobacco leaf per acre cultivated increase dramatically, especially in the western highlands. It was this higher yield per acre that accounted for a slightly lower rate of contraction in production when compared to the one in cuerdas planted. This was crucial for tobacco growers, who were still able to eke out a living, even if they needed to reduce the number of cuerdas dedicated to tobacco.

CONCLUSION

Tobacco cultivation in Puerto Rico from 1899 to 1940 experienced periods of expansion and contraction for various reasons. On the eve of the American occupation of the island, Puerto Rico's tobacco sector was well established and had been operational for centuries. The inclusion of Puerto Rico in the tariff structure of the United States opened the American market to the island's tobacco. The interest in the island's tobacco because of its particular characteristics and general quality, combined with the absence of an import tariff to the United States and the influx of American capital into the industrial phase of the tobacco industry, dramatically accelerated the expansion of tobacco cultivation after 1898.

By 1910, tobacco had become the second-most-important commercial crop for export, employing thousands of agricultural laborers throughout the island, and because of insular taxation policies tobacco had become a major revenue producer for the island's government. Until 1917, the cultivation of tobacco, both in terms of cuerdas planted and in terms of production, grew slowly and steadily. The end of the First World War opened markets around the world for American tobacco, and Puerto Rican tobacco growers rapidly increased plantings to meet demand. Tobacco cultivation grew significantly after 1917 and peaked in 1927 with a crop of over 50 million pounds. The economic consequences of this bumper crop would be aggravated by the economic depression that began in 1929. Because most of the tobacco leaf produced on the island was exported to the United States, the Puerto Rican tobacco economy was intimately linked to economic and cultural changes in mainland markets. Accordingly, the stock market crash of 1929 greatly affected the island's tobacco sector because of a decline in demand. At the same time, smokers' tastes had shifted from larger, heavier cigars to smaller, lighter cigars and cigarettes, a preference that continued as economic hardship made the purchase of more expensive cigars more difficult.

By the 1930s, Puerto Rican tobacco had faced a major economic depression, the shifting of consumer preferences, and three major hurricanes that caused great devastation to the tobacco crop. Although there was some recovery of the tobacco sector from 1933 to 1938 due to federal aid programs and wider credit availability, its value fell to levels of the early twentieth century, and the tobacco economy would never again recover to the levels of production or importance in the local economy achieved during the 1920s.

CHAPTER 2

Life in the Tobacco Regions
of Puerto Rico

For most of the highland farms, tobacco is the keystone upon which hinges the entire agricultural structure.

—John P. Augelli

The development of the tobacco leaf market and its importance as a commercial product is an important beginning in understanding the complex puzzle of how Puerto Ricans in the highland regions were affected by an expanding economic sector. The opportunities for participation in the colonial government structures that are discussed in the later chapters of this book occurred because tobacco cultivation became a viable economic activity, one that provided sustenance for families in the highlands. Because small-scale farmers cultivated the great majority of the tobacco leaf grown in Puerto Rico, the study of their families and farming operations provides an opportunity to analyze how larger economic processes affected people at the most local of levels. Therefore, this chapter analyzes demographic and economic data to discuss the profound social and economic transformations that occurred in the tobacco regions after 1898. This chapter also compares the tobacco regions of the island with the sugar regions in order to engage with several of the salient debates in the historiography of early twentieth-century Puerto Rico. Sugar cultivation, as explained earlier, has dominated the discussions of the effects of U.S. colonialism and capital investment on the island, although there were other important commercial products that had tremendous effects. Coffee regions are also included in these comparisons, perhaps to a lesser extent, but the purpose remains to add complexity to the agricultural narrative of the island.

Known as the "poor man's crop," tobacco could be cultivated on very small tracts of land, required no major capital investments in machinery, and had a relatively short growing season. Farmers in the highlands generated the greatest share of their cash income from the sale of tobacco leaf, often after just one growing season. Because tobacco could be cultivated efficiently on small parcels of land, a farmer could dedicate a percentage of the available farmland to food crops for domestic consumption that could then be sold at the local markets. More important for the well-being of a tobacco-farming family, tobacco occupied the land for only several months out of the year, freeing well-fertilized land for subsistence crops such as corn, rice, and green beans, among others. Thus, farmers in the tobacco regions relied on tobacco cultivation for cash income and were also able to produce food crops for family sustenance or for sale in local markets. Families were attracted to both of these possibilities and population increased in the tobacco regions at rates that were greater than in other areas of the island, especially during the apex of tobacco cultivation during the 1920s.

Some scholars have argued that the traditional Puerto Rican family was seriously threatened in the rural areas due to displacements caused by expanding agricultural production in the early twentieth century, and that this was related to the supposed out-migration of males from highland communities who sought employment in coastal sugar-producing enclaves. Empirical evidence suggests that this was not the case and that population movement between regions was predominantly a family phenomenon not only in tobacco regions, but also in sugar and coffee zones.[1] A relative parity was maintained between adult male and female populations in each region during the early twentieth century, although the tobacco regions maintained the most balanced sex ratio among adults of the three main agricultural regions. There was certainly some level of out-migration of working males, but the continued parity in the sex ratio (the number of males for every 100 females) of the adult population aged twenty and over from 1910 to 1940 suggests that families were the major component of interregional migration. Another indicator of the predominance of families in all the agricultural regions was the maintenance of a relatively large number of children (under ten years of age) in relation to adult women of childbearing age (fifteen to forty-four years of age). These child/women ratios were highest in the tobacco regions compared with sugar- and coffee-producing areas. Balanced sex ratios and a high number of children in a region are indicative of families living in that region. It is apparent that in the tobacco regions, and to a lesser extent in the sugar and coffee regions, family ties remained strong throughout the early decades of the twentieth century.

Another debate in the historiography of early twentieth-century Puerto Rican rural history has revolved around the social and economic impact of investment patterns by American absentee individuals and corporations. Several interrelated themes have been explored in this regard. The first theme is the changing level of owner-operated farms as opposed to farms run by managers or those that were leased to tenants. Many scholars have accepted the sugar-focused interpretation of the impact of American capital on land owner-ship patterns and have projected it to all agricultural regions, transforming the Puerto Rican landowner into a wage earner or a renter. In 1947, however, a research team led by Julian H. Steward compiled substantial quantitative and qualitative data in a tobacco-growing municipality they called "Tabara." The data indicated that during the twentieth century, there was an increase in the number of small farms and a decrease in the number of large farms in Tabara, a clear indicator that land concentration was not occurring.[2] The empirical evi-dence presented in this chapter supports their findings and indicates that the number of owner-operated farms increased in the tobacco regions from 1910 to 1940, and that there were a larger number of owner-operated farms in the tobacco regions than in the sugar or coffee regions.

A second and related issue is the supposed loss of land by Puerto Rican farmers who were displaced by absentee U.S. corporations, a paradigm that has not been tested empirically in most studies that have asserted this.[3] It is evi-dent that there was a high number of landless families throughout the Spanish colonial period, and this continued to be so after the United States occupied the island in 1898. Differences existed, however, in land tenure patterns between discrete agricultural sectors, in particular sugar, coffee, and tobacco. One way of testing this is to measure the number and relative percentage of Puerto Rican rural families who owned no land of their own during the early twentieth century, and how this changed from decade to decade. It is evident that, although the percentage of landless families increased in all of the agri-cultural regions from 1910 to 1940, it increased by a smaller margin in the tobacco regions than in the sugar or coffee zones. This is due to increased opportunities for purchasing land in the tobacco regions—after all, tobacco could be cultivated even on the smallest of farms—opportunities that did not exist as readily in the coffee or sugar regions.

Clearly, tobacco cultivation was important for the well-being of the fami-lies living in the highland regions. Tobacco provided cash income, but per-haps most importantly, its cultivation did not eliminate the production of secondary commercial crops or subsistence crops for family consumption. Additionally, there were more opportunities for land ownership in the tobacco regions than in other agricultural regions. The political and scientific involvement of tobacco farmers and their families in programs that secured their sector does not seem unusual or surprising when the consequences of their involvement would protect their land, their income, and their food supply.

Demographic Changes

The population in the western and eastern highland tobacco regions experienced high rates of growth between 1899 and 1940. In 1899, the population in the municipal districts comprising these regions was 386,814. By 1940, it had more than doubled to 798,832. Eastern highland districts experienced more dramatic changes than the western highland tobacco municipalities. (See tables 2.1 and 2.2.) This was largely due to the fact that tobacco cultivation expanded at a much more rapid pace in the eastern highlands than in the western highlands and drew more internal migrants to the region. It is interesting to note, however, that the rate of growth in the western highlands was highest between 1930 and 1940, when the tobacco sector began its decline. As discussed in the previous chapter, it was at this time that technological advances in tobacco cultivation had made larger yields per acre possible in the lower quality soil of the western highlands. The higher demand for brighter tobacco together with lower population increases may have made the western highlands attractive for families looking for better economic opportunities.

It is useful to compare demographic changes in the tobacco regions with those occurring in the other two major agricultural regions on the island, the sugar and coffee zones. In 1899, a significant number of the island's

TABLE 2.1

POPULATION IN THE TOBACCO REGIONS, 1899–1940

	1899	1910	1920	1930	1940
Tobacco Regions	386,814	462,433	555,518	671,842	798,832
Eastern Highlands	194,773	257,218	319,232	405,557	488,186
Western Highlands	192,041	205,215	236,286	266,285	310,646

Sources: Data for 1899 from War Department, *Report on the Census of Porto Rico, 1899* (Washington, DC: Government Printing Office, 1900), 164–169. Data for 1910 from Bureau of the Census, *Thirteenth Census of the United States Taken in the Year 1910. Statistics for Porto Rico* (Washington, DC, 1913), 1208–1224. Data for 1920 from Bureau of the Census, *Fourteenth Census of the United States Taken in the Year 1920.* Volume 3, *Population* (Washington, DC, 1922), 1208–1214. Data for 1930 from *Census 1930*, 147–154. Data for 1940 from Bureau of the Census, *Sixteenth Census of the United States: 1940. Reports for Puerto Rico*, Bulletin No. 2: *Characteristics of the Population* (Washington, DC, 1942), 31–40.

TABLE 2.2

TOTAL PERCENTAGE CHANGE IN POPULATION AND YEARLY RATE OF
POPULATION GROWTH IN TOBACCO REGIONS, 1899–1940

	Percentage change	*Yearly rate of growth*
Eastern Highlands		
1899–1910	32.1%	2.8%
1910–1920	24.1	2.2
1920–1930	27.0	2.4
1930–1940	20.4	1.9
Western Highlands		
1899–1910	6.9%	0.7%
1910–1920	15.1	1.4
1920–1930	12.7	1.2
1930–1940	16.7	1.6

Sources: See table 2.1.

coffee farms were destroyed by Hurricane San Ciriaco. In the aftermath of the destructive storm and the U.S. invasion and occupation of 1898, capital investment surged into the sugar and tobacco sectors, both having been of secondary importance to the island's economy prior to 1898. Accordingly, in the first decade of the twentieth century population in the coffee regions declined slightly, while population in the tobacco and sugar regions increased significantly. (See table 2.3.) Between 1910 and 1920 the overall percentage population increases in all three regions were similar. However, from 1920 to 1930, when the tobacco sector peaked in importance, both in terms of value and productive output, the population in the tobacco regions grew almost 21 percent, while the population in the sugar regions grew approximately 17 percent. In the coffee zones, population increased by 11 percent. In the eastern highlands, the most important tobacco zone of the two, the population grew by 27 percent during the 1920s. (See table 2.4.) It is clear that people moved to municipalities in the eastern highland regions to take advantage of opportunities presented by expanded markets for tobacco leaf, and they did so at a greater rate than to other areas of the island. Even during the 1930s, when the tobacco sector contracted due to the impact of the Great Depression and the consumer shift from cigars to cigarettes, the population in the

TABLE 2.3

POPULATION BY AGRICULTURAL REGION, 1899–1940

	Tobacco region	Sugar region	Coffee region
1899	386,814	346,310	322,732
1910	462,433	424,890	319,301
1920	555,518	510,913	377,091
1930	671,842	599,535	417,419
1940	798,832	738,904	493,365

Sources: Data for 1899 from Census 1899, 164–169. Data for 1910 from Census 1910, 1208–1224. Data for 1920 from Census 1920, 1208–1214. Data for 1930 from Census 1930, 147–154. Data for 1940 from Census 1940, 31–40.

tobacco regions continued to increase, but at a slower rate than in the sugar cane–growing municipalities.

Changes in the working population also reflected the economic cycles in the agricultural sectors of the island. Ideally, the working population should include those between the ages of fifteen and forty-four. However, age categories in published census reports from 1899 to 1940 prevent such a precise comparison. The working population figures for 1899 and 1920 include those who are ages twenty-one and older. During the 1930s, the working population definition was changed to include those ages twenty and older. Data for 1910 are not available in a comparable age category, so the figures for 1910 have been omitted for tables detailing the working population. In this study, therefore, the working population is defined as adults who are ages twenty and older.

In the tobacco regions, there was an increase of 34.9 percent in the working population between 1899 and 1920, while the working-age population in the sugar regions increased 48.7 percent and in the coffee districts by 24.3 percent. (See table 2.5.) This working-age population increased slightly more in the tobacco regions than in the sugar and coffee zones during the height of tobacco production from 1920 to 1930. As noted in the previous chapter, the tobacco sector experienced radical fluctuations during the 1930s with an overall decline in production. Paralleling this economic instability, growth of the working population in the sugar regions was greater than in tobacco municipalities. Expansion or contraction in the working populations as a response to demand for labor in agricultural regions in different time periods

TABLE 2.4

TOTAL PERCENTAGE CHANGE IN POPULATION AND YEARLY RATE OF
POPULATION GROWTH BY AGRICULTURAL REGION, 1899–1940

	Percentage change	*Yearly rate of growth*
Tobacco Region		
1899–1910	19.5%	1.8%
1910–1920	20.1	1.9
1920–1930	20.9	1.9
1930–1940	18.9	1.8
Sugar Region		
1899–1910	22.7%	2.1
1910–1920	20.2	1.9
1920–1930	17.3	1.6
1930–1940	23.2	2.1
Coffee Region		
1899–1910	−1.1	−0.1%
1910–1920	18.1	1.7
1920–1930	10.7	1.0
1930–1940	18.2	1.7

Sources: See table 2.3.

suggests the facility of labor mobility among regions, as well as knowledge among farmers and agricultural workers about economic conditions throughout the island. When times were tough in tobacco country, for example, people moved to other regions, returning to the tobacco regions when conditions improved.

The conclusion that interregional migration was a family phenomenon in the agricultural regions of the island, regardless of crop, is supported by an analysis of the changes in the working population by sex and in the sex ratio. In the tobacco regions from 1899 to 1920, the male working population grew 39.4 percent while the female working population grew 30.6 percent, with a slight differentiation over the twenty-one-year period. (See table 2.6.) This suggests that during the initial expansion of tobacco as a commercial crop, slightly more men moved to the regions to explore economic opportunities.

TABLE 2.5

WORKING POPULATION BY REGION AND BY SEX, 1899–1940

	Tobacco regions		Sugar regions		Coffee regions	
	MALE	FEMALE	MALE	FEMALE	MALE	FEMALE
1899	86,136	90,449	76,582	81,584	68,305	69,210
1920	120,113	118,160	116,583	118,580	83,894	87,048
1930	149,838	145,415	142,432	142,168	95,552	99,250
1940	189,970	182,765	184,716	183,366	119,899	122,185

Sources: Data for 1899 from *Census 1899*, 164–169, 172–173, 243–245. Data for 1910 from *Census 1910*, 1208–1224. Data for 1920 from *Census 1920*, 1208–1214. Data for 1930 from *Census 1930*, 147–154. Data for 1940 from *Census 1940*, Bulletin No. 2, 31–40.

By way of comparison, over the same time period in the sugar regions, the male working population increased 52.2 percent and the female working population increased 45.3 percent. It was only in the coffee region that the female working population increased at a greater rate, but this was only marginal and reflected a slightly higher rate of out-migration of men from the depressed coffee districts. Between 1920 and 1940, growth of male working populations was slightly higher in relation to females in the tobacco and sugar regions. In the coffee zones, the working population grew evenly between the sexes from 1920 to 1930, although from 1930 to 1940 males increased at a slightly higher overall percentage (25.5 percent) than females of working age (23.1 percent).

The sex ratio for the tobacco regions in 1899 was 96 (96 males for every 100 females), compared to 95 for the sugar region and 99 in the coffee region. (See table 2.7.) By 1920, there were 102 men per 100 women in the tobacco regions and the sex ratio was 98 in the sugar-producing municipalities. In the coffee zones, the corresponding figure was 96. These sex ratios suggest that slightly more men than women moved out of the coffee region into tobacco and sugar municipalities, where employment opportunities were more prevalent because of economic expansion. The increase in the number of men per women continued until 1940 for all three regions. By 1930, there were 103 men per 100 women in tobacco regions; 100 in the sugar region; and there was no change in the coffee region. By 1940, the number of men per 100 women was 104 (tobacco), 101 (sugar), and 98 (coffee).

TABLE 2.6

PERCENTAGE CHANGE IN WORKING POPULATION BY
REGION AND BY SEX, 1899–1940

	Tobacco region			Sugar region			Coffee region		
	MALE	FEMALE	TOTAL	MALE	FEMALE	TOTAL	MALE	FEMALE	TOTAL
1899–1920	39.4%	30.6%	34.9%	52.2%	45.3%	48.7%	22.8%	25.8%	24.3%
1920–1930	24.7	23.1	23.9	22.2	19.9	21.0	13.9	14.0	14.0
1930–1940	26.8	25.7	26.2	29.7	29.0	29.3	25.5	23.1	24.3

Sources: See table 2.5.

TABLE 2.7

SEX RATIO (MALE TO FEMALE) OF WORKING
POPULATION BY REGION, 1899–1940

	Tobacco region	Sugar region	Coffee region
1899	96	95	99
1920	102	98	96
1930	103	100	96
1940	104	101	98

Sources: See table 2.5.

Although the differences are slight, these data are important because of the insights they provide into the demographic history of Puerto Rico in the early twentieth century, especially with respect to the internal migration of people to and from different economic subregions of the island. According to the extant historiography of Puerto Rico and the sugar narrative paradigm indicated earlier in this study, the influx of American capital into the sugar sector supposedly resulted in the migration of large numbers of men from depressed mountain regions to the sugar zones in search of employment opportunities in the expanding economy. Yet an examination of the data indicate that the sex ratio in the sugar region was slightly lower than in the tobacco regions and slightly higher than in the coffee regions between 1920

TABLE 2.8

CHILD-TO-WOMAN RATIO BY REGION, 1899–1940

	Tobacco region	Sugar region	Coffee region
1899	1,650	1,424	1,456
1920	1,700	1,454	1,503
1930	1,402	1,177	1,171
1940	1,324	1,169	1,237

Sources: Data for 1899 from *Census 1899*, 164–169, 172–173, 243–245. Data for 1910 from *Census 1910*, 1208–1224. Data for 1920 from *Census 1920*, 1208–1214. Data for 1930 from *Census 1930*, 147–154. Data for 1940 from *Census 1940*, Bulletin No. 2, 31–40.

Note: For 1899 and 1920, the ages for women are 18 to 44. For 1930 and 1940, the ages for women are 15 to 44. Children are those under 10 for all years.

and 1940. If prior interpretations asserting that males left the municipalities of the *cordillera central* were accurate, a distorted sex ratio in favor of working-age males should have been found in the sugar zones of the island. In fact, this was not the case. In 1920, the sex ratio favoring males was highest in the tobacco regions, not in the sugar-producing zones.

Fairly similar sex ratios were found in the major agricultural regions of the island in the first four decades of the twentieth century. The largest differentiation was found in 1930 between tobacco (103) and coffee regions (96). There were also comparable yearly rates of increase in the working population of both sexes, and although there were differences among regions and between decades, the working population of both sexes grew at similar rates between 1899 and 1940. These data do not imply that men did not migrate from one zone to another in search of employment. Instead, they suggest that families migrated from one region to another more often than men alone.

An examination of the child-to-woman ratio, which is the number of children (under ten years of age) per 1,000 women (between the ages of fifteen and forty-four), provides further evidence of the predominance of families in all of the agricultural regions. (See table 2.8.) The tobacco regions had the highest number of children in relation to women of childbearing age from 1899 to 1940, which suggests that more families migrated to tobacco regions than to sugar and coffee regions. The lower child/woman ratio in the sugar region, together with the higher rates of growth among the male working population, suggests that there were indeed men who were moving alone in search of work. However, the differences between the sugar and coffee regions are not very dramatic in the context of the sugar society that has been described in the prevailing literature.

Population changes in the tobacco regions from 1899 to 1940 reflected the economic processes occurring in the tobacco sector of Puerto Rico. As the tobacco sector expanded, with increased importance for commercial exports, the population grew as well. When the tobacco sector contracted due to market pressures both on the island and in the United States, population growth slowed.

INCOME AND EXPENSES ON TOBACCO FARMS

Tobacco cultivation remained a viable economic endeavor from 1910 until 1940 for farmers with plots of all sizes, even with the overall decline in the tobacco sector from 1930 to 1940. Tobacco farmers earned most of their cash income from the sale of tobacco, although they cultivated subsistence crops as well. Since land was only dedicated to tobacco for part of the year, the tobacco crop was usually followed by the planting of corn, green beans, rice, and sweet potatoes.[4] Some of these crops were sold on local markets, but most were used for family consumption. An examination of the income and expenses of the average tobacco farm between 1936 and 1938 illustrates how, by combining cash earnings from tobacco sales and the sale or consumption of food crops, families in the tobacco regions lived better than their counterparts in the sugar and coffee regions, even though families in the tobacco regions often earned less cash income than families in the other economic zones.

The average weekly income for families living in the tobacco regions for 1936 was $8.60, lower than the $10.07 for families in coffee regions, and much lower than the weekly income of $16.20 for families in sugar regions.[5] The average annual income in 1936 for tobacco farms was $421.59, slightly lower than the annual income in coffee farms of $426.92 but significantly lower than the income of sugar farms at $804.94 for the year. (See table 2.9.) To make ends meet, families in all agricultural regions earned income from many sources. Because all regions had job opportunities for day laborers, many family members, including women and children, would work off of the farms that were their principal residences during their particular slow seasons. Wages as a source of family income were most important in the sugar regions where pay rates were generally higher than in tobacco and coffee zones. However, it is clear that wages were not an important source of income for

TABLE 2.9

AVERAGE ANNUAL INCOME OF FAMILIES BY
SOURCE AND BY TYPE OF FARM, 1936

| Type of farm | Annual income per family | Source of income | | | |
		WAGES	PRODUCTS CONSUMED	PRODUCTS SOLD	OTHER INCOME
Tobacco	$421.59	$51.86	$100.76	$222.96	$46.01
Sugar	804.94	112.00	105.70	491.99	95.25
Coffee	426.92	32.41	73.84	198.05	122.62

Source: Manuel A. Pérez, *Living Conditions among Small Farmers in Puerto Rico*,
Research Bulletin on Agriculture and Livestock, Bulletin No. 2 (San Juan, PR:
Bureau of Supplies, Printing, and Transportation, 1942), 13, 52.

farm owners in any of the agricultural regions, since they derived the greatest
benefits from land cultivation and sale of their products.

Families also earned income from other sources, such as land or animal
rentals, and these were most important in the coffee regions. (See figure 2.1.)
Sugar farms made more cash income from the sale of agricultural products
(which included sugar, secondary crops, wood and coal, and animal products)
than tobacco and coffee farms.[6] However, to determine the actual benefit of
agricultural products to a particular farm or sector, the income from the cash
sales must be added to the income derived from the consumption of home-
grown products. A slightly higher percentage (77 percent) of the annual income
earned by families on tobacco farms was derived from agricultural products,
both sold and consumed, compared to sugar farms (74 percent), although this
was significantly greater than the 64 percent found on coffee farms.

Cultivation expenses determined net profits or losses for small farms in
each of the agricultural regions of the island. Roberto Huyke and Ramón
Colón Torres, officials of Puerto Rico's Agricultural Experimental Station,
conducted the first detailed study of the cost of tobacco cultivation during
the 1937–1938 crop year. For this study, accounting books were distributed
among farmers in the tobacco-growing municipalities of Caguas, San
Lorenzo, Aguas Buenas, Cidra, Cayey, Comerío, Aibonito, and Barranquitas
in the eastern highlands, and Orocovis in the western highlands.[7] The greatest expense for tobacco farms was labor, especially for the owners of larger
farms that could not meet their labor needs with family or extended family

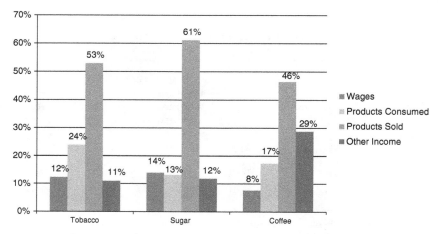

FIGURE 2.1 Percentage of Average Annual Income of Families by Source and by Type of Farm, 1936.

members. (See table 2.10.) Fertilizer expenses were significant, as tobacco needed constant fertilizing throughout the cultivation season to ensure that the leaf would be of good quality. Once all of the expenses were added and deducted from the total income of the farm, these tobacco growers reported a net loss of $22 per cuerda of tobacco. However, the average value of the farm products consumed by the tobacco farmer and his family for that same year was $315, and these included milk, eggs, meat, and minor crops.[8] To determine the total benefit reaped by tobacco farmers from their land, the value of the farm products consumed by the family must be added to the total cash income from the sale of produce, in which case the tobacco farmer generated a yearly net income of $292.96, according to these data.

The distribution of expenses on farms was similar in all of the agricultural regions in Puerto Rico. Food was the largest expense for all families, even with the benefits derived from subsistence crops. (See table 2.11.) Families in tobacco regions had the highest food expenses of all agricultural regions, and families in sugar regions had the lowest. This was due, in part, to higher transportation costs incurred by food distributors in the mountainous regions where tobacco was cultivated. Infrastructural development was much more advanced in the sugar zones since the level of sucrose of recently cut sugar cane dropped in proportion to the length of time it took to press the cane from the time it was cut. Therefore, well-constructed roads were of extraordinary importance in the sugar regions to ensure the maximum yield of refined sugar from the sugar cane.[9] Additionally, sugar producers needed

TABLE 2.10

AVERAGE CULTIVATION INCOME AND EXPENSES ON
TOBACCO FARMS, 1937–1938

Description	Cost per cuerda	Cost per quintal
Expenses	$116.05	$12.95
Labor	64.44	7.19
Fertilizer	15.58	1.74
Rent of curing ranch	9.76	1.09
Purchase of seedlings	7.04	
Insecticides	3.69	
Animal rental	6.74	0.75
Rent of farm	3.30	
String for curing	4.75	0.19
Other	3.79	0.42
Income	94.01	10.49
Net loss	(22.04)	(2.46)

Source: Roberto Huyke and R. Colón Torres, "Costo de producción de tabaco en Puerto Rico, 1937–38," Boletín de la Estación Experimental Agrícola 56 (1940): 10–11.

well-built all-weather roads to move bulky sugar from mills to ports. Tobacco leaf did not need to be quickly transported to cigar factories, since the quality of the leaf would not be affected by delays in transportation. Thus, because of higher internal transportation costs, food prices in the tobacco regions were higher than in the sugar regions, making the dollar benefit of food grown for subsistence on tobacco farms greater than on sugar farms.

The income and expenses of farmers who cultivated tobacco, compared to those in sugar and coffee farms, demonstrate that although overall earnings from the sale of tobacco leaf were lower than from the sale of sugar or coffee, tobacco farmers derived other benefits from their farms, such as secondary agricultural products to sell and food for family consumption as noted previously. Cultivation expenses were lowest in the tobacco sector, accounting for 10 percent of total expenses, compared to 14 percent for sugar farms and 13.4 percent for coffee farms. Lower cultivation expenses, combined with greater overall farm benefits, allowed tobacco cultivation to remain economically viable between 1910 and 1940 despite the decline of the tobacco sector after 1930.

TABLE 2.11

DISTRIBUTION OF EXPENSES BY TYPE OF FARM, 1937

	Tobacco	Sugar	Coffee
Food	55.3%	42.1%	50.0%
Farm operation expenses	10.4	14.0	13.4
Clothes	9.9	7.7	8.7
Health	7.1	5.9	5.5
Recreation and transportation	7.0	6.7	7.5
Payment of debts	4.3	10.2	6.0
Miscellaneous	3.1	4.3	4.7
Purchase of property	1.6	5.5	1.6
Taxes	0.8	1.4	1.3
Help to relatives	0.5	2.2	1.3
Total expenses	100	100	100

Source: Pérez, Living Conditions, 57.

Number of Farms and Land Use

From 1910 to 1940, the tobacco regions had the greatest number of farms of the three main agricultural zones. Before analyzing the changes in the number of farms, however, a brief explanation of the census figures for 1920 is necessary. The number of farms in the 1920 census is dramatically lower in all agricultural regions compared to the 1910 and 1930 figures. These radical fluctuations between census years suggest that there may be methodological inconsistencies in the enumerators' instructions on how to count farms. These inconsistencies compromise the validity of the number of farms counted in the 1920 census, and therefore, any comparison between 1920 and either 1910 or 1930 would be suspect. There are other indicators that the number of farms may have been undercounted in 1920. First, a calculation of the yearly rate of growth in the number of farms per region shows the same dramatic fluctuations. From 1899 to 1910, the yearly rate of growth in the number of farms for tobacco regions is 4.3 percent. From 1910 to 1920, there is a yearly rate of decrease of 2.8 percent, and then from 1920 to 1930 there is a 3.1 percent increase annually. It is unlikely that the number of farms would have increased, then decreased, then increased again so dramatically. If the figures

TABLE 2.12

NUMBER OF FARMS BY REGION, 1910–1940

	Tobacco region	Sugar region	Coffee region
1910	26,736	19,656	15,039
1920	20,101	13,238	11,243
1930	27,242	14,477	14,611
1940	30,104	13,650	15,820

Sources: Data for 1910 from *Agriculture Census 1910*, 66–71. Data for 1920 from *Agriculture Census 1920*, 392–399. Data for 1930 from *Census 1930*, 212–215. Data for 1940 from *Agriculture Census 1940*, 36–37.

for 1920 are eliminated and the yearly rate of growth is calculated between 1899 and 1930, it is a more reasonable (but still significant) 1.6 percent per year.

Second, inexplicable and dramatic fluctuations are found in the percentage change in the number of farms per size. In the tobacco regions, for example, according to census data the number of farms under 10 cuerdas decreased by 44 percent from 1910 to 1920, followed by an increase of 83 percent from 1920 to 1930. Again, it is unlikely that such variations would occur. A comparison between 1910 and 1930 demonstrates an increase of 2.8 percent in the number of farms in the tobacco regions under 10 cuerdas. Although the figures for 1920 appear to be unreliable, they will be included in the data tables for comparison purposes among regions in that year. The changes between 1910 and 1920 will not be discussed. Instead, 1910 and 1930 will be used as comparative years.

The number of farms in the tobacco regions increased from 26,736 in 1910 to 27,242 in 1930 and then to 30,104 in 1940. (See table 2.12.) In comparison, the number of farms in the sugar region decreased between 1910 and 1930 from 19,656 to 14,477, a decrease of 26.3 percent, and decreased yet again to 13,650 in 1940, a fall of 5.7 percent. The number of farms in the coffee regions decreased from 15,039 in 1910 to 14,611 in 1930 (a 2.8 percent decline), but increased by 8 percent to 15,820 in 1940. From 1910 to 1940, the number of tobacco farms increased by 12.6 percent, while the number of sugar farms decreased 30.6 percent. There was a slight increase of 5.2 percent in the number of farms in the coffee region over the same period. It is clear that farms were more readily available in tobacco regions than in the other regions, and that farmers were taking advantage of that opportunity, a conclusion supported by the increase in population in the tobacco regions.

The increase in the number of farms in the tobacco regions between 1920 and 1930 was caused by the overall expansion of tobacco production during the 1920s. Additionally, the number of tobacco farms continued to increase from 1930 to 1940, even as the tobacco sector contracted. One explanation for this increase may be that farmers took advantage of U.S. government–sponsored programs developed under the Agricultural Adjustment Administration that provided benefit payments for tobacco growers, thereby guaranteeing a minimum income regardless of market conditions.

Another factor that may be used to explain the increase in the number of tobacco farms during the 1930s was the expanded credit availability for the cultivation of tobacco, together with the organization of agricultural cooperative associations in the tobacco regions. Finally, the nature of tobacco cultivation, with its low land requirements and need for little capital investment, made tobacco farming more economically viable than the production of sugar cane, which required much more land to turn a profit, or a newly established coffee farm, which had a five-year minimum initial gestation period until seedlings would mature and become significant producing coffee bushes.

Land use in tobacco farms was more diversified than on sugar and coffee farms. After a decade of rapid expansion in the tobacco sector during the 1920s, the census figures for 1930 indicate that less than 10 percent of all improved farmland in the tobacco regions was planted in tobacco, although there were significant differences between municipalities. For example, farmers in Aibonito, a municipality in the eastern highlands, dedicated over 30 percent of their land to tobacco, while those in Orocovis, a nearby municipality in the western highlands, only dedicated 7.7 percent to tobacco. These differences may have been related to the extent of arable land found on each district's farms. In the sugar and coffee regions, the percentage of land dedicated to each main cash crop was much higher in comparative perspective for 1930. Almost 38 percent of all improved land was dedicated to the planting of coffee in the coffee regions and 28.4 percent to sugar in the sugar regions.[10]

Diversification of land use meant that tobacco farmers could use their land in more productive ways than those farmers in sugar or coffee lands. First, tobacco provided cash income from smaller parcels of land than was the case on sugar or coffee farms, an obvious benefit for farmers with small parcels of land or for those with limited resources. Second, because small extensions of land were planted in tobacco, more land could be dedicated to secondary crops, such as plantains, which could be consumed by the family or sold on local markets. Finally, greater land availability on tobacco farms permitted the raising of cattle, pigs, goats, or chickens, which provided eggs, dairy products, and meat for family consumption.

LAND TENURE

Writing on the particular characteristics of tobacco farms across the highland region and the projected future of the tobacco sector after 1940, one observer noted that "the geographical location [of tobacco farms], together with the prevalence of many small farms, make the consolidation into large estates difficult, if not impossible." He also wrote that there was "practically no absentee ownership in the agricultural phase of the tobacco industry."[11] This meant that unlike in the dominant sugar sector, the cultivation of tobacco remained almost entirely in Puerto Rican hands during the early twentieth century, an especially significant conclusion in light of the level of political involvement of tobacco growers throughout this time period.

The tobacco regions had the greatest number of farms operated by owners of all three major agricultural regions for 1910 and 1930. In 1910, owners operated 20,906 farms in the tobacco regions, and in 1930 this figure rose to 21,968, an increase of 5.1 percent. The number of owner-operated farms decreased in the sugar region from 16,137 in 1910 to 11,893 in 1930, a decrease of 26.3 percent. In the coffee regions, the number of farms fell by 5.5 percent from 12,472 in 1910 to 11,782 in 1930. (See table 2.13.) Additionally, a higher percentage of the total land in farms was owner-operated in the tobacco regions than in the sugar or coffee regions from 1910 to 1930, although all three regions experienced a decrease from 1910 to 1930. In 1910, in the tobacco regions, 72.8 percent of the total land in farms was operated by owners, although the comparable figure decreased to 68.9 percent in 1930. In the sugar regions, the percentage of the land in farms that were owner-operated decreased from 65.6 percent in 1910 to 44.1 percent in 1930, and in the coffee regions from 70.4 percent in 1910 to 56.6 percent in 1930.

The increase in the number of farms operated by owners in the tobacco regions suggests a pattern of land fragmentation occurring between 1910 and 1930, the period when the tobacco sector was rapidly expanding. This conclusion is supported by the increase in the number of small farms in the tobacco regions. Between 1910 and 1930, the number of farms under 9 cuerdas in the tobacco regions increased from 12,979 to 13,337, a modest overall rise of 2.8 percent. (See table 2.14.) This is striking, however, when compared to the decrease in farms under 9 cuerdas in the sugar (39 percent) and coffee (12.7 percent) regions. During this same time, the number of farms in the tobacco regions between 10 and 19 cuerdas increased significantly by 24 percent, compared with a slight decrease of 0.8 percent in the sugar regions and an increase of 16 percent in the coffee regions. It is clear that in the tobacco regions there were greater relative opportunities for participation in the

TABLE 2.13

NUMBER AND PERCENTAGE OF FARMS, AND PERCENTAGE OF LAND OPERATED
BY OWNERS AND MANAGERS BY REGION, 1910–1940

	Number and percentage of farms					
	OWNERS		MANAGERS		PERCENTAGE OF LAND	
	NUMBER	PERCENTAGE	NUMBER	PERCENTAGE	OWNERS	MANAGERS
Tobacco Region						
1910	20,906	78.2%	522	2.0%	72.8%	13.2%
1920	17,716	88.1	580	2.9	79.3	10.1
1930	21,968	80.6	1,222	4.5	68.9	22.3
1940	22,474	74.7	432	1.4	64.9	19.3
Sugar Region						
1910	16,137	82.1%	554	2.8%	65.6%	25.2%
1920	11,606	87.7	496	3.7	69.7	19.8
1930	11,893	82.2	1,350	9.3	44.1	48.5
1940	10,916	80.0	441	3.2	46.5	42.9
Coffee Region						
1910	12,472	82.9%	312	2.1%	70.4%	20.8%
1920	9,844	87.6	418	3.7	79.1	15.6
1930	11,782	80.6	1,470	10.1	56.6	37.8
1940	13,030	82.4	562	3.6	59.9	30.8

Sources: Data for 1910 from *Agriculture Census 1910*, 66–71. Data for 1920 from *Agriculture Census 1920*, 392–399. Data for 1930 from *Census 1930*, 210–213. Data for 1940 from *Agriculture Census 1940*, 36–37.

sector as independent producers than in sugar or coffee regions, despite the proliferation of the *colonato* (independent sugar farmers) in the sugar-producing zones of the island during the first decades of the twentieth century.[12]

A small number of manager-operated farms were found in all agricultural districts, although there were significant differences in the percentage of land

TABLE 2.14

NUMBER OF FARMS BY SIZE (IN CUERDAS) AND PERCENTAGE CHANGE
IN REGIONS, 1910–1930

	Number of farms, 1910	Number of farms, 1930	Percentage change, 1910–1930
Tobacco Region			
9 and under	12,979	13,337	2.8%
10 to 19	4,793	5,954	24.2
20 to 49	4,609	4,791	3.9
50 to 99	1,969	1,760	−10.6
100 to 174	878	770	−12.3
175 to 499	683	502	−26.5
500 and over	195	128	−34.4
Sugar Region			
9 and under	11,754	7,167	−39.0%
10 to 19	3,023	3,000	−0.8
20 to 49	2,508	2,313	−7.8
50 to 99	1,100	977	−11.2
100 to 174	508	434	−14.6
175 to 499	519	417	−19.7
500 and over	244	169	−30.7
Coffee Region			
9 and under	8,045	7,020	−12.7%
10 to 19	2,520	2,941	16.7
20 to 49	2,276	2,417	6.2
50 to 99	1,015	1,016	0.1
100 to 174	510	563	10.4
175 to 499	518	542	4.6
500 and over	155	112	−27.7

Sources: Data for 1910 from *Agriculture Census 1910*, 60–65. Data for 1930 from *Census 1930*, 216–219.

in farms that they operated in each region. The percentage of land in farms that were manager-operated in 1910 in the tobacco regions was 13.2 percent, compared to 25.2 percent in the sugar region and 20.8 percent in the coffee regions. By 1930, the percentage of land in farms operated by managers had increased to 22.3 percent in the tobacco regions, to 48.5 percent in the sugar region, and to 37.8 percent in the coffee region. (See table 2.14.) Farms that were operated by managers in the tobacco regions were owned either by established, prosperous landowners (U.S. residents and citizens, or Puerto Ricans), or to a lesser extent, by tobacco manufacturing corporations. The lower percentages of land in farms that were manager-operated between 1910 and 1930 in the tobacco regions, suggest that larger farms were not as prevalent in the overall land tenure structure of the region as they were in the sugar or coffee regions.

There were two types of tenants in the tobacco economy. Most tenants were farmers who were hired by owners of larger farms to cultivate part of the land they owned in sharecropping arrangements. Under these agreements the owner contributed seed, animals, and a curing barn (if there was one on the property), and they assumed one-half of the expenses for fertilizers, insecticides, bundling cord, and any other materials. The tenant contributed all of the labor and the remaining half of production expenses. In return, the tenant received one-half of the crop.[13]

A smaller number of "tenants" were those farmers who had entered into a *venta con compacto de retroventa* (a theoretical sale with right to buy back the land), also called *hipoteca, refacción, y arrendamiento* (mortgage, cultivation loan, and lease) in legal documents. This was not really a land sale but a credit arrangement whereby a farmer transferred the title of land as a guarantee in return for seasonal operating capital. When the farmer paid back the loan, the title was transferred back to him. These "tenants" were usually responsible for the entire cost of cultivation, but the entire crop after harvest was theirs to sell. Thus, although they theoretically were tenants cultivating land owned by someone else, in reality they were farming land that they considered to be their own. This credit system was the continuation of an institution for securing and guaranteeing loans that was already widespread during the nineteenth century.

The percentage of tenant-operated farms was higher in the tobacco regions than in the sugar or coffee regions in both 1910 and 1930. (See table 2.15.) In 1910, 19.9 percent of all farms in the tobacco regions were tenant-operated, compared to 15 percent in both the sugar and coffee regions. By 1930, the percentage of farms that were tenant-operated had decreased to 14.9 percent in tobacco regions, 8.5 percent in sugar regions, and 9.3 percent in the coffee

TABLE 2.15

FARMS OPERATED BY TENANTS BY REGION, 1910–1940

	Number of farms	Percentage of farms	Percentage of land
Tobacco Regions			
1910	5,308	19.9%	14.0%
1920	1,805	9.0	10.6
1930	4,052	14.9	8.8
1940	7,198	23.9	15.9
Sugar Region			
1910	2,965	15.1%	9.2%
1920	1,136	8.6	10.5
1930	1,234	8.5	7.3
1940	2,293	16.8	10.6
Coffee Region			
1910	2,255	15.0%	8.8%
1920	981	8.7	5.4
1930	1,359	9.3	5.5
1940	2,228	14.1	9.3

Sources: Data for 1910 from Agriculture Census 1910, 66–71. Data for 1920 from Agriculture Census 1920, 392–399. Data for 1930 from Census 1930, 210–213. Data for 1940 from Agriculture Census 1940, 36–37.

region. The percentage of the land in farms operated by tenants was also higher in tobacco regions than in sugar and coffee regions from 1910 to 1930. In tobacco regions, 14 percent of the land in farms was operated by tenants, compared to 9.2 percent in sugar regions and 8.8 percent in coffee regions. By 1930, the percentage of tenant-operated land in farms had decreased to 8.8 percent in tobacco regions, 7.3 percent in the sugar regions, and 5.5 percent in the coffee region. The larger percentage of tenant-operated farms in the tobacco regions indicates that as the tobacco sector expanded from 1910 to 1930, the relative opportunities for participation in the sector for farmers who were unable to purchase land remained more open than in sugar and coffee regions.

A discussion of land use and ownership must include a consideration of the role of those agricultural laborers who owned no land of their own. Agricultural laborers were different from tenants because tenants usually had contracts stipulating the use of a parcel of land. Although tenants were landless in that they did not own the land that was farmed, they had the right of commercial cultivation. Yet agricultural laborers were sometimes permitted to "plant a small area in food crops for home use" by their employers, thus reaping nonwage benefits for their labor.[14] Tenants were also responsible for some type of payment for usufruct rights over land, either in cash or kind rent, or by providing a portion of expenses for cultivation. Agricultural laborers, in most cases, "do not pay rent since they usually live [as squatters] in houses built by themselves on somebody else's land, or in houses provided free by the landowners [who hired them]."[15] These men, women, and sometimes children who were hired seasonally were paid daily wages. A study conducted by the Department of Labor in 1936 noted "the busy season of the tobacco and cane plantations lasts for about six months, and that of the coffee farms for about three months. Coffee workers go to the sugar and tobacco regions and tobacco workers go to the cane regions after the busy season in their own district is over. Tobacco and cane laborers also go to the coffee regions to work during the picking season."[16]

As expected, the number of agricultural laborers found working in each of the major agricultural sectors varied according to the expansion or contraction of each sector. For the cultivation of tobacco and coffee, there was a constant increase in the number of workers employed between 1910 and 1930, then a sharp drop from 1930 to 1940. (See table 2.16.)[17] Tobacco and coffee both declined in importance throughout the 1930s, and accordingly the loss of employment for agricultural workers in the cultivation of these crops is not surprising. Sugar remained an employment alternative for wage laborers, and some tobacco and coffee workers surely migrated to sugar areas in search of employment. The number of sugar laborers increased continuously from 1910 until 1940, even during the crisis years of the Great Depression.[18]

Of the three major agricultural regions, tobacco regions had the lowest number of agricultural laborers, as well as the lowest percentage of families that owned no land, between 1910 and 1940. (See table 2.17.)[19] The sugar region, in contrast, had the most laborers and the highest percentage of landless families. The percentage of landless families in the tobacco regions increased from 61.5 percent in 1910 to 73.5 percent in 1940, compared with 68.4 percent in 1910 and 85.3 percent in 1940 in the sugar regions.

Two possible factors may have impacted land ownership. First, the data for the tobacco regions suggest that the possibility of becoming a landowner

TABLE 2.16

NUMBER OF AGRICULTURAL LABORERS PER CROP, 1910–1940

	Tobacco	Sugar	Coffee
1910	6,188	76,601	29,720
1920	28,118	79,261	37,776
1930	29,839	84,112	40,088
1940	10,010	111,835	15,334

Sources: Data for 1910 from Bureau of the Census, *Thirteenth Census of the United States Taken in the Year 1910*. Volume 4, *Population 1910, Occupation Statistics* (Washington, DC: Government Printing Office, 1913), 295–300. Data for 1920 from *Fourteenth Census of the United States Taken in the Year 1920*. Volume 4, *Population 1920, Occupations* (Washington, DC: Government Printing Office, 1922), 1288. Data for 1930 and 1940 from Bureau of the Census, *Sixteenth Census of the United States: 1940. Reports for Puerto Rico*. Bulletin No. 3, *Occupations and Other Characteristics by Age* (Washington, DC, 1942), 54–59.

TABLE 2.17

PERCENTAGE OF LANDLESS FAMILIES BY CROP, 1910–1940

	Tobacco regions	Sugar region	Coffee region
1910	61.5%	68.4%	67.5%
1920	75.5	81.0	78.3
1930	70.9	80.7	71.8
1940	73.5	85.3	74.8

Sources: Data for 1910, 1920, and 1930 from *Census 1930*, 124, 132. Data for 1940 from *Census 1940*, Bulletin No. 3, 9, 21–22.

was greater in the highlands than in the sugar regions. Second, the comparatively larger increase in landless families in the sugar regions from 1910 and 1940 may have been the result of families moving from tobacco regions to sugar zones in search of work. In all likelihood, both factors were important. The same phenomenon may be observed when comparing the sugar region to the coffee region, where the percentage of landless families increased from

67.5 percent in 1910 to 74.8 percent in 1940. Although the percentage of land-less families in the sugar regions was comparatively greater than that found in either the tobacco or coffee regions, it is important to note that all three regions had more landless families in 1940 than they did in 1910.

Conclusion

The rural areas of Puerto Rico during the early twentieth century have been discussed by most of the extant historiography as if they were one homoge-nous unit. The arguments made in relation to the development of the sugar sector, such as absentee ownership, displacement of families, and high rates of male migration have been applied to other agricultural sectors without sys-tematic study of each region. In the tobacco sector, the paradigms used to describe the sugar sector were not evident and cannot be applied analytically.

There were similarities, of course, between the tobacco, sugar, and coffee regions, such as rapid population growth, the continued importance of the family unit, the increase in the number of landless families, and the high per-centage of family income spent on food products. But there were also marked differences in social and economic patterns among the three. First, the over-all cash earnings of tobacco farmers were much lower than the earnings of sugar and coffee farmers. This limited the cash wealth that tobacco farmers could potentially accumulate from their activities in comparison with sugar or coffee farmers. Second, cultivation expenses were the lowest in tobacco regions. Thus, farmers in the tobacco regions of Puerto Rico had greater opportunities to participate as independent producers in a booming agricul-tural market than their counterparts in the sugar and coffee regions because of lower start-up costs. Third, in the tobacco regions, landowners (as opposed to managers or tenants) cultivated the greatest share of the crop and were responsible for the largest number of cuerdas under cultivation as compared to the other agricultural sectors. There were more farmers who owned land in tobacco regions in 1940 than in 1910, even after a decade of diminishing returns from tobacco earnings after 1930. All of this suggests that farmers in tobacco regions had greater relative opportunities to eventually own their own land than farmers in sugar or coffee regions.

A crucial factor that must be taken into account when calculating the economic benefits derived by farmers was the amount of food that a family could produce on their farms. Food items were the largest expense for any rural family. This was especially true for families in tobacco regions because the high costs of transportation increased the prices of food, most of which came from other regions of the island. The amount of food a family could produce on their farm lessened the amount of cash that would have to be spent on the purchase of food items. For farmers in tobacco regions, who had the lowest cash earnings of any of the agricultural regions, the availability of land to cultivate subsistence crops was a guarantee that at least a minimum standard of living would be maintained throughout the year.

Because of the nature of tobacco cultivation, with its limited land requirements and lower expenses, farmers and their families were able to live off their land even when the tobacco crop did not turn a profit. It was the importance of the secondary agricultural items produced both for the local market and for family consumption, in addition to the cash-earning potential of tobacco, that made tobacco farming such an attractive economic alternative for the thousands of farmers in the eastern and western highland regions of Puerto Rico.

CHAPTER 3

Politics

TOBACCO GROWERS AND AGRICULTURAL ORGANIZATIONS

The Association has not made, nor will it make, political commitments to any great party, nor will it impose on any of its associates any political credo; but it will ally its resources with those parties that carry our associates in their party tickets . . . with the primary objective of seeking the well-being of our agriculture and, by extension, of our country. [Our members will] freely disavow political allegiances when incompatible with the health and prosperity of our agricultural class.

—Resolution approved in the General Assembly of the Asociación de Agricultores Puertorriqueños, 1928

The expansion of tobacco cultivation that transformed many of the highland regions of Puerto Rico also provided an arena for Puerto Rican tobacco growers to negotiate three discrete areas of imperial control discussed in detail in this second group of chapters. The first and most important was access to the political structures that could effect changes for the local population. Through their affiliation with the Asociación de Agricultores Puertorriqueños (AAP), tobacco growers became a political force, securing access to the highest levels of the administration on both the island and the mainland. The second, and a direct consequence of the first, was the demand for adjustments in federal legislation that would be beneficial to those in the island's primary economic sector, agriculture. Finally, to support the continued expansion of agriculture and to improve living conditions on the island, Puerto Ricans secured the legislation and financial allocations that permitted the constant transfer of technology as well as scientific experimentation and education.

Tobacco farmers systematically became involved in democratic organizations in an attempt to exert control over their economic interests and to improve their social, economic, and political positions. The right of free association, demanded by Puerto Ricans and guaranteed by the new U.S. colonial state, allowed Puerto Rican farmers to join the insular AAP as well as local agricultural societies. This chapter discusses the participation of tobacco growers in protests, political campaigns, and lobbying efforts in Washington and San Juan to demand fair prices for their product, economic incentives, and social programs. In return, insular and federal officials responded to such pressure by altering legislation, providing economic relief, and including Puerto Ricans in their decision-making. Tobacco growers' participation in, and negotiation with, all levels of the insular and federal governments demonstrate that, rather than being victims or passive observers, they were collaborators and activists who struggled to shape their own lives.

THE *LIGAS AGRÍCOLAS* AND COOPERATIVE SOCIETIES

Ligas agrícolas, local agricultural societies that served as the farmers' advocates to government officials, existed during the Spanish administration of the island. After the U.S. occupation, however, and especially after Puerto Ricans were granted U.S. citizenship in 1917, the number of tobacco growers that became affiliated with ligas agrícolas increased rapidly. The insular government encouraged such affiliation, and the establishment of ligas agrícolas in every municipality became official agricultural policy. In fact, Manuel Camuñas, the first commissioner of the Department of Agriculture and Labor, argued that ligas agrícolas should be considered an important element of agricultural modernization. "Rural organization," he wrote in his 1917 annual report, "should be a preferred object of the law and should cover the needs of country life, in order to make agricultural pursuits agreeable, beneficial, and profitable." The state's cooperation in the establishment of agricultural societies was "the best means to carry out the social and economical purposes of rural organization."[1] Additionally, Camuñas hoped that once farmers were affiliated with ligas agrícolas, they could be persuaded to create cooperative societies to take advantage of cultivation credit made available through the recently enacted Federal Farm Loan Act of 1916. Although the act was not extended to Puerto Rico at this time, lobbying efforts in Washington were already under way and Puerto Rican farmers, insular legislators, and agricultural administrators expected the extension to be approved. The strategy, therefore, was to establish the infrastructure demanded by the Federal Farm Loan Act on the island so that when the act was ultimately extended, farmers would benefit immediately.

As expected, the tobacco growers who initially became intensely involved in the ligas agrícolas were those who had already been active prior to the U.S. invasion of 1898. These growers tended to be owners of large parcels of land, who would often rent part of their land for others to farm or hire managers to operate their farms. The Solá brothers, tobacco growers and businessmen from Caguas, are a good example. Marcelino and Modesto Solá owned large tobacco farms and several businesses under the moniker Solá Hermanos. In 1876, Solá Hermanos founded a commercial-agricultural society to make loans to smaller growers and to find good markets for tobacco. The brothers and their descendants appear in the membership rosters of the liga agrícola in Caguas. They also participated in the establishment of the agricultural experiment station in Caguas and the founding of the AAP, and were active in town politics.[2] In his work on tobacco growers, Juan José Baldrich convincingly argued that the great landowners became involved in agricultural societies because they were the most threatened by the influx of American capital. This may be true for men such as José L. Pesquera, Agustín Fernández, and Tomás Rodríguez, large-scale tobacco growers who were early members of the AAP. Pesquera and Fernández later served as presidents of the Comisión para proteger el tabaco de Puerto Rico, an institute dedicated to the well-being of the tobacco industry.[3] Regardless of their initial motivation for involvement, it is clear that these men, and many others like them, were crucial to the establishment of and the continued efforts at organizing the agricultural associations.

The challenge to the agricultural administrators of the insular government and to the landowners who were already involved was how to incorporate the growing number of tobacco farmers. These farmers were generally owners of small parcels of land, had little technical knowledge of scientific cultivation methods, and were skeptical of the benefits of affiliation. A review of official government and agricultural publications suggests that agricultural agents constantly struggled with selling the idea of cooperation to the farmers. Agricultural officials reported that the "mission of organizing the country encountered at first distrust and apathy" and a "lack of earnestness in farmers due to discouragement caused by economic crisis."[4] To facilitate the process of organization, and to help combat this "lack of earnestness" among small-scale tobacco farmers, the Bureau of Agriculture within the Department of Agriculture and Labor assigned an agronomist and a deputy inspector to each agricultural district. These agents were charged with, among other duties, promoting involvement in the ligas agrícolas and encouraging the establishment of cooperative societies for the purchase of all cultivation materials, for the sale of their farm products, and for the securing of credit.[5] The agricultural agents worked closely with those farmers who were already members of ligas agrícolas to visit unaffiliated farmers and present public lectures on the benefits of affiliation. Simply stated, by 1917 the agents and the active farmers began a publicity campaign to create ligas agrícolas throughout the island.

The campaign was boosted by rapidly changing economic conditions. After the First World War, when the market for tobacco expanded, supply could not meet demand. By 1920, prices paid to farmers for tobacco reached 52 cents per pound (up from 30 cents per pound in 1919), the highest it would ever be.[6] These high prices accelerated investment in tobacco planting, and supply increased so rapidly in Puerto Rico that the market could not absorb the additional product. Just a year later, prices plummeted to a little over 18 cents per pound.[7] Tobacco farmers held on to their product with the hope that shortages would once again lead to increased prices. However, tobacco buyers circumvented Puerto Rican growers and obtained the tobacco they needed from Cuban growers. This created an economic crisis for most Puerto Rican tobacco farmers, who were unable to repay the cultivation loans they had secured and which were guaranteed against their harvest. The crisis, together with the possibility that buyers could manipulate prices by bringing in tobacco from other islands, was the incentive growers needed to become involved and join agricultural leagues. So many farmers had dedicated land to tobacco that it was no longer the owners of larger tobacco farms who were interested in affiliation.[8] Thirty-six ligas agrícolas were established between 1919 and 1920. Almost 60 percent of the ligas and almost half of all members were in tobacco-growing municipalities. (See table 3.1.)

Involvement in ligas agrícolas paved the way after 1920 for the establishment of cooperative societies, membership-based organizations that operated as marketing agencies for tobacco.[9] The cooperative associations would handle the storage, delivery, and management of the crop until its sale. All of the members' tobacco would then be marketed and sold in bulk.

The first attempt at establishing a cooperative association occurred in 1920 when members of the ligas agrícolas in Comerío, Jayuya, Caguas, and San Lorenzo decided to combine their product and sell it directly to the market. Although the cooperative secured prices that were higher than those paid to unaffiliated growers in those municipalities, the prices were lower than expected due to the tactics of the Puerto Rican Leaf Tobacco Company (PRLTC), the largest manufacturer in the island and a subsidiary of the American Tobacco Company.[10] Instead of purchasing all the available stock in Puerto Rico, the PRLTC buyers purchased only a part of it, acquiring the rest from tobacco growers in Cuba. Cuban tobacco paid a low tariff when imported to Puerto Rico, so tobacco buyers could do all the processing in Puerto Rico and then export the finished product to the United States.

TABLE 3.1

AGRICULTURAL LEAGUES IN TOBACCO
REGIONS, 1920

Municipality	Founding date	Members
Aguas Buenas	March 28, 1920	84
Aibonito	January 11, 1920	80
Arecibo	January 25, 1920	355
Barceloneta	March 7, 1920	61
Barranquitas	January 25, 1920	40
Bayamón	September 11, 1919	45
Caguas	January 18, 1920	250
Camuy	April 4, 1920	27
Ciales	March 17, 1920	54
Comerío	March 9, 1919	50
Corozal	March 2, 1920	58
Hatillo	March 21, 1920	45
Isabela	April 5, 1920	38
Jayuya	November 29, 1919	200
Juncos	March 7, 1920	100
Morovis	March 7, 1920	15
Orocovis (Barros)	January 18, 1920	110
Quebradillas	May 8, 1920	66
San Lorenzo	February 29, 1920	203
Utuado	October 11, 1919	315
Yabucoa	May 23, 1920	67
Total in Puerto Rico (36)		4,245
Total in tobacco regions (21)		2,101
Percentage of members in tobacco regions		49.5%

Source: Governor 1920, 522.

Because the tobacco product would be coming from Puerto Rico, instead of Cuba, it would be tariff-free when it entered the United States. To prevent recurring low prices due to Cuban imports, the tobacco growers of the Liga Agrícola de San Lorenzo and the Liga Agrícola de Comerío joined another early cooperative in Cayey, the Asociación de Cosecheros de Tabaco de Puerto Rico, and sent representatives to Washington in support of a bill that would raise the tariff of tobacco imported to Puerto Rico to 35 cents a pound.[11] A higher tariff would mean that tobacco buyers would no longer find it profitable to go to alternative sources and would pay fair prices for Puerto Rican tobacco. When the bill was later ratified, it became known as the *ley de sellos* because, in addition to the tariff increase, it also demanded that each exporter and manufacturer use a stamp on the package to indicate the percentage of native and foreign tobacco in a cigar.[12]

The success of these growers in securing higher prices and the ley de sellos, together with a campaign led by the newly established AAP, an island-wide farmers' association, created excitement among the farmers for affiliation into cooperative societies, including tobacco banks, purchasing cooperatives, and marketing associations. In addition, the Federal Farm Loan Act was extended to the island in 1921 and cooperatives were now able to apply for cultivation loans from a Federal Land Bank. Farmers needed credit to run their farms, regardless of the size of the operation. Tobacco growers, like other farmers in Puerto Rico, would get a *contrato de refacción* from a lender. This agricultural contract advanced a determined sum of money at a particular interest rate based on the expected sale price after the harvest. Because prices paid to the farmer were fixed in the contract and were irrespective of real market prices at harvest time, many farmers found themselves either in debt after the harvest was sold or unable to begin the following year's cultivation without another loan. Supporters of cooperatives argued that if tobacco farmers were to set up cooperative banks, then they would have greater control over their finances. With the extension of the Federal Land Act to Puerto Rico, tobacco banks, as these cooperatives were called, could secure loans from a Federal Land Bank and then lend to individual farmers at lower interest rates than the ones offered by speculators and companies. As a result, the number of tobacco growers affiliated with cooperatives dramatically increased after 1921.

Tabacaleros de Comerío, Inc. was organized on August 15, 1925, with $10,260 in capital and fifty-seven shareholders.[13] The cooperative held 2,954 quintales of tobacco valued at $126,736.85. A year later, it recorded a profit of $1,591.41, a return of over 15 percent. Most municipalities in the tobacco-growing regions of Puerto Rico followed suit. Two hundred fifty tobacco growers established a cooperative in Morovis on May 23, 1926. That same month, another 200 growers met in Caguas and contributed $100,000 to incorporate Tabacaleros de Caguas.[14] Growers in Naranjito organized their Banco Tabacalero with $6,000, and Tabacaleros de San Lorenzo, Inc. had $10,000 from forty-seven shareholders when they began, with a stockpile of 3,000 quintales of tobacco leaf valued at $113,165.06.[15] Tabacaleros de Aibonito, Inc. originally had sixty shareholders and an initial operating capital of $12,000, which they invested in 3,360 quintales of tobacco that was later valued at $356,477.55. In addition, part of their initial capital was used to build a warehouse to hold over 10,000 quintales of tobacco.[16] The 102 founding shareholders of Cayey, incorporated as Tabacaleros de Cayey, Inc., built a warehouse and began operating with $11,000 in capital.[17] Shareholders in Cayey invested in 8,447 quintales of tobacco valued at $362,315.25. Banco Tabacalero de Utuado was established with $3,000 in capital.[18] The tobacco growers of Corozal set up their bank on August 15, 1926.[19] The Tabacaleros de Bayamón was established in 1927 and they quickly advertised in *El agricultor puertorriqueño*, the magazine of the farmers association.[20] That same year, growers in Manatí, Barceloneta, and Morovis decided to join forces and establish one cooperative association that represented the growers of all three municipalities.[21] In short, cooperative societies were in operation in all the largest tobacco-producing municipalities during the 1920s.

Enthusiasm alone, however, would not be enough to guarantee the success of the cooperative associations. In 1927, the tobacco crop yielded a dramatic 50 million pounds, double what the market could absorb. This led to severe price declines, from approximately 38 cents a pound in 1926 to 19 cents a pound in 1927. Although there was modest recovery in 1928 and in 1930, prices never came close to 1926 levels again. In addition, the rapid shift in smokers' preferences from expensive cigars to cheap cigarettes meant that the cheaper grades of tobacco sold more than the expensive ones. The switch to less expensive cigarettes had devastating consequences for the cooperatives, whose members took great pride in the high quality of their tobacco and relied on selling the higher priced grades of leaf to balance their books at the end of the season. Many tobacco cooperative societies struggled financially into the 1930s, when the tobacco industry in Puerto Rico began its downward spiral.

In response to the tobacco crisis of 1927, tobacco growers became interested in the possibility of establishing insular cooperative societies and approached the AAP for assistance. The members of the AAP resolved that the executive board should designate someone to study the possibility of establishing an insular cooperative. This study included a meeting with farmers from all tobacco-growing municipalities. As a result, and based upon the recommendation of this study, the Cooperativa Insular de Tabacaleros de Puerto Rico, an insular tobacco cooperative that combined five existing local cooperative societies, was established in 1928.[22] By 1929, the Tabacaleros de Puerto Rico, as it was known, was meeting regularly and was being visited by insular agricultural administrators and representatives from the insular legislature.[23]

Tabacaleros de Puerto Rico was an attempt to create a sophisticated financial organization by becoming involved in every aspect of the production and distribution of tobacco leaf.[24] Tabacaleros would assist their members from the very beginning of the cultivation process by purchasing all materials needed, such as seeds, fertilizers, and farming tools. The cooperative would then promote cultivation methods that would guarantee a high-quality product. Once the tobacco was harvested, the cooperative would assist their members in the curing, storage, and classification of the leaf. Finally, the cooperative would package the leaf to sell to the market, advertise in industry publications, and organize transportation to deliver the leaf once sold. Tabacaleros would support existing tobacco banks, lobby elected officials both in Puerto Rico and the United States, and maintain relationships with agents from the federal banks. This was the most comprehensive mission for a cooperative society thus far. Although it was successful in helping its members secure better financial returns, it did not have an effect on the overall decline of the tobacco sector.

Perhaps the most successful cooperative society was the Puerto Rico Tobacco Marketing Cooperative Association. La Marketing, as it became known, was founded in 1934 to find new markets for Puerto Rican tobacco, improve the living conditions of tobacco farmers, and secure needed services for their members. "It is our mission to concern ourselves with the progress of our tobacco industry, to adequately contribute to the improvement of our agricultural economy, and to inspire and assure the man who works in the tobacco field."[25] The Commission to Protect the Tobacco Industry of Puerto Rico granted La Marketing a $24,000 loan to establish a bank with the assistance of the Federal Farm Credit Bank of Baltimore and the Baltimore Bank for Cooperatives.[26] By 1940, La Marketing was the largest cooperative society in Puerto Rico, with 4,832 registered members and capital totaling $66,324.00.[27] La Marketing provided the most comprehensive member services of any cooperative society on the island, including life, fire, and hurricane insurance and seed distribution programs. Crucial for the financial survival of small-scale tobacco farmers, La Marketing provided agricultural loans at no more than a 5.4 percent interest rate, lower than the typical 7 to 10 percent interest rate available for most agricultural loans. La Marketing also supplied cultivation materials, such as zinc, cloth, insecticides, and fertilizers, to its membership in order to facilitate healthy tobacco crops.[28] Finally, the cooperative consistently paid members, on average, 8–10 percent higher prices for tobacco than what buyers paid throughout the island.[29]

The expansion of the tobacco sector and the resulting economic changes provided opportunities for farmers to become involved in democratic processes at both the local and insular level, some available through government efforts, others created by themselves. The process through which tobacco farmers became involved in ligas agrícolas and cooperatives, as evident in the data presented above, demonstrates that Puerto Ricans were aware of the economic and political power they could yield if they were affiliated, and then took the necessary actions to actively participate and improve their economic returns. Such participation, however, was not particular to tobacco growers. Sugar planters, coffee farmers, and fruit and vegetable producers were also members of ligas agrícolas and cooperative societies. Farmers throughout the island, like the tobacco growers, recognized that their power would be greatly expanded if they united. It was through the activities of the AAP that farmers gained the most political leverage in the colonial structure.

THE ASOCIACIÓN DE AGRICULTORES PUERTORRIQUEÑOS

The AAP was established in June 1924, "in a moment of deep crisis for the agriculture of the country."[30] Héctor Scoville, a prominent fruit exporter, called a meeting of farmers to discuss the effects of a possible quarantine of Puerto Rican fruit. Eighty-one farmers representing cane, tobacco, and fruit cultivation came together to foster the mutual assistance and protection of all members and to bring together all "agricultural forces for the purpose of obtaining scientific agriculture based on modern methods [of cultivation]."[31] In addition, the AAP committed itself to "promoting, implementing, and developing, on the farmer's initiative and with the Government's cooperation, credit and production cooperatives."[32] The AAP was interested in not only supporting the farmers, but also securing the progress of the rural areas of Puerto Rico. Its mission statement also included the demand to create a solid rural infrastructure that would include roads, schools, medical services, mail routes, telegraph service, public safety, and hygiene. The AAP would be "a defender of agricultural interests, a servant to the farmers, a promoter of the union of all those who work the land, a sentry of his rights and the spokesman of his being."[33]

Foremost in their attempt to reach these goals was the organization of local AAP committees in every municipality. Founding members of the AAP, among them tobacco growers Rafael Arce Rollet from Caguas and Pablo Morales Cabrera from Toa Alta, visited municipalities throughout the island to explain the goals of the AAP and to discuss the importance of joining the organization.[34] Those farmers who were already involved with the *ligas agrícolas* were enthusiastic about the AAP.[35]

It is not clear from the minutes of the organization what fee members would pay to join the organization, although it is certain that a contribution was expected. In the first general assembly, a resolution was passed that allowed the Executive Board to determine a contributive amount for each municipality based on the agricultural resources of the locality. It would then be the responsibility of the local committees to decide on the membership fee for their particular municipality. The idea was that the membership fee collected by the local committee would be more than the contributive amount imposed by the executive board, and the remainder of the money would remain in the coffers of the local committee for expenses.

It is a testament to the importance given to the AAP by insular and federal government officials that a year after the AAP was established, both the resident commissioner in Washington, Felix Córdova Dávila, and the governor, Horace Mann Towner, attended a regular meeting of the AAP on July 12, 1925. Governor Towner addressed the participants, expressing his support for the goals of the AAP. The participation of members of the insular and federal governments in AAP meetings and events was welcomed and encouraged by the AAP, and their remarks were often published in the magazine of the AAP, *El agricultor puertorriqueño.*

Several months after that initial visit, on December 20, 1925, in the southern city of Ponce, the AAP held the first annual general assembly in which members analyzed economic and political issues affecting farmers, discussed problems specific to a particular crop, and organized lobbying efforts, both in Washington and with local politicians. The AAP had sixty local committees and 6,000 members by this time. Fifty-five of those local AAP committees were represented at the general assembly.[36] The main issue before the membership in 1925 was concern over a scheduled visit to Washington by Governor Towner and several local legislators. The AAP was concerned that these officials would "deceive the federal authorities with their tales of grandiose progress of the island."[37] Members argued that since "los poderes no están en Puerto Rico, están en Washington," a commission of farmers representing the AAP should join the governor and "truly represent the economic situation in the island."[38] This commission should also lobby for the extension of federal economic laws that would be favorable to Puerto Rico, in particular, the Curtis-Aswell project, which was being debated in the

U.S. legislature at the time and would allow the creation of cooperative marketing societies and, more importantly, would give cooperatives the power to
limit production.[39] It was also determined that the commission should ask for
federal sanctions so that the 500-acre law would be respected.[40] Finally, the
commission should negotiate AAP's affiliation with the American Farm
Bureau Federation.[41] The AAP requested that Governor Towner support the
commission. So determined were the members to be successful in their petition, that the organization committed itself to a negative public relations
campaign in the event that the governor ignored the request.[42] Governor
Towner heeded the request, and such a campaign was not necessary. The AAP
membership contributed over $2,600 to cover the expenses of the trip.[43]
(See table 3.2.) The AAP commission visited Washington in April 1926 and
met General Frank McIntyre, chief of the Bureau of Insular Affairs, and
Secretary of War Dwight F. Davis, the men heading the U.S. departments
responsible for the administration of Puerto Rico.

The AAP publicized every detail of the commission's visit to Washington
in *El agricultor puertorriqueño*. The members of the commission presented
their formal report at the general assembly meeting held on July 11, 1926.[44]
The fact that a commission of Puerto Rican farmers was able to meet with the
Committee of Insular Affairs, General McIntyre, and representatives of the
Department of Agriculture suggests that rather than a one-sided colonial
relationship, there was participation from the Puerto Rican population
affected by federal laws. The record of the conversations among all the parties
concerned show remarkable candidness and a no-holds-barred attitude on
the part of the AAP representatives to make the situation in Puerto Rico
known to U.S. officials. For example, Enrique Landrón spoke of the extreme
levels of poverty on the island. He then criticized the level of taxes paid by the
Puerto Rican taxpayer when compared with the American taxpayer, arguing
that for Puerto Ricans this amount represented a hardship and a heavier burden than for their American counterparts.[45] Later in their visit, the commission met with Lloyd S. Fenny from the Bureau of Rural Economies to lobby
for an agricultural survey of the island.[46] The Bureau of Agricultural
Economics of the federal Department of Agriculture eventually conducted
and paid for the survey.

Visits to Washington and to U.S. politicians by members of the AAP
became a regular occurrence, and such access to American legislators and federal administration officials was crucial for a colonial people with no voting
representation in the main legislative body. In 1926, the AAP requested that
any time the Committee for Insular Affairs decided to hold hearings regarding Puerto Rico, the AAP should be notified. A few months later, the AAP

TABLE 3.2

CONTRIBUTIONS FOR EXPENSES
FOR WASHINGTON TRIP, 1926

Adjuntas	$50
Aguadilla	100
Aibonito	50
Bayamón	80
Caguas	200
Cayey	50
Comerío	100
El agricultor puertorriqueño	25
Guayanilla	50
Individual donations	890
Isabela	55
Lajas	100
Lares	50
Manatí	100
Mayagüez	175
Ponce	320
P.R. Leaf Tobacco Co.	100
San Germán	100
Toa Baja	10
Yauco	100
Total	$2,705

Source: Minutes, AAP (May 25, 1926).

received a letter from Edgar A. Kieso, chairman of the Committee for Insular Affairs, stating that he would grant a public hearing to any commission that came from Puerto Rico.[47] Puerto Ricans also demanded access to the executive levels of government, as evident in a 1927 meeting involving José L. Pesquera, President Calvin Coolidge, and Secretary of War Davis, reported in detail to the AAP.[48] The constant conversations between Puerto Ricans and American officials demonstrate that, rather than making decisions without consultation, there was a willingness to discuss repercussions and examine alternatives.

It appears that in many of these negotiations, Puerto Rican farmers bypassed the insular government and directly dealt with U.S. administrators in Washington. The 1920s were chaotic years in the political life of the island, with constant realignments of political alliances according to status, current fiscal issues, or personalities.[49] Access to federal administrators and legislators, therefore, had the added benefit of sidestepping particular political agendas.

The AAP leadership, with the support of the general membership, lobbied both insular and federal politicians and bureaucrats to secure the funds, laws, or commitment it needed to carry forward its agenda. It had great success. In 1928, an extraordinary session of the AAP was held to discuss the devastation after Hurricane San Felipe II hit the island on September 18, causing a great deal of destruction to many agricultural districts. It was decided that a cable would be sent to Washington describing the dire situation of the island and to "solicit that the American Congress approve legislation to liberally extend credit to Puerto Rican farmers to save the only source of wealth for the country."[50] A few months later, the AAP received a visit from Senator Hiram Bingham, chair of the Committee on Territories and Insular Possessions, to witness the effect of the hurricane, and relief funds followed shortly thereafter.[51]

A resolution was passed during the 1930 general assembly to solicit the U.S. Congress to immediately approve the extension of the Smith-Lever and Purnell laws to Puerto Rico.[52] The Smith-Lever Law would create agricultural extension services, and the Purnell Law would provide support to the agricultural experiment stations. Both programs enjoyed widespread support from the farmers, and both laws were extended to Puerto Rico shortly thereafter. An AAP commission traveled to Washington in 1931 to solicit additional funds for economic recovery after San Felipe. Its efforts resulted in the creation of a Rehabilitation Commission with an appropriation of $6,000,000 in agricultural rehabilitation loans, $2,000,000 for repairs to schools and roads, and $100,000 for the purchase and distribution of seed to farmers.[53] In addition, the commission lobbied successfully for temporary tax reductions for those affected by the hurricane. These examples demonstrate that farmers were not only involved at all levels of the island's governmental structure, but had learned how to skillfully negotiate the policies of the U.S. government that directly affected their interests.

The AAP agenda was not only concerned with agricultural issues. The AAP also dealt with various other matters that affected everyday life in rural

Puerto Rico, including improvement in roadways, fair and uniform valuation of rural property, workers' compensation programs for farmers, regulations for women and children's labor, the creation of a rural police force, and the construction of new schools.[54] From the meeting minutes of the AAP and the articles and reports published in *El agricultor puertorriqueño*, it is clear that the members of the AAP were heavily involved in economic issues. For example, in 1925, the AAP asked local committees to gather farmers to protest unjust appraisals of rural property, which would lead to higher taxes. The insular government, facing a budgetary crisis, had decided property appraisals should occur throughout the island. Residents would then pay taxes according to the new valuations assigned to their properties. The AAP expected that these values would be much higher than in the past, placing an additional burden on the already struggling farmers. The AAP began a campaign to criticize the property reappraisals, declaring that the association would not "support any government [expenditure] earmarked for improvements exclusively in the urban zones, forgetting the needs of the countryside."[55] In addition, the AAP drafted a detailed proposal for the legislature in which they specified how any reappraisal should be conducted: land values should be the same within categories (i.e., all tobacco lands should have the same value, all sugar lands the same, etc.); corporations should not have special appraisals; farmers should be represented in all taxation committees; and any new taxation should only be imposed once all property had been reappraised.[56] The plan was presented to the insular legislature at the end of 1926.[57] Although the AAP did not succeed in suspending the reappraisals, subsequent communications between insular government officials and the AAP demonstrate that the development of the rural areas remained central to government policy.

The AAP was equally involved in the political arena, although the official AAP mission statement held that it was not a political organization. In 1927, the AAP became involved in several political campaigns, supporting candidates who were friendly to farmers. An attempt at creating a political platform was made that same year. At the general assembly on March 25, 1928, the membership agreed that the AAP should support "their men" in the upcoming elections for the insular Senate and the House of Representatives. These men would serve with the "principal objective to promote the wellbeing of the agricultural sector, and by extension of the country, free of political compromises when [legislation] is incompatible with the prosperity of the agricultural class."[58] The AAP went as far as declaring that it would put all of its economic resources and political influence at the service of the political party that best represented the interests of the farmers.[59]

Evidence of the complex relationship between the AAP and the insular and federal government can be found in the pages of *El agricultor puertorriqueño*. The AAP openly criticized the governor, other insular elected officials, and the federal government when decisions seemed unfair. This candor may seem remarkable within the context of a colonial government, but it is evidence of the democratic space created by Puerto Ricans within the colonial system to effectively comment on critical issues facing them in their daily lives. Editorials in *El agricultor puertorriqueño* called both the insular and federal government uncaring, abusive, unfair, and willing to sell out the farmers when politically convenient.[60] An example from the AAP's efforts on behalf of tobacco growers is illustrative of the influence of the AAP in the insular legislature. Governor Towner's administration was not well liked. After the 1927 tobacco harvest, when it became apparent that tobacco growers were facing financial difficulties, the AAP requested that the governor convene an extraordinary session of the legislature to discuss possible solutions. Governor Towner declined the request. The editors of *El agricultor puertorriqueño* criticized the governor for refusing to deal with the tobacco crisis and accused him of being unethical: "Of he who directs the displacement of Puerto Ricans, with the criminal complicity of the political fanfare, nothing can be expected except an indirect contribution to the bankruptcy of Puerto Ricans. Governor Towner's administration should receive no gratitude for any rebuilding of our meager riches. Instead, he leaves us a mortgage of fifty million . . . with which he capriciously manipulated our political establishment."[61]

Governor Towner and the legislature had to respond. The result was Law #53, enacted on March 23, 1928, which created the Commission for the Protection of Puerto Rican Tobacco.[62] The Commission would fall under the jurisdiction of the insular Department of Agriculture and Labor and would be financed by the issuing of a $3,000,000 bond. It would then be supported by a contribution of 1 cent per pound of tobacco grown, processed, or sold in Puerto Rico, to be paid by farmers, manufacturing companies, and tobacco buyers. The commission was charged with providing credit for tobacco cooperatives, acting as the intermediary between growers and buyers, and regulating the acreage of tobacco plantings. The law also required that all "persons, firms or corporations that are dedicated to the financing of the cultivation of tobacco . . . must be authorized to do so with a license issued by the commission."[63] Those operating without said license would be fined $100 to $1,000 per infraction. Governor Towner vetoed the law. It was once again enacted by the insular legislature on February 18, 1929, only to be vetoed again in a "new destructive action" by the governor.[64] This time, however, the governor's veto did not stand, and the commission was established.

FIGURE 3.1 "La Justa Revancha . . . y el Porvenir Indeciso de Algunos
Comisionados." *Source*: *EAP* 7, no. 11 (June 15, 1929): cover page.

The influence of the AAP on local legislators was crucial in the enactment
of this law, but the displeasure of the AAP only grew as it became clear that
Governor Towner intended to staff the commission with friendly appointees
and not "bona fide tobacco growers," as the AAP had demanded. A cartoon
published in June 1929 eloquently demonstrates the type of pressure applied
to local officials. (See figure 3.1.) José L. Pesquera, president of the AAP, is in
charge of a catapult that has sent Governor Towner on a direct toss to
Washington. Witnessing this momentous event is E. Landrón, president of
Tabacaleros de Puerto Rico, holding the hard stick of punishment and shak-
ing his finger at the Towner-appointed commissioners, saying, "Now we're
going to fix you up!" Also present is Francisco M. Zeno, executive director of
the commission, who looks through a telescope to make sure Governor
Towner has really left. A group of farmers cheers them on, yelling, "Be tough
with them!" and "Well done!"

Governor Towner relented. The final appointees included five tobacco
growers chosen from a list of fifteen candidates submitted to the governor by
the AAP on behalf of a general assembly of tobacco growers. The AAP and the
tobacco growers had argued that only tobacco men could appropriately represent the interests of the tobacco sector, and the inclusion of these men on

the commission was a triumph for the AAP and for tobacco growers through-out the island. Unfortunately, the commission was unable to meet the goals of the law, mostly because the required contribution proved too costly for already struggling farmers. In addition, tobacco manufacturers actively resis-ted the application of licensing fees, which would have guaranteed operating funds for the commission.[65] Although it remained operational for a few more years, the commission was ineffective and was dissolved.

The AAP continued its struggle on behalf of tobacco growers, and in 1935 it pressured the legislature to establish the Tobacco Institute, an organization dedicated to conducting scientific research that would address tobacco's culti-vation problems.[66] The institute was also charged with assisting farmers in the implementation of improved cultivation methods. Unlike the Commission for the Protection of Puerto Rican Tobacco, the Tobacco Institute was funded by the insular legislature as a budget line item. Additional funding was acquired through the levying of a 15-cent tax on each quintal of tobacco sold in Puerto Rico. The institute would have a full-time director, to be appointed by the governor from a list of candidates submitted by the AAP. In 1937, when Governor Winship submitted nominations for the director's position, the AAP protested, stating that the nominees were not bona fide farmers and it would not recommend the farmers cooperate until the "nominations are cor-rected."[67] The Tobacco Institute set up a facility that included agronomy and chemistry departments, it regularly published scientific findings in both the local and American press, and it lobbied the insular legislature for additional funding and for laws that would protect the Puerto Rican tobacco industry.[68]

During the decade of the 1930s, when the AAP reported a record 10,000 members, it became a "champion of the nation." It equated agricultural pros-perity with the success of the Puerto Rican nation. In 1932, the AAP created a Regional League for the Consumption of Native Products to encourage the population to stop buying imported products and "go native."[69] Front and center was a campaign to establish "Patriotic Fridays," when no Puerto Rican would eat imported food. From January 1, 1933, the campaign would add Wednesdays, and from July, Mondays would also be included. The pages of *El agricultor puertorriqueño* have many examples of advertisements printed in support of this campaign.

The AAP was a leader in the campaign to establish cooperative associations. In 1927, a meeting was dedicated to a discussion of how to create momentum for the cooperative movement in Puerto Rico. It was "urgently necessary" to support the establishment of cooperatives and even more so "for all social classes to join [them] as a matter of patriotism."[70] Subsequent editorials in *El agricultor puertorriqueño* frequently advocated for the organization of all farmers, especially tobacco farmers, into cooperatives to negotiate for better prices, cheaper cultivation materials, and fairer credit standards. The magazine regularly reported the activities of tobacco cooperatives, updating figures on the membership and capital available, and announcing meetings or particular campaigns to drum up attendance and support.[71]

El agricultor puertorriqueño was the main propaganda instrument for the AAP. Billed as "useful and necessary for the farmer as is his tractor, his plough, or his yoke," *El agricultor puertorriqueño* cost 5 cents per issue or $3 per year.[72] The editors often commented on the hot topic of the time, whether it was absentee landowners, the latest insular political scandal, or the nutritionally poor diet of the typical Puerto Rican farmer.[73] The magazine published letters from farmers, legislators, and insular and federal government bureaucrats, as well as interesting news from the United States and around the world. There were also articles on nutrition, agricultural techniques, botany, and literature, and advertisements for farm equipment, fertilizer, college courses, and insurance. Perhaps the most important section of the magazine was titled "Market and Prices," and it listed the latest prices paid to farmers for products such as sugar, tobacco, and citrus fruits.

Many farmers contributed articles to the *El agricultor puertorriqueño*. These articles dealt with a variety of topics, from tobacco cultivation techniques to larger agricultural issues, such as banking and credit.[74] The ever-changing tax code received plenty of coverage, and the magazine usually included copies of official forms, surveys, or names and contact information of those who should be called for questions.[75] Farmers also commented on the living conditions and general well-being of the population of the countryside.[76]

The AAP's support of tobacco growers included reports in *El agricultor puertorriqueño* of meetings, incessant comments on the status of the crop, and the publication of every minute transaction during the buying season.[77] Through the magazine, the AAP disseminated information to tobacco growers regarding global market conditions, including the quantity and quality of tobacco grown in places as far as India and the Philippines, and commenting on potential buyers of Puerto Rican tobacco. Foreign and American tobacco buyers visited the island on a regular basis to determine the quality and availability of the product and to buy tobacco after the harvest. Among these were representatives from the American Cigar Company, Rosenstadt and Waller, American Tobacco Company, Congress Cigar Company, Stern Mendelsohn Co. Inc., Durlach Bros., Webster Cigar Co., and Union Cigar Co. *El agricultor puertorriqueño* regularly reported the quantity of tobacco in the hands of these buyers as a way to disseminate information on current stock and to make market predictions.

The AAP continued to increase its membership throughout the years, and it exists to this day. Farmers established the AAP to address cultivation problems on the island and to act as the public voice of the farmer in the insular and federal legislature to guarantee the enactment of laws beneficial to the agricultural sector. The AAP was consistently successful, particularly in its efforts to support tobacco growers. Through their affiliation with the AAP, tobacco growers became a political force, and this culminated in the establishment of the Commission for the Protection of Puerto Rican Tobacco in 1929 and the Tobacco Institute in 1936. The shining moment of collaboration between the AAP and the tobacco growers was the coordination of the *no siembra*, a no-planting protest organized by tobacco growers to reduce the size of the tobacco crop and thus affect prices in their favor.

Tobacco Growers, the Asociación de Agricultores Puertorriqueños, and the No Siembra

The first report of any intent to limit the tobacco crop occurred in the AAP general assembly of 1925, where it was reported that the farmers of Comerío had agreed to leave the second picking of tobacco in the field.[78] Each tobacco-growing season had two pickings: the first one was of a better quality leaf and garnered the best prices; the second picking was of lower quality and therefore worth less. Tobacco buyers would often wait for the second picking to occur before buying product, thus creating a glut of tobacco in the market and paying lower prices for both the first, higher quality tobacco and for that of the second picking. In deciding not to carry out the second picking of tobacco, farmers were looking to stabilize prices by reducing the quantity and increasing the quality of tobacco in the market. Less and better tobacco would mean higher prices. The AAP supported the Comerío decision and sent a copy of the final resolution as approved in the general assembly to the local committees in tobacco-growing municipalities.[79]

In January 1926, *El agricultor puertorriqueño* reported that meetings had been held in many tobacco municipalities to discuss whether the second picking of the tobacco crop should occur.[80] Most growers who belonged to cooperative societies supported the no-pick agreement, with the exception of the growers of Utuado. A month later, members of the cooperatives in Cayey, San Lorenzo, Comerío, and Aibonito met with E. B. Thomas, director of the Federal Bank, and Carlos Chardón, commissioner of agriculture and labor, to discuss the financial repercussions of a reduced crop if the buyers held out. It was agreed that the Federal Bank would extend the necessary credit to pay off outstanding loans so that the cooperatives could hold on to their tobacco as long as necessary.[81] Fortunately, tobacco prices remained high that season, averaging $35 to $40 per quintal, and the no-pick strategy was not necessary.

In 1927, however, tobacco acreage expanded greatly, resulting in a massive crop of 50 million pounds. The market had absorbed 30 million pounds in 1926, and the AAP believed that such an increase would be disastrous. In addition, 25 percent of the 1926 crop still remained in the hands of tobacco manufacturers, reducing the quantity of tobacco that they would buy by at least that much. Fearing a dramatic drop in prices, the AAP and the tobacco growers affiliated with it decided that drastic action needed to be taken. The first resolution to reduce the acreage planted in tobacco for the 1928 season occurred during the AAP general assembly in July 1927, followed by an agreement from the tobacco cooperatives in a meeting that took place a month later.[82] At that meeting, representatives from the tobacco cooperatives agreed that acreage should be reduced by 50 percent and that all tobacco growers should meet in every municipality to sign a contract of reduction. In addition, growers agreed to form a committee that would ensure compliance. The cover of the October 15, 1927, issue of *El agricultor puertorriqueño* proclaimed, "The planting of tobacco is reduced."[83] The efforts for the 1928 crop were not successful: the reduction was minimal; prices stayed low; and the amount of tobacco in the hands of manufacturers remained considerable.

Yet another resolution was passed to attempt to limit the 1929 planting. Citing the low prices paid for the last two crops and the great amount of tobacco that was still in the hands of American buyers, the AAP wholly supported the reduction in tobacco acreage. The AAP tried to force the hand of farmers who were not interested in reducing plantings by meeting with representatives from the Federal Bank so that all agricultural loans would carry a commitment from the grower to reduce plantings.[84] For the next few months, the campaign to reduce the tobacco planting became front and center news in *El agricultor puertorriqueño*. Some members, like tobacco grower M. Meléndez Muñoz, wrote letters of support for the reduction. A member who was a "known tobacco grower from Manatí" wrote, "It was calculated that there are more than 500,000 quintales of tobacco in existence. Estimating that the market needs 250,000 quintales, we have enough to cover the next two years."[85] The campaign was moderately successful: many members voluntarily reduced their plantings for 1929, but prices were ultimately not dramatically affected. Another year of reductions would be necessary.

Wondering if a reduced planting would actually solve the problem, the AAP criticized the tobacco buyers for making their purchases in July, when loan payments were due. With loan payments looming over them, farmers were willing to sell their product for whatever price was offered. The AAP argued that this manipulation needed to be stopped.[86] The AAP also criticized the tobacco growers who had not reduced their planting, and called for their participation as the only way to guarantee higher prices.[87] Tobacco growers who had not joined a cooperative society were urged to do so as the only safeguard against the abuses of the buyers. By 1931 the campaign had wide support among cooperative members, who decided that the 1932 season should be one of no siembra or no planting at all. *El agricultor puertorriqueño* described the tobacco growers' campaign as being "life or death for tobacco agriculture": "Never had the spirit of collective action been manifested with such vehemence by the tobacco growers, who, tired of suffering from the abuse of those who monopolize the buying, are willing, for the first time in the history of the country, to defend themselves through a quasi-revolutionary civic movement, with the goal of preventing tobacco plantings this year."[88]

Because support for the no siembra was not universal, the AAP continuously published editorials, articles, and letters in defense of the campaign.[89] If there was any mention in the press about growers planting tobacco, the AAP would immediately respond. For example, there had been reports in the press that some growers in Caguas and Aguas Buenas had prepared their land for cultivation. "Prominent tobacco growers" from Caguas responded to the allegation by writing a letter to a local newspaper stating that "we are convinced that no planting this year is necessary . . . and we want to make public our commitment to cooperate with the success of the campaign."[90] José L. Pesquera, president of the AAP and a tobacco grower, explained that some farmers in Caguas and Aguas Buenas expected the no siembra to be changed to a limited planting. They had thus prepared their land in the event such a change would be made. Pesquera also reported that 1,200 tobacco growers met in Caguas, most of whom supported the no siembra.[91] A Special Committee of the AAP visited those farmers who had not signed on for the no siembra to explain the importance of joining a cooperative society and supporting the campaign. As tobacco growers joined the no siembra, they were congratulated in the pages of *El agricultor puertorriqueño*. "These honorable friends are worthy of our most heartfelt congratulations for their noble and patriotic attitude in rectifying their mistake."[92]

As protection against the possibility of a tobacco shortage, the Puerto Rican Leaf Tobacco Company expanded the planting on their lands in Cayey.[93] This resulted in a violent escalation of the no siembra campaign, as tobacco growers burned PRLTC warehousing ranches in protest. Other fires followed in towns where support for the no siembra was widespread and where the cooperatives were well established. Curing ranches, warehouses, and even recently harvested tobacco were burned. Under pressure from the PRLTC and other tobacco growers affected by the fires, the insular state intervened, arresting those suspected of arson. Police involvement stopped the burnings, and the no siembra campaign continued without incident through the remainder of the 1932 season.

Although the no siembra reduced the acreage planted and the tobacco available for the 1932 season, it did not have the dramatic effect hoped for by the AAP and the tobacco growers who supported it. It was, however, successful in creating a "national conscience" for tobacco growers, who participated in an island-wide struggle to assert control over their economic sector.[94] The no siembra also demonstrated the extent of the collaboration between the AAP and the tobacco growers, and the commitment of the AAP to fight for its constituents, even if the struggle was outside of the legislative chambers.

Conclusion

Farmers in the tobacco region, through their affiliations in local and insular-level organizations, actively participated in the expansion of an economic sector that benefited them. At the local level, tobacco growers joined local ligas agrícolas, invested in cooperative societies, and demanded legislation to safeguard their economy. Tobacco growers attended meetings, drafted proposals and letters, voted in support of or against resolutions, and passionately debated the status of their industry. Together with many farmers in Puerto Rico, tobacco growers created political capital by establishing the Asociación de Agricultores Puertorriqueños and contributing to *El agricultor puertorriqueño*. The AAP accepted its self-appointed role as the public voice of the farmers in the insular and federal legislatures, successfully lobbying for legislation that was not only beneficial to the agricultural economy, but that would foment the development of the rural areas and demonstrate the government's commitment to raising the standard of living of all rural residents.

The new political system, colonial to be sure, ironically created space for these political and economic organizations to exist and flourish, space that Puerto Ricans quickly and enthusiastically filled with ligas agrícolas, cooperatives, committees, and institutes. Governors, presidents, senators, and other administrators were visited by the representatives of Puerto Rican tobacco growers, publicly challenged, and criticized. Insular and federal officials responded to such challenges, as evident in the case of Governor Towner's approval of Law #53 creating the Commission for the Protection of Puerto Rican Tobacco, or of Senator Bingham's visit to the island after Hurricane San Felipe. Puerto Ricans were hardly powerless within the colonial structure;

they rapidly learned how to negotiate the new governmental structure and efficiently used the freedom of the press and the ability to affiliate to effect change. Rather than observing from a distance and being victims of a tyrannical colonial government, Puerto Ricans were involved in every level of government. Their activities had a direct impact on both insular and federal policies and legislation and affected their everyday lives.

CHAPTER 4

Law

THE EXTENSION OF FEDERAL AGRICULTURAL CREDIT LEGISLATION TO PUERTO RICO

The one and a half million American citizens that reside in Puerto Rico believe that all legislation that specifically extends to the States of the Union certain benefits, excluding Puerto Rico, constitutes an unjust privilege against our island. . . . This exclusion is as illogical as it would be illogical to adopt a measure for the States of the Union, "except New York, South Dakota or Tennessee." . . . We argue that the most rudimentary principles of justice and equality demand that all the measures adopted to assist banks, industry, and agriculture, and to alleviate unemployment in the current emergency, should be extended to Puerto Rico. . . . We are not begging for charity. We are only claiming our rights. . . . We are prepared to solve our own problems as long as we can count with the same means and resources that are provided to other American citizens.

—José L. Pesquera's testimony to the
U.S. Senate Committee on Finance, 1932

Access to the colonial political structure allowed tobacco growers, together with other Puerto Rican farmers, to demand the extension of beneficial agricultural legislation to the island. The early part of the twentieth century was a time of dramatic changes in the agricultural economy of the United States, resulting in agricultural legislation designed to protect the living standard of American farmers. Puerto Ricans were well aware of these changes and the resulting legislation, and argued that it would only be fair for these benefits to be extended to the island, an argument made all the more powerful after 1917, when Puerto Ricans were granted U.S. citizenship. Of particular interest to Puerto Rican farmers were the government programs and legislation that created an institutional credit infrastructure, one that offered long-term loans and short-term production credit at lower interest rates than noninstitutional or private lenders. Puerto Rican farmers deemed such legislation crucial to the well-being of the agricultural sector and successfully lobbied in San Juan and Washington for the extension of those laws to the island.

Although tobacco cultivation did not require the large capital investments needed for sugar cultivation, small-scale tobacco farmers depended on agricultural credit to finance cultivation and cover their living expenses until their crops could be marketed after the harvest.[1] Agricultural credit for tobacco cultivation came mostly from noninstitutional sources, such as refaccionistas (loosely translated as "financiers"), local leaf traders, or, to a lesser extent, corporations that manufactured cigars or cigarettes, often at interest rates as high as 30 percent.[2] American and Puerto Rican agricultural administrators and government officials, as well as representatives of the agricultural sector, constantly decried the "lack of adequate credit facilities"—by which they meant institutional sources, such as banks or cooperatives—and often called their poor development "one of the main problems of Puerto Rican agriculture."[3] To address this problem, the insular and federal governments, under pressure from agricultural organizations and farmers throughout the island, worked to establish an agricultural credit structure that would benefit Puerto Rican farmers.[4]

The insistence by tobacco farmers and insular government officials to extend federal agricultural laws to the island, and the resulting legislation, created a sophisticated institutional credit structure that provided long-, middle-, and short-term credit for tobacco cultivation. Puerto Ricans were betting that this new credit structure, an extension of the one established in the United States, would increase the profitability of not only tobacco leaf, but also the entire agricultural sector of the island. Tobacco planters in the early twentieth century were quick to take advantage of these opportunities, and they not only requested credit in greater numbers than all other types of farmers on the island, but they also received the largest share of available institutional production credit. By 1936, tobacco farmers utilized about 46 percent of the institutional credit on the island, and in comparison, sugar farmers, producers of the most important agricultural commodity, used 41.6 percent.[5]

Tobacco growers, through their affiliation with the Asociación de Agricultores Puertorriqueños (AAP), skillfully maneuvered the political terrain both in Washington and San Juan to secure what they defined to be their guaranteed right as citizens of the United States: the ability to provide economic sustenance for their families. Their success demonstrates the effective negotiation of the legislative process and the colonial bureaucracy both in the island and the mainland to effect economic change. Additionally, their willingness to participate in federal agricultural credit programs demonstrates a commitment to improving their standard of living, regardless of whatever colonial structures may be responsible for making those programs available.

Non-Institutional Credit

The greatest share of small-scale tobacco farmers obtained credit from *refaccionistas*, who were often well-established tobacco growers, owners of large farms, or local merchants who traded in agricultural products such as fertilizer, animal feed, and equipment.[6] A refaccionista would provide currency, fertilizer, or other materials in exchange for a promise of the farmer's tobacco crop. This agreement between the grower and the financier was very formal and included a detailed contract called the *contrato de refacción*.[7]

In a contrato de refacción, the financier and the farmer would agree upon a specific amount of money to cultivate a defined number of cuerdas in tobacco. The funds would be disbursed either on a regular basis—that is, weekly, bimonthly, or in specified installments—or "as needed." The refaccionista, as the supplier of the production credit, would be involved in the actual cultivation process: he was allowed, under contractual agreement, to make unannounced visits to the tobacco fields he was financing and could "recommend" ways to spend the capital he loaned.[8] In exchange for this credit the farmer would deliver the tobacco to the refaccionista after the harvest. At this point, the financier would classify it into grades and give the grower a receipt that would reflect "a deduction ... made from delivery weights for anticipated losses in drying and fermenting of 10–12 percent."[9] The refaccionista, according to insular law, would have a lien on the crop until he determined that all contractual stipulations had been met. The farmer received no such protection. The financier then cured and fermented the tobacco leaf and arranged for its sale. Only after the sale was arranged would the farmer be cleared of his loan obligations.

In addition to local landowners or merchants, local tobacco leaf dealers, corporate leaf buyers, and tobacco manufacturing corporations could also act as refaccionistas. Local leaf dealers were usually located close to the tobacco farms and acted as "commissioned intermediaries between [American and international] leaf dealers and [local] financiers."[10] When a local dealer acted as a refaccionista, he also received the tobacco leaf after the harvest and maintained warehouses where the leaf was classified according to grade, where potential buyers visited to inspect the leaf, and where the leaf was packed for shipment after its sale.

Loans from tobacco leaf dealers were similar in structure to those of the refaccionistas: the tobacco farmer would receive money on a week-by-week basis in exchange for a formal contractual obligation of the tobacco crop at the end of the harvest.[11] Unlike the merchants, leaf dealers would settle a farmer's account when the tobacco was delivered, not when it was later marketed.

There were a few leaf dealers who traded in fairly large volume. These dealers were usually located in urban centers, like San Juan or Caguas, had a number of employees, and had connections with all the American buyers that came to the island. In addition, although leaf dealers often paid better farm prices for tobacco, all of the other main costs—for transportation, warehousing, curing, and fermenting—would be the responsibility of the farmer, thus canceling any benefit that a slightly higher price per quintal would have brought.

Owners of larger farms often dealt with volume traders, since their capital needs were greater and volume traders were capable of providing larger loans. An example is found in a contrato de refacción, dated December 1927, between Julio Esteves Solá, owner of 286 cuerdas in Aguas Buenas, Cupey, and Trujillo Alto, and Fernando Álvarez Cabeza, a leaf dealer and refaccionista from San Juan.[12] Álvarez Cabeza loaned Esteves Solá $11,250 to cultivate 150 cuerdas of tobacco in his properties ($75 per cuerda). The contract stipulated that Esteves Solá would receive the money in small amounts "as needed" and that employees of Álvarez Cabeza would have access to all tobacco fields at any time deemed necessary. Esteves Solá was allowed to sell his tobacco to a third party, but he would incur a penalty of $1 per quintal. The loan would be due in June 1928, roughly six months after the contract date. There was no rate of interest specified in the contract, although there was a $150 charge for expenses.

Tobacco manufacturing companies also acted as refaccionistas, as was the case with C. W. Boom, owner of a cigar factory in Caguas, the largest tobacco-growing municipality of the eastern highlands.[13] In one contrato de refacción dated December 2, 1927, Boom agreed to lend $800 to Manuel Quiñones and Belén Alverio, owners of almost 60 cuerdas in Caguas, to cultivate 10 cuerdas of tobacco ($80 per cuerda).[14] The funds would be disbursed weekly throughout the duration of the growing season. A few days later, Boom signed another contrato de refacción with Dionisio Maldonado and Juana Laguna, owners of 15 cuerdas in Guaynabo.[15] The couple secured a loan for $750 to cultivate 10 cuerdas of tobacco ($75 per cuerda). Both of these contracts specified a 9 percent interest rate and an additional $100 for expenses, and would be payable in one year's time.

Refaccionistas also entered into contracts with farmers that included capital for other disbursements, such as mortgage payments and rent expenses. Rafael Ocasio and Juana Cruz, owners of a 14-cuerda farm in Caguas, signed a "Contrato de refacción, hipoteca y arrendamiento" (production credit contract, mortgage, and lease of land) with Isidoro Álvarez González, also from Caguas.[16] Their contract was quite complicated but perhaps typical. The couple's farm was first mortgaged for $1,700 in 1924; the contract does not specify the lender for the first mortgage. In early 1927, the couple secured a second mortgage for $1,900 from Isidoro Álvarez González, which they had not yet been able to pay. In this contract, dated December 14, 1927, they agreed to give Álvarez González the title to the property in Caguas in lieu of payment. Álvarez González agreed to lease the farm back to Ocasio and Cruz for four years, at a price of $150 per year, and gave the couple the option to buy the farm at the end of the four years for $1,900.[17] In addition, Álvarez González lent them $700 to cultivate 10 cuerdas of tobacco. The money would be disbursed in several payments: $300 payable immediately and then $20 per week for twenty weeks, roughly the length of the tobacco-growing season. The contrato de refacción would be due in May 1928.

There is no doubt that contratos de refacción could be problematic for farmers. The same person who acted as the lender was also the buyer of the harvest and the marketer of the final product, thereby having an extraordinary amount of control over the price paid to the farmer for his tobacco irrespective of actual market prices at harvest time. Once the tobacco was taken to the financier's warehouse, he classified it according to grade. Instead of paying the farmer according to the price fixed by the New York tobacco market on a particular date for that particular grade, the refaccionista calculated the stock he had on hand and what he expected to receive from other borrowers, and then he determined the price to be paid to the farmer.

The contract between C. W. Boom and Manuel Quiñones and Belén Alverio to cultivate 10 cuerdas of tobacco cited above is an example of this. The average farm price paid for tobacco leaf was 25.07 cents per pound and the average yield per cuerda was 669 pounds during the harvest of 1928. Quiñones and Alverio cultivated 10 cuerdas of tobacco, which would have yielded 6,690 pounds of tobacco leaf at the end of the harvest. If Boom took the standard deduction of 10 percent of the total weight to account for weight loss after curing, then the total weight recorded for payment to Quiñones and Alverio would have been 6,021 pounds. At a price of 25.07 cents per pound, this would amount to a payment of $1,509.46. The debt owed Boom totaled $972 ($800 principal, plus $72 in interest, plus $100 for expenses), assuming that no other expenses were added for the processing of the leaf. This would leave a profit of $537.46. If Quiñones and Alverio spent the average 40 percent of their income on labor, their final net profit from the cultivation of tobacco would be $322.46 (21 percent of the farm value of the crop).[18] It is safe to make the assumption that the couple also spent the average of 39 cents per day for food for their family, totaling another $142.35 for the year.[19] The remainder of the money, $180.11, would have to settle whatever other debts the family had incurred, either for other cultivation materials for secondary crops, home supplies, and clothing. In the event that there was money left after the repayment of all debt, it would need to last for one year until new contratos de refacción could be signed prior to the following tobacco season. Most tobacco growers were once again in debt before the next tobacco season began.

In contrast, Boom became the owner of 6,021 pounds of leaf tobacco, which according to average prices of 46.96 cents per pound in the export market of 1928, would be valued at $2,827.46. Boom almost doubled his investment with a profit of $1,318. In the crop year of 1928, there was a difference of almost 22 cents per pound (87 percent) between the price paid to farmers and the price paid for tobacco in the market. Clearly, if tobacco prices paid to farmers had been based on the average price of tobacco in the export market, farmers would have increased their earnings. Instead, being the lender as well as the buyer and marketer of the leaf allowed the refaccionista to set a price based on his existing stock and other tobacco still owed under contratos de refacción, thus keeping the farm price at levels that were well below actual market prices. For lenders, providing agricultural production loans was very good business indeed.

A cartoon, published in the agricultural magazine *El agricultor puertorriqueño*, is an eloquent portrayal of the relationship between the tobacco farmer and the refaccionista. (See figure 4.1.) In this cartoon, the farmer on the left side is perhaps coming from the harvest; he is dirty, unshaven, and wearing simple clothing, with a basket of tobacco leaf under his arm. The leaf is green and raw; it has not yet been cured. The *intermediario* or refaccionista in the center is flushed with the indicators of wealth, such as jewels, girth, and fancy clothes. Sitting on almost-bursting bags of money, he buys the leaf from the farmer, paying 25 cents per pound. The intermediario, who has presumably turned the leaf into cigars, then sells the finished tobacco product to the gentlemanly consumer on the right with a significant markup, 25 cents for two cigars. The consumer who is purchasing the finished product is a clean-shaven, nicely dressed man, with surplus money that allows him to partake in a small luxury. The contrast between the farmer and the consumer is as dramatic as the contrast between the raw leaf and the cigar. This cartoon not only comments on the financial benefits enjoyed by the refaccionista but also on a chemical transformation that is symbolic of a social transformation. What began as a green leaf, under the feet of the farmer, chemically transforms under the girth of the intermediary, who can cure and ferment it into the beautiful, fragrant, and very valuable leaf that will, in turn, be transformed into a consumable product, a cigarette, pipe filling, or cigar.

It should be no surprise, then, that farmers attempted to change the equation and literally move some of those bags of money to their side. Farmers, of course, were free to approach different buyers to secure better prices, but as demonstrated by the contratos de refacción cited above, most contracts included a clause exacting a significant penalty if a sale to a third party was made. For already cash-poor farmers, any penalty, regardless of how small, was a great economic hardship. Some lenders would also charge the farmer for warehousing costs, transportation to the new buyer's facilities, and any other expense deemed necessary by the lender.[20] In fact, financing was so problematic that some farmers reported losses amounting to between $3.50 and 7.50 per quintal of tobacco.[21] Faced with a never-ending debt cycle and a noncompetitive credit market, farmers attempted to improve their financing opportunities through legislative reform. With the vocal support of

FIGURE 4.1 "Transformación Social del Tabaco." *Source: El agricultor puertorriqueño* 3, no. 11 (June 1927): 20.

the insular government, farmers pressured the federal government for the extension of agricultural credit laws recently enacted in the United States to alleviate farmers' economic stresses.

INSTITUTIONAL CREDIT STRUCTURES

The development of the institutional banking and credit structure in Puerto Rico is intimately tied to the development of similar institutions in the United States. Farmers in Puerto Rico were continuously updated regarding the latest laws enacted by the U.S. Congress through newspaper and magazine articles and advertisements, radio broadcasts, and personal visits by government agents and agricultural organizers. Understanding the benefits of these laws, farmers constantly and successfully lobbied for their extension to the island.

The initial U.S. legislation of importance to Puerto Rican farmers was the Federal Farm Loan Act of July 1916.[22] This act established twelve Federal Land Banks that would make long-term first mortgages to farmers at low interest rates.[23] The U.S. Treasury supplied the original capital for these banks, but they were designed as financial cooperatives where borrowers would eventually become the owners of the institution. To this end, borrowers were required to purchase stock in the bank equal to 5 percent of their loan amounts. The Federal Land Banks captured 10 percent of the farm mortgage market in fewer than ten years of operations, but this rapid expansion was due in part to incredibly high lending rates in particularly high-risk areas.[24] Defaults on Federal Land Bank loans in these areas brought a shift to more conservative and stringent lending policies.

In Puerto Rico, Governor Arthur Yager, farmers, and the insular legislature lobbied in Washington for the extension of the Federal Farm Loan Act to the island, which Puerto Ricans, who had just been granted U.S. citizenship, now saw as their right. As part of this effort, the recently created Department of Agriculture prepared an extensive survey of the economic conditions of Puerto Rico and a study of the advantages that farm loan legislation would have on the farmers of the island.[25] The arguments were persuasive, but there was concern over the mandatory stock purchase option that had been so problematic for American farmers. Nevertheless, on October 1, 1922, the Federal Land Bank began operations in San Juan.[26] Mortgages from the Federal Land Bank were granted for up to $10,000 at 6 percent interest and lasted for twenty years. In its first four years of operations, the Federal Land Bank approved 3,778 loans totaling in excess of $11 million.[27]

The main problem with the Federal Land Bank programs in the United States and in Puerto Rico was that the only credit provided by the institution was long-term financing. Although it was helpful to farmers who could mortgage their properties to pay for farm expenses, the true nature of the credit problem for both American and Puerto Rican farms was the absence of options for short-term production credit. As early as 1913, the U.S. Congress determined that the "real cause for inadequate financing was due in part at least to the fact that the commercial banking machinery of the country was ill-adapted to making certain loans for the periods required by the farmer."[28] Because farmers needed credit for short to intermediate periods, for the six months of a tobacco harvest or for one year to make farm improvements, banking institutions were created to accommodate such needs. The Agricultural Credit Act of March 1923 established twelve Federal Intermediate Credit Banks (FICB) to provide loans to cooperative associations, banks, and other credit institutions.[29] Those credit associations or local credit institutions would redistribute the money provided by the FICB to individual farmers according to need. It would be up to the farmers to form cooperative organizations that could be funded through the FICB and then apply for individual loans to the associations. The FICB would be fully owned by the government, thereby eliminating the added expenses of mandatory stock purchases in order to secure a loan. Unfortunately, private banks seldom asked the FICB for loan monies, mostly because smaller banks looked at the FICB as competition, not as a partner.[30] Ultimately, this kept farmers in the United States and Puerto Rico from accessing monies available from the FICB for seasonal production.[31]

The Agricultural Act of 1923 addressed some of the problems with the Federal Land Bank legislation of the previous decade. Under Title III of the act, the maximum loan amount from the Federal Land Bank was raised to $25,000 from $10,000.[32] To address continuing concerns over access to short-term credit, the act allowed the secretary of agriculture to make short-term production loans directly to farmers. With the enactment of this act, the structures were set in place to provide access to long-, intermediate-, and short-term credit. In 1924, Title I of the law, which dealt with the establishment of the FICB, was extended to Puerto Rico and was heralded as a "blessing from heaven" by the agricultural press.[33]

To take advantage of FICB monies, Puerto Rican tobacco farmers, who were already involved in ligas agrícolas, immediately founded cooperative organizations in San Lorenzo, Comerío, Cayey, and Aibonito, a process analyzed in the previous chapter.[34] A few years later, there was at least one cooperative organization in each of the major tobacco-growing municipalities, and in 1927, farmers in Puerto Rico attempted to consolidate these into one insular cooperative association, a decision approved and heralded by the Asociación de Agricultores Puertorriqueños.[35] It is evident that tobacco farmers were aware of the benefits of credit available under federal programs and that they took the necessary steps to avail themselves of that credit.[36]

By December 1925, the other provisions of the Agricultural Credit Act had not yet been extended to Puerto Rico. E. B. Thomas, director of the Porto Rico Branch of the Federal Land Bank of Baltimore, met with representatives of the Asociación de Agricultores Puertorriqueños to discuss the other sections of the act, in particular Title III, which would raise the limit of the Federal Farm Bank loans to $25,000.[37] This meeting occurred at the same time that the Federal Land Bank was reevaluating its loan policies due to high foreclosure rates in the United States. Farmers in Puerto Rico, who were aware of the problems and who were afraid of defaulting on their Federal Land Bank loans at the same high rates as American farmers, were asking for blanket extensions to all loans made to Puerto Rican farmers. Such requests could not have come at a worse time, since both the insular legislature and the farmers' association were intensely campaigning for the extension of the Agricultural Credit Act in its entirety to the island. An editorial in *El agricultor puertorriqueño* encouraged farmers to repay their loans without an extension: "The extensions will perhaps be granted, but it would greatly affect the solid credit that the farmers have earned with the Federal Bank . . . this allows us to ask for a greater credit amount that will reach $25,000."[38] Unfortunately, the defaults could not be prevented and the new loan maximum under Title III of the Agricultural Credit Act was not made available to Puerto Rican farmers.

Although tobacco farmers were willing to deal with institutional credit, noninstitutional systems were still very much in place and were either supplemented with or used in lieu of institutional credit. The case of José Muñoz López, owner of a 90-cuerda tobacco farm in San Lorenzo, is an interesting example of the difficulties with the Federal Land Bank program and the availability and utilization of noninstitutional credit. Although the exact date of the transaction is not known, Muñoz López secured a twenty-year mortgage from the Federal Land Bank of Baltimore for $3,015.68. Because he was having trouble paying the Federal Land Bank, and wanted to avoid a default, Muñoz López obtained a second mortgage in 1927 for $1,000 from Pedro Orcasitas Muñoz, another local landowner.[39] The new mortgage was payable in one year, at the rate of 1 percent interest per month plus $200 for expenses. Federal Land Bank loans meant increased capital, but Puerto Rican farmers, like those in the United States, were having trouble maintaining the expected payment schedule.

After the market crash of 1929, delinquent loans and foreclosures increased both in the United States and in Puerto Rico. As a response, the U.S. Congress enacted emergency measures intended to provide the necessary credit to continue agricultural production. First, the loan conditions of Federal Land Banks were amended to make short-term credit easier to obtain for cooperative associations. In Puerto Rico, the Federal Land Bank of Baltimore offered production loans from six months to three years. To prevent heavy losses the borrowers could only secure loans worth 75 percent of the expected crop.[40] Additional production loans were granted by the Federal Rehabilitation Commission, managed through the "Porto Rican Hurricane Relief Commission," which had been established after the devastating Hurricane San Felipe II struck the island in 1928. These rehabilitation loans, as specified in an official memorandum from the federal agency published in *El agricultor puertorriqueño*, were granted to individual farmers who suffered significant damage to their crops, farms, or other buildings (such as curing ranches) because of the hurricane.[41] Loan limits were set at $25,000 and payments were made on a monthly basis.

Federal agricultural legislation continued to evolve and became more sophisticated as it responded to the changing reality of farmers in the United States. Puerto Rican farmers closely followed these reforms. The Federal Farm Board was created under the Agricultural Marketing Act of 1929 to provide funds to stabilize prices through marketing programs, such as compiling data on prices, existing stock, and domestic and foreign demand for agricultural products.[42] The Federal Farm Board would make these data accessible to agricultural producers so that farmers would be well informed when they sold their products in the market. The Federal Farm Board also encouraged the establishment of marketing cooperatives and provided funds to build structures that would help in the distribution of agricultural products, including warehouses to store tobacco.[43] This was particularly important since the Federal Farm Board made loans to any cooperative association. Like previous laws, the Agricultural Marketing Act was not immediately extended to Puerto Rico, to the great disappointment of the farmers on the island.

On March 15, 1930, *El agricultor puertorriqueño* included a cartoon titled "The Struggles in Washington and the Injustice of an Allocation . . . !!," which depicted the distribution by the Federal Farm Board of its $500 million congressional allocation. (See figure 4.2.) A dapper Benjamin Alling, the U.S. attorney general, calmly supervises a Federal Farm Board representative who distributes healthy bunches of hay to different states of the union. Ohio has his hands up, waiting for delivery; Florida and Alabama are next in line. On the left-hand side of the illustration, Maine is leaving the scene and Iowa is walking away, hay on his shoulder, while whistling a happy tune. On the bottom left, there is an emaciated mule, standing in for Puerto Rican agriculture. She is hurting; she has small bandages on her rear hip and leg and a large one tied around her front ankle. She appears exhausted, hungry, and lethargic to the extreme that she can barely lift up her head. At the end of the flimsy rope that hangs around her neck is Félix Córdova Dávila, the resident commissioner at that time.[44] Córdova Dávila, wearing the typical Puerto Rican *pava*, or peasant's hat, points a very large accusatory finger at the attorney general and says: "Hey Attorney, tell that riff-raff to give me a handful too, 'cause my animal is the one that needs it most!" The attorney general pays no attention, while that Farm Board riff-raff scornfully looks at Córdova Dávila as he hands off the bundle to a prosperous Ohio.

This cartoon was yet another tool used by farmers in Puerto Rico to pressure the U.S. federal government into extending the Agricultural Marketing Act to the island, and was printed after months of lobbying by both farmers and insular officials in Washington and San Juan. As early as October 1929,

FIGURE 4.2 "Los Forcejeos en Washington y la Injusticia de un Reparto . . . !!"
Source: El agricultor puertorriqueño 9, no. 5 (March 15, 1930): cover page.

a group of AAP members visited Governor Theodore Roosevelt Jr. to demand that he lobby on behalf of Puerto Rican farmers for the extension of the act.[45] Such efforts had yielded no results other than a vague promise of including Puerto Rico in the relief allocations. The leadership of the AAP and many insular officials decided that the lobbying campaign for the extension of the marketing act needed to be stepped up. This cartoon and many other scathing editorials in both the agricultural and local press, together with a visit to President Herbert Hoover by a delegation of farmers and insular officials, resulted in the extension of the law to Puerto Rico in October 1930.[46] The details of the law and the expected benefits to the island's farmers were celebrated in the pages of *El agricultor puertorriqueño*.[47]

Even when the laws were extended in their entirety to the island, the local population could be unhappy with the results. Barely a month after the Federal Farm Board programs had been approved for Puerto Rico, representatives of the Asociación de Agricultores Puertorriqueños asked Governor Roosevelt and Resident Commissioner Félix Córdova Dávila to lobby in Washington for an additional $1 million in loan money. Although "grateful" to the U.S. Congress for the initial approval of $6 million for loans, the amount only funded 3,000 of the 5,000 applications in the system.[48] An additional appropriation would be necessary if all of the applicants were to be funded. The determination with which Puerto Rican farmers constantly pressured the insular and federal legislators to act on their behalf was remarkable. There was no reluctance and no intimidation on the part of the farmers and their representatives when dealing with colonial authorities in San Juan or in Washington.

Puerto Rican farmers understood the colonial legislative structure and how to operate within it, but they were not only looking toward the mainland to solve production credit problems. Puerto Rican farmers called their insular legislators to task and reminded them that their loyalty was to the island, not to the mainland. In a general assembly of the Asociación de Agricultores Puertorriqueños of 1930, the membership approved Resolution #29, which asked the insular legislature to set the interest on loans at 9 percent. In addition, the members passed Resolution #37, which would establish a commission to study the feasibility of establishing the "Agricultural Bank of Puerto Rico."[49]

Further evidence that Puerto Rican farmers applied pressure to effect changes in financial decisions that affected them can be found in 1931, when the Puerto Rican branch of the Federal Land Bank of Baltimore put a blanket stoppage on all loans granted to farmers. Farmers throughout Puerto Rico quickly and publicly criticized the seemingly arbitrary nature of the decision.

As a response, representatives of the bank visited the island to address their concerns.[50] Representatives met with Governor Roosevelt, Commissioner of Agriculture Edmundo Colón, and the president of the Asociación de Agricultores Puertorriqueños, José Pesquera. After their visit, the bank decided to reinstitute borrowing for those farmers who would qualify and made its decision public with a letter published in its entirety in *El agricultor puertorriqueño*. The AAP made a commitment to meet with farmers throughout the island to make everyone aware of the results of the visit with the bank directors.

Further changes to U.S. agricultural legislation once again affected Puerto Rican farmers as the Great Depression continued. The Reconstruction Finance Corporation (RFC), which was created on January 22, 1932, was responsible for making agricultural loans to banks, insurance companies, mortgage companies, and local credit unions for the financing of both long- and short-term loans. The RFC would also establish twelve regional agricultural credit corporations, one in each of the Federal Land Bank districts; Puerto Rico would be included in the RFC corresponding to Baltimore.[51] This branch was assigned $3 million for production loans, and Puerto Rico would be able to take advantage of these. Local realities, however, fueled demands for additional assistance. That same year, the island was devastated by Hurricane San Ciprián. Farmers demanded that both the insular and federal governments assist the agricultural sector with additional emergency funding. As a response, the federal government created the Puerto Rico Rehabilitation Commission to offer second mortgages on agricultural property.[52]

Perhaps no other legislation had as much effect on Puerto Rican tobacco growers as the Agricultural Relief Act of 1933, part of Franklin D. Roosevelt's relief program to help stabilize the U.S. economy. The Agricultural Relief Act was an extensive agricultural program that attempted to stabilize agricultural markets through relief payments to farmers, crop reduction to support prices, and access to credit. Several pieces of legislation quickly followed. The Emergency Farm Mortgage Act of May 12, 1933, dealt with the problem of delinquent mortgage loans by providing the necessary funds to refinance all mortgages held by companies other than Federal Land Banks. A reduction in the interest rate was mandated to 4.5 percent in the United States and 5 percent in Puerto Rico; these were later reduced again to 3.5 percent and 4 percent respectively.[53] In addition, extensions on all Federal Land Bank loans would be granted to all borrowers facing repayment difficulties. The maximum amount for a loan was increased from $25,000 to $50,000 and, most important, Federal Land Banks were now authorized to make loans directly to farmers.[54] By 1935, the Federal Land Bank had become the most important mortgage lender for tobacco farmers in Puerto Rico, and the second most important lender for coffee and sugar farmers. (See table 4.1.) Just two years later, the Federal Land Bank was the most important mortgage lender for farmers in all three major crops. However, individual lenders still held a large share of the mortgages for tobacco and sugar farms.

The Farm Credit Act enacted on June 16, 1933, specifically addressed the problem of access to short-term credit for cultivation by establishing a production credit corporation in each of the Federal Land Bank districts. Although the production credit corporations did not themselves lend money to farmers, they were charged with promoting the organization of farmers' credit associations and supervising those associations' financial operations. The United States would be divided into twelve federal districts, each with a Federal Land Bank, a Federal Intermediate Credit Bank, a Corporation of Production Credit, and a Bank for Cooperatives. Puerto Rico would fall under District #2, and would be served by the Baltimore organizations.

The Annual Report of the Commissioner of Agriculture and Commerce of 1933–1934 devoted an entire section to the Farm Credit Act and its effects on the farmers of Puerto Rico.[55] Carlos Chardón, commissioner at the time,

TABLE 4.1

PERCENTAGE OF MORTGAGES HELD BY TYPE OF LENDER, 1935 AND 1937

Lender	1935			1937		
	TOBACCO	SUGAR	COFFEE	TOBACCO	SUGAR	COFFEE
Federal Land Bank	36.7%	26.7%	29.8%	46.2%	54.3%	43.5%
Hurricane Relief Commission	8.7	6.0	34.8	5.4	3.8	27
Individual lenders	33.3	48.7	16.8	44.3	38.5	19.7
Commercial banks	4.7	3.8	6.4	2.5	0	0
Other	16.7	14.8	12.2	1.6	3.4	9.8
Total	100%	100%	100%	100%	100%	100%

Source: Division of Agricultural Economics, Agricultural Extension Service, *Annual Report of the Division of Agricultural Economics of the Agricultural Extension Service, 1934–1935* (San Juan, PR: Bureau of Supplies, Printing, and Transportation, 1935), 145.

stated that "due to, in great part, the efforts of the insular Department of Agriculture and Commerce . . . all credit programs [under the Farm Credit Act] had been made available on the island. To such aim, the Commissioner traveled to [Washington] in November 1933, presenting to the authorities the case of Puerto Rico and the need on the island to establish the different credit agencies of the Farm Credit Administration."[56] During his visit to Washington, Commissioner Chardón met with George H. Stevenson, president of the Production Credit Corporation of Baltimore, and with Dr. F. H. Bomberger, president of the Bank for Cooperatives, both of whom assured him of their commitment to establish said agencies in Puerto Rico within the shortest time frame possible.[57] These promises were kept, and the Puerto Rico Production Credit Association and the Bank of Cooperatives were established on the island less than a year later.

As a show of good faith, Miles H. Fairbanks began operations of the Production Credit Corporation of Baltimore in Puerto Rico on March 1, 1934. Other local Production Credit Associations quickly followed, all established to take advantage of these new financing opportunities. (See table 4.2.) Although more than half of the total capital available (63 percent) was divided among five sugar cane Production Credit Associations, the largest single allocation was made to the one tobacco Production Credit Association, which received 24 percent of the available capital. Considering that typical loans averaged 9 to 12 percent interest, these production loans, at 5 percent fixed interest, were seen as a godsend by farmers across the island.[58]

Loans made by the Bank for Cooperatives in Puerto Rico would finance the construction of necessary buildings, including factories and warehouses, for the processing of agricultural products. The life of a loan would be from five to ten years, at an interest rate of 4.5 percent.[59] Additionally, loans would be made for one year at 4 percent interest to assist in the marketing of products. Considering that the single largest physical expense for a tobacco grower was the building of an appropriate curing barn, these loans were crucial to the financial solvency of tobacco farms. Tobacco cooperatives applied for loans to build ranches that their members could use for a nominal fee.

The final law tied to the Agricultural Relief Act, and the most important in terms of cash benefit for small farmers in Puerto Rico, was the Agricultural Adjustment Act (Public Law 73–10 of May 12, 1933), which was an attempt to regulate prices by limiting the available quantity of a particular agricultural product. The bill included "provisions for adjusting production, regulating markets, protecting consumers compensating cooperators, expanding exports, removing market surpluses and obtaining revenue in order to raise farm purchasing power."[60] Although many agricultural commodities were included in

TABLE 4.2

PRODUCTION CREDIT ASSOCIATIONS ESTABLISHED IN PUERTO RICO IN 1934

Name	Agricultural product	Capital
Asociación de Créditos Refaccionarios de Cafeteros	coffee	$50,000.00
Asociación de Créditos Refaccionarios para Frutas	citrus and pineapple	250,000.00
Asociación de Créditos Refaccionarios de Cosecheros de Tabaco	tobacco	400,000.00
Asociación de Créditos Refaccionarios del Norte Central	sugar cane	150,000.00
Asociación de Créditos Refaccionarios del Norte	sugar cane	200,000.00
Asociación de Créditos Refaccionarios del Noroeste	sugar cane	200,000.00
Asociación de Créditos Refaccionarios del Este Central	sugar cane	200,000.00
Asociación de Créditos Refaccionarios del Sur	sugar cane	250,000.00
Asociación de Créditos Refaccionarios del Sureste	sugar cane	200,000.00

Source: "Organización de la Administración de Créditos Agrícolas," *EAP* 14, no. 1 (Jan. 1934): 4.

the Agricultural Adjustment Act, tobacco growers greatly benefited from its economic programs, whether in the United States or in Puerto Rico.

The program was based on providing parity payments to farmers who left land unplanted. For American tobacco, the goal was to reduce plantings by 30 percent. A specific quota would be set for each planter based on his total acreage, past production, and resources available to cultivate his land. To make sure tobacco farmers' income was not further reduced, benefit payments would make up the difference in receipts. These subsidies could be made in the form of rent for unused land, adjustments on the market price of tobacco, or deficiency payments for tobacco production that fell below the specified allotment.[61] If farmers wanted to receive benefit payments, they signed contracts adhering to their allotments. Farmers who did not sign contracts, or who grew tobacco over their quota, would be taxed from 25 percent to 33 percent of the market price.[62] The act also created the Agricultural Adjustment Administration (AAA), a federal agency that would be responsible for establishing and managing the program.

In Puerto Rico, where the tobacco sector was still recovering from the bumper crop of 1927, the AAA provided a structure wherein tobacco farmers could reduce plantings without sacrificing income. Shortly after the AAA was passed by the U.S. Congress, the director of the Tobacco Program of the AAA in Washington, Dr. J. B. Hutson, visited Puerto Rico. During his meeting with Commissioner Chardón, he made a commitment to do everything possible to extend AAA benefits to Puerto Rico. In March 1934, James Bernard Gibbs was appointed to supervise AAA allotments on the island.[63]

Over 11,000 tobacco farms extending over 30,000 cuerdas were affected by AAA contracts when the Agricultural Adjustment Act was extended to Puerto Rico.[64] Because the 1933–1934 planting was already in the ground when the law was applied to the island, adjustments were made to the benefit payment structure. Farmers who either destroyed or greatly reduced the second planting of 1933–1934 would receive $10–15 for each destroyed cuerda of tobacco, depending on its classification. For the crop years 1934–1935 and 1935–1936, the payment would be increased and farmers would receive $30 for each unplanted cuerda and another payment at the end of the harvest for 30 percent of the value of the crop that would have been planted. Interestingly, this is the same amount as American tobacco farmers were receiving.

The tobacco regions were assigned almost all of the available AAA allotments in Puerto Rico from 1934 to 1939. The eastern highland region, in particular, received three-quarters of the available tobacco allotment during that time.[65] Such widespread participation in the AAA program resulted in improved financial returns for tobacco farmers. (See table 4.3.) Although in some years the difference in income was a little over 1 percent, in other years AAA payments meant a 48 percent increase in income, a significant difference for anyone involved in commercial agriculture.

AAA subsidies were funded through a tax levied on processors of agricultural products. In 1936, the Agricultural Adjustment Act was declared unconstitutional by the Supreme Court of the United States because the processing tax was placing undue pressure on one group of farmers to benefit another. The Soil Conservation and Domestic Allotment Act of 1935, which made benefit payments to farmers who planted soil conservation crops instead of market crops, covered some of the payments made by the AAA until a second Agricultural Adjustment Act was approved on February 16, 1938

TABLE 4.3

FARM PRICE FOR TOBACCO AND AAA PAYMENTS, 1933–1940
(PRICES IN CENTS PER POUND)

Crop year	Farm price	Farm price including AAA payments	Difference in income	Percentage of increase in income due to AAA payment
1933–1934	14.18	18.81	4.63	32.7%
1934–1935	17.22	17.41	0.19	1.1
1935–1936	15.32	22.79	7.47	48.8
1936–1937	14.96	15.59	0.63	4.2
1937–1938	11.81	12.36	0.55	4.7
1938–1939	16.86	19.98	3.12	18.5
1939–1940	13.87	15.74	1.87	13.5

Source: Roberto Huyke and R. Colón Torres, "Costo de producción de tabaco en Puerto Rico, 1937–38," Boletín de la Estación Experimental Agrícola 56 (1940): 5, 8.

(Public Law 75–430). Because this act paid for subsidies through a general tax, it was acceptable to the Supreme Court.

Although many more legislative changes would occur between 1935 and 1940, agricultural credit legislation took a back seat to far-reaching programs of land reform. The Resettlement Administration (1935), later incorporated into the Farm Security Administration (1937 and 1938 in Puerto Rico), and the Puerto Rican Reconstruction Administration (1935) made funds available for farm ownership, resettlement programs, and subsistence cultivation.[66] The Bankhead-Jones Farm Tenant Act (1937) made loans available for land and equipment purchases, and production credit became the responsibility of the Emergency Crop Loan Office.[67] However, the change in Puerto Rico from an agricultural economy to an industrial one that began in 1940 shifted the financial interest of the federal and insular legislators from agricultural concerns to capital incentives for corporate investment.

Conclusion

The majority of tobacco farmers obtained credit from noninstitutional sources, such as refaccionistas, lenders who were local landowners, merchants, or leaf traders. Refaccionistas, in addition to being production credit providers, also acted as buyers and marketing agents of the leaf they had financed, thereby exerting a tremendous amount of control over the price paid to farmers. Interest rates for contratos de refacción varied, from 9 percent to 15 percent or higher, and often included additional charges for warehousing, transportation, or simply "expenses." This arrangement led to abuses on the part of the lenders, and the farm price paid to tobacco farmers was barely enough to cover expenses. In fact, many tobacco growers were in debt before the tobacco season began, and this debt did not include whatever production credit may have been acquired later.

It is no wonder, then, that federal and insular administrators, American observers, and agricultural representatives bemoaned the credit structure of the island, calling it "evil" and "dirty." Because the situation was equally difficult for farmers in the United States, the federal government had, since 1916, been involved in enacting agricultural legislation to improve the standard of living of American farmers. Most of the legislation had to do with the establishment of credit institutions that would provide the necessary money for farmers to cultivate their crop, improve their land and buildings, and finance their homes. It was due to pressure from the agricultural sector of the island and the insular government that these laws were extended to Puerto Rico.

By 1940 there was a well-established institutional credit structure in Puerto Rico made up of federal and insular banking institutions and commercial private banks.[68] Credit was available at reasonable rates and for any length of time that a farmer needed. The Farm Credit Administration, through the Federal Intermediate Credit Bank of Baltimore and the Puerto Rico Production Credit Association, provided short- and intermediate-term credit. The Federal Land Bank of Baltimore, and its subsidiaries in San Juan, provided long-term credit. The Baltimore Bank for Cooperatives provided operating capital and commodities loans for cooperative associations to lend to their members at nominal interest rates. It is perhaps surprising that with all this activity, only a small number of Puerto Rican farmers were taking advantage of federal credit programs.

In a study of small farms conducted by the Department of Labor and the Puerto Rican Reconstruction Administration in 1936, only 1 percent of the farms studied obtained financing from commercial banks.[69] Noninstitutional lenders still served as the principal source of credit for small tobacco, sugar, coffee, and minor crop farms, even after twenty years of available institutional credit. Fifty-three percent of tobacco farms reported that they received credit from refaccionistas.[70] It appears that institutional credit programs, although well intentioned, only served those farmers who had a track record with other banks, were in a stable financial situation, or perhaps were the largest producers.

For example, Manuel Soto Aponte, a tobacco grower in Caguas, signed a contrato de refacción for $2,000 with American Colonial Bank of Puerto Rico to cultivate 60 cuerdas of tobacco in 1927. One thousand dollars was paid immediately and another $1,000 was paid in December. It is interesting to note that the interest rate was set at 9 percent and that the harvested tobacco had to be delivered to warehouses specified by the bank.[71] Both of these contract stipulations were no different from the ones found in the contratos de refacción from noninstitutional lenders cited above. It is apparent from the similarities in the contracts that there was much more connection between the institutional and noninstitutional credit establishments than previously thought. If credit could be obtained under similar terms from either institutional or noninstitutional establishments, then farmers may have decided to request credit from already familiar lenders, and this could partly explain why participation rates in institutional credit systems remained so low.

It is also not unusual for farmers to look toward institutions, both public and private, for long-term credit needs, but to prefer noninstitutional credit sources for short and intermediate credit. In his discussion of the use of store credit in the United States, Jesse E. Pope argues that informal credit can thrive, regardless of the availability of formal credit institutions, and that, "This is due partly to the convenience of the system, partly to the failure of farmers to realize that in paying the 'credit prices' of the storekeeper, they are paying him a rate of interest higher than they would have to pay the bank and partly to the fact that the storekeeper can give credit to farmers who would be unable to obtain it from the bank."[72]

Like these farmers in the United States, farmers in Puerto Rico were hesitant to adopt banking practices if their immediate needs were being met through merchants or other noninstitutional sources of credit. Puerto Rican participation in credit programs nevertheless meant that they were interested in taking advantage of whatever programs were available to them. Tobacco growers, in particular, benefited greatly from credit and parity payments, extending the viability of their chosen crop at least until the shift in development strategies of the 1940s.

CHAPTER 5

Technology

MODERN AGRICULTURE, HOME
MANAGEMENT, AND RURAL PROGRESS

*The interest of the public in the work of the Station, and the general
desire awakened in the intelligent farmer to improve his methods and
procedure, have created a demand for more and more cooperation on the
part of the Station with the planters and even the industrialists of the
island, in the form of direct help in the immediate solution of their
everyday problems.*

—F. A. López Domínguez, director of the Insular
Agricultural Experiment Station, 1926

As was the case with the negotiation of the colonial political structure and the
demands for beneficial legislation, Puerto Ricans were involved in a constant
transfer of agricultural technology between the island and the mainland. The
development of tobacco as a profitable export product after the U.S. occupation of Puerto Rico occurred, in large part, because scientists, tobacco corporations, tobacco farmers, and the insular and federal governments supported the
science of tobacco, from research to the practical application of scientific discoveries on the cultivation fields. This practical application of scientific knowledge also extended into the rural home. In an attempt to improve their living
conditions, Puerto Rican housewives learned the latest techniques in food
preservation, nutritional information, the importance of sanitation and
hygiene, child-rearing strategies, home improvement, and sewing.

The word "housewives" is used throughout this chapter to refer to the
women in the rural areas who participated in the home demonstration
programs discussed herein. The problems associated with using such a word
are many, and I use the word "housewives" recognizing the limitations of the

category. Women in the fields of Puerto Rico, especially women in the tobacco regions, often participated in all the farming chores, including clearing, fertilizing, planting, weeding, and harvesting. They were much more than caretakers and homemakers; they were workers, farmers, and some were landowners. However, in all the literature and reports of the period, the women are referred to as "housewives," and it will be useful to keep that construct to discuss the programs and the impact of those programs.

Because government officials believed that the main obstacle to the continued expansion of the agricultural sector was a lack of sophistication in farming techniques, they looked to science to provide solutions.[1] Puerto Rican and American scientists, already focused on the particular problems of sugar, were called upon to begin a careful agronomic study of the tobacco plant and its cultivation, including its life cycle, its susceptibility to pests and diseases, and efficient planting techniques.

The insular government actively disseminated such information since science would only be useful if translated into actual changes in agricultural techniques. To accomplish this, insular authorities, with the assistance of the federal government and the support of the Asociación de Agricultores Puertorriqueños (AAP), established the Department of Agriculture and Labor and funded the development of agricultural experiment stations. These institutions were responsible for both agricultural research and its application in the field. Tobacco growers, like other farmers throughout the island, became involved in scientific study by attending lectures and demonstrations where new agricultural techniques were presented, lobbying the insular legislature for funding for tobacco research, and ultimately applying new techniques on their farms. Insular legislators, at the insistence of tobacco growers and other members of the AAP, lobbied the U.S. Congress for the extension to Puerto Rico of laws that would support agricultural science. When government agencies were unable to meet the research needs of the tobacco sector, growers pressured the insular legislature to establish independent institutions dedicated to tobacco research, such as the Comisión para Proteger el Tabaco de Puerto Rico and the Instituto de Tabaco. These organizations were established with the financial support of the insular government and the cooperation of the federal and insular scientific communities.

The large tobacco-processing corporations were also interested in improving tobacco through seed selection and in obtaining higher yields per cuerda, which would guarantee a steady and uniform supply of the product they needed. Like tobacco growers, corporations became involved in scientific inquiry when the insular government's funding proved inadequate. They invested in the establishment of experimental fields, hiring tobacco specialists, and collaborating with the Agricultural Experiment Station and the Department of Agriculture in ongoing research and practical experimentation.

But the insular government of Puerto Rico, which included both Americans and Puerto Ricans, in conjunction with the federal government, saw the need to expand and modernize the agricultural sector as much more than a mere economic necessity; it was an opportunity to improve the harsh living conditions found in rural Puerto Rico in the early twentieth century. Government officials believed that an increase in agricultural production would alleviate chronic unemployment in the countryside. This meant not only the expansion of export crops but an increase in fruit and vegetable cultivation, which could contribute to the well-being of the family by providing necessary nutrition and a potential source of cash income. Equally important was a commitment to modernizing rural areas, where people lived in "appalling poverty and disease."[2] The majority of the rural population was illiterate and nutrition was inadequate, as most suffered from a "monotonous and debilitating diet."[3] It was in the home where the improvement of rural life would begin.

These concerns were in line with the mission of the Asociación de Agricultores, which also saw science and technology as a way to improve conditions in the rural areas. Government officials put forth a two-pronged rural development plan based on the rational and practical application of cutting-edge scientific knowledge. First, scientists affiliated with the Department of Agriculture, the University of Puerto Rico, and the Agricultural Experiment Station conducted research to find ways that agricultural products could be cultivated efficiently with minimum production costs for the farmer and maximum yields. A program of instruction for farmers consisting of live demonstrations at experimental farms, visits to individual farms, and media outreach (including print and radio after 1920) was established to bring the latest research to the fields. Second, home economics professionals, mostly women, created programs of instruction for women that promoted efficient home management and the family's well-being.

The science of tobacco provided an arena for extensive cooperative relations among tobacco interests, scientists, and the insular and federal governments. The development and practical application of the science of tobacco, something that was actively demanded by Puerto Ricans, indicates that Puerto Ricans negotiated yet another area of the U.S. empire—technological knowledge—to maintain the viability of the economic sector that provided sustenance for their families. Furthermore, the acquisition and application of scientific knowledge was not exclusive to the tobacco fields, as women in the tobacco regions participated in the management of their families' health and well-being by adopting home economics strategies.

THE BEGINNINGS OF SCIENTIFIC INQUIRY
AND EXPERIMENTAL STATIONS

The interest in scientific research was not new to post-1898 society. The last three decades of the nineteenth century were characterized by an unprecedented interest in scientific study.[4] During this period, the Spanish Crown canceled all import taxes levied on machinery and other cultivation tools and reduced duties on many agricultural products. In addition, agricultural leaflets began circulating throughout the island describing new agricultural techniques. The efficacy of printed leaflets as a method to disseminate agricultural information among a mostly illiterate population is questionable, at best, and it was clear that new strategies would need to be implemented for the knowledge to impact the largest numbers of farmers on the island.

The interest in agricultural technology and the desire to widen the availability of such technology occurred at the same time as the Spanish Crown loosened trade restrictions, creating new market opportunities for Puerto Rican products. Agricultural technology could provide the increase in production necessary to meet the possible demand resulting from expanded trading. In 1876, Puerto Rican agriculturalists petitioned colonial authorities for the enforcement on the island of a *Real Orden* that mandated agricultural instruction via the establishment of agricultural schools and experimental farms.[5] This royal decree specified that the colonies would be assisted by royal authorities in order to comply with the mandate. Although the Crown agreed to cede land to the Puerto Rican government, the project was officially suspended in 1883 due to lack of funds.

In 1887, the Crown once again received a petition to establish two agricultural stations (one in Bayamón and the other in Mayagüez) dedicated to the study of plants, insects, land, and water, the training of foremen to work in the fields, and the distribution of cultivation machinery. Both stations were also charged with the study of tobacco in order to improve the quality of the crop.[6] The plan was approved in 1888 and the stations began operating shortly thereafter. Unfortunately, lack of funds forced the closing of the stations by 1897, and all materials and equipment were sold in a public auction in 1898.[7] The interest in scientific inquiry remained, however, and when investment in agriculture after the American occupation resulted in new possibilities for scientific study, Puerto Rican farmers were enthusiastic about participation.

The U.S. Department of Agriculture established an agricultural station in Mayagüez in 1901, and the scientists who worked there were mostly interested in experiments designed to find new agricultural products appropriate for Puerto Rico's climate and topography. The diversification of Puerto Rico's agricultural sector was of no interest to established sugar planters, who wanted to see investments in sugar-specific research.[8] Accordingly, the Porto Rico Sugar Growers Association founded the Experiment Station of Río Piedras, an agricultural research facility that would deal with sugar cultivation issues.[9] The station was established on 200 cuerdas of land in Río Piedras bought from Francisco Robledo y García on July 25, 1910.

Although the station in Río Piedras was focused on sugar, there was much pressure from farmers throughout the island for scientists to conduct research on other crops, such as tobacco, citrus, and coffee. In fact, J. T. Crowley, the director of the station during its initial years, indicated that many farmers wanted to establish substations dedicated to research on nonsugar crops, and he commented on the "cordial spirit of cooperation" he found among them.[10] Because the station was on land that bordered Caguas, the largest tobacco-growing municipality at the time, tobacco was the second major research project for the station, and systematic studies of tobacco problems began in 1912.[11] A year later, George B. Merrill, an entomologist on the station's staff, conducted a comprehensive experiment that focused upon insects plaguing tobacco farms out of a substation in Aibonito, another center of tobacco cultivation.[12]

In 1914, the Board of Commissioners of Agriculture decided that the station should not belong solely to sugar planters and that it should be an organization of the insular state. Accordingly, the station was donated to the insular government with a mandate that there "must be a general broadening of the station activities to include other Puerto Rican crops."[13] The transfer was approved by the legislature of Puerto Rico with the enactment of Law #13 on March 28, 1914. The law also changed the station's name to the Insular Agricultural Experiment Station (IAES).

THE SCIENCE OF THE FARM: EXPERIMENTAL STATIONS, THE DEPARTMENT OF AGRICULTURE, AND TOBACCO RESEARCH

Research on tobacco expanded immediately and there was an increase in the number of scientists dedicated to the study of all aspects of the tobacco sector, from seedbed plantings to the manufacturing process. John A. Stevenson, a tobacco pathologist, studied the problem of cigar mold, which tended to appear several days after manufacture.[14] R. T. Cotton studied the life cycle of the tobacco flea-beetle, considered "the worst enemy to tobacco."[15] A year later, Cotton was in charge of planting an experimental tobacco plot on IAES grounds.[16] In 1917, tobacco scientists were busy studying *lapas*, limpets or suck-flies, and detailed a plan of action to treat the problem.[17] In short, tobacco became as central a project for the IAES as research on sugar cane, and this reflected the increasing importance of tobacco as a commercial product for export.

The Organic Act of March 2, 1917, created the Department of Agriculture and Labor.[18] It divided the island into twelve agronomical districts with a sub-inspector in charge of each district. With this act, responsibility for the agricultural sector fell into the hands of the insular state, as the commissioner of agriculture and labor clearly understood. He observed: "The legislature [must] now shape an organization of [agricultural] services . . . in order that the best practices shall be established in accordance with the conditions of the country for increasing and improving production, bettering the existing practices, and introducing new ones that shall contribute to the economic development of the island."[19] The department took their charge seriously, and a strong relationship between the Department of Agriculture and the IAES was cemented when Joint Resolution #18, signed on November 30, 1917, transferred the jurisdiction of the IAES to the insular Department of Agriculture and Labor.[20]

The transfer made administrative sense since there had been a great deal of cooperation between scientists at the IAES and those at the U.S. Department of Agriculture and the Bureau of Plant Industry, Soils, and Agricultural Engineering. This cooperation was ongoing, with scientists repeatedly traveling between insular and federal stations for training, demonstrations, and experiments. For example, during 1919, a joint experiment was conducted with Harry Ardell Allard, a scientist in the Office of Tobacco Investigations of the Bureau of Plant Industry, Soils, and Agricultural Engineering.[21] E. E. Barker, a scientist in the Department of Plant Breeding of Cornell University, was in Puerto Rico in 1920 to conduct seed selection experiments throughout the tobacco zones.[22] American scientists also served as IAES staff. While George N. Wolcott served as the staff entomologist at the station, he conducted the first studies on the *gusano de candela*, a tobacco split worm, in 1922.[23]

Puerto Rican scientists were equally involved in all aspects of tobacco research at the station. J.A.B. Nolla joined the IAES staff in the early 1920s and by 1926 was in charge of the tobacco field laboratory.[24] Carlos Chardón, perhaps the most important agricultural researcher, who later became an influential economic policy maker, began his tenure as a public officer by working on tobacco experiments at the IAES.[25] Puerto Rican scientists were involved in scientific inquiry as project leaders, as auxiliary staff, and in high-level administrative positions. Such extensive participation in the scientific life of the island by both American and Puerto Rican scientists demonstrates that federal agricultural agencies were as interested in the modernization of agricultural practices as insular ones, and that scientists on the island and the mainland were in constant communication about projects, findings, and practical application in the fields.

The collaboration between the Department of Agriculture and Labor and the IAES was crucial to the application of scientific findings throughout the rural areas. The two institutions not only delved into all aspects of scientific study, but they were actively involved in the campaign to organize farmers throughout the island. Each of the agricultural divisions of the Department of Agriculture and Labor—sugar, tobacco, and citrus—was assigned an agronomist and deputy inspector. Among their duties were the popularization of "modern agricultural methods" and the urging of farmers to establish cooperative societies and loan associations.[26] By 1920 agricultural inspectors had made 1,984 visits to the northern areas and 1,777 to the southern areas of the island.[27] They noted living conditions, the number of cuerdas dedicated to each crop, the average yield per acre, and prices that were paid for crops. Inspectors also advised and instructed farmers on the latest methods for pest control and the most productive application of fertilizers, and offered ideas on how to effectively market their crops. Finally, inspectors conducted live demonstrations and discussed the latest scientific findings. (See table 5.1.) It is interesting to note that over 50 percent of all lectures were delivered in tobacco districts. Almost half of the more than 13,000 people who attended these lectures did so in tobacco regions. It is likely that those in attendance were tobacco growers enthusiastic about scientific discoveries that would potentially improve the quality and quantity of their crops. Better product would, the growers hoped, earn higher prices in the market.

Tobacco improvement continued to be a major component in the work of the Insular Agricultural Experiment Station as well. New breeds, better understanding of cultivation and curing methods, and up-to-date knowledge of how to combat insects and diseases contributed to the development in the field laboratories of a more uniform crop, higher yields per acre, and better product quality.[28] IAES administrators were committed to the dissemination of scientific findings through "intimate and continuous contact" with farmers throughout the island.[29] The results of all experiments were published in their entirety in the monthly *Bulletin of the Agricultural Experiment Station*, published in Spanish and English, and excerpted in local magazines and newspapers. In addition, shorter essays and advice columns were widely

TABLE 5.1

LECTURES HELD IN TOBACCO-GROWING MUNICIPALITIES
AND ATTENDANCE, 1920

Municipality	Number of lectures	Attendance
Aguas Buenas	5	159
Aibonito	3	98
Arecibo	8	731
Barceloneta	4	222
Barranquitas	1	60
Caguas	12	448
Camuy	5	236
Cayey	1	90
Ciales	1	50
Comerío	2	400
Corozal	6	245
Hatillo	5	328
Humacao	2	26
Isabela	12	606
Juncos	9	290
Las Piedras	2	65
Morovis	1	200
Orocovis	2	108
Quebradillas	6	322
San Lorenzo	14	610
Utuado	16	909
Total in Puerto Rico	228	13,048
Total in tobacco regions	117	6,203
Percentage in tobacco regions	51.3%	47.5%

Source: Ramón Gandía Córdova, Acting Commissioner of Agriculture and Labor, *Report of the Commissioner of Agriculture and Labor of Porto Rico, 1920. From the Report of the Governor of Porto Rico, 1920, pages 503–566 inclusive* (Washington, DC: Government Printing Office, 1920), 518–519.

disseminated among farmers by station scientists working at the local substations. By 1920, the bulletin had a circulation of over 600 copies, more than 400 of them in Spanish. A year later, the number of Spanish subscriptions had doubled.[30]

Beginning in 1920, a change in attitude became evident in the scientific community and in the governmental agencies that dealt with agriculture. Scientists, as well as the government officials affiliated with them, recognized that agricultural research and the application of scientific findings would only guarantee a healthy crop, and that true modernization and steady agricultural development would require the involvement of other agencies and the improvement of the island's economic and physical infrastructure. Scientists in the Insular Agricultural Experimental Station, with the support of the Department of Agriculture and Labor, lobbied for an expanded role and for conducting studies that would improve economic and social conditions throughout Puerto Rico. The high cost of transporting agricultural goods from the interior of the island to maritime shipping facilities; the establishment of adequate agricultural credit structures; the shortage of fuel, wood, and other materials for rural construction; and the lack of organizations to facilitate the marketing of agricultural products, were as much factors in the ability of tobacco growers to make a living as the type of seed planted.[31] Additionally, the nutrition, sanitation, hygiene, and comfort of the rural population was under scrutiny. This marked the beginning of the expansion of the mission of the IAES, from an organization purely dedicated to agricultural research to one interested in the modernization of rural areas and the generalized development of Puerto Rican agriculture. These interests and concerns would be echoed by the newly established AAP, which, as previously indicated, included in its mission statement a commitment to the improvement in the quality of life in the rural areas of Puerto Rico.

The decade of the 1920s was one of outreach and growth for the Insular Agricultural Experiment Station. Increased interest on the part of farmers throughout the island resulted in the creation of an outreach program in which scientists visited working farms to teach farmers new cultivation techniques. Because of the challenge of disseminating information to a large number of illiterate farmers, especially those from the older generation who had not benefited from increased literacy after 1898, field visits and demonstration farms became the most effective tools for outreach.[32] Demonstration farms were either built independently by the IAES or were set up in private farmland donated by local farmers or by tobacco corporations. For tobacco growers, these farms were an opportunity to see for themselves the success of modern methods of cultivation such as protecting seedbeds with cloth, using appropriate quantities of fertilizers, and utilizing adequate leaf curing and storage methods. Those unable to travel to the demonstration farms took advantage of field visits by IAES scientists and Department of Agriculture specialists. These men and women visited thousands of farms and gave hundreds of Sunday lectures throughout the island. They demonstrated new planting techniques, answered questions about government programs and explained changes in relevant legislature, and discussed market conditions for particular crops. Farmers' participation in such programs was constant and demonstrated a willingness to experiment with better cultivation methods and modern, scientific techniques that could provide better returns on their investments. The 1929–1930 IAES report noted that "farmers have availed themselves to a greater extent of the opportunities of service offered by the Station."[33]

A brief discussion of the changes in the average yield of tobacco leaf per cuerda in the tobacco regions from 1910 to 1940 illustrates the impact that IAES programs had on tobacco cultivation. Tobacco specialists at the IAES had defined the depletion of minerals from soil used in tobacco cultivation and the poor quality of tobacco seed throughout the island as two immediate problems to be addressed by research at the station. Experiments with different types and proportions of fertilizers as well as plant breeding experiments began in 1916 and continued through 1938.[34] The goal was to increase yield per cuerda to an average of 800 pounds so that acreage in tobacco could be reduced and vacant fields could then be used for other crops such as vegetables, tubers, or fruits.[35] In addition, "new varieties of greater yielding capacity, good quality, and resistance to diseases [would] allow the farmer to restrict his plantings to his better lands without reducing his total production."[36]

IAES scientists, who had achieved success in field experiments, shared the new techniques with farmers across the tobacco regions. In 1910, the average yield per cuerda in the tobacco regions was 515 pounds of tobacco leaf per cuerda. After thirteen years of experimentation, the IAES report of 1923 stated that tobacco cultivation had become more profitable and that the "selection of more productive varieties, better cultural methods for the seedbeds and field plantings, use of fertilizers and adoption of control methods to check disease and insect damage have done wonders."[37] By 1940, average yields had increased to 698 pounds per cuerda, an increase of 35 percent from 1910. (See table 5.2.) Because tobacco-cultivated soil does not miraculously replenish itself, it is reasonable to assume that the improvement in yield was due to changes in the use of fertilizers, seeds, or other general cultivation methods. In addition, 82 percent of all tobacco-growing municipalities increased their

TABLE 5.2

YIELD PER CUERDA IN THE TOBACCO REGIONS, 1910–1940
(IN POUNDS PER CUERDA)

	1910	1920	1930	1940
Eastern Highlands				
Aguas Buenas	432	583	662	814
Aibonito	552	502	685	791
Barranquitas	378	528	666	784
Bayamón	33	546	573	628
Caguas	565	648	670	864
Cayey	561	644	672	828
Cidra	465	706	607	837
Comerío	400	502	565	723
Corozal	529	434	514	606
Gurabo	454	489	537	682
Humacao	535	629	462	587
Juncos	545	424	402	576
Naranjito	306	431	540	606
San Lorenzo	187	467	515	868
Toa Alta	668	402	495	620
Yabucoa	620	567	344	580
Average for Eastern Highlands	482	562	589	747
Western Highlands				
Arecibo	723	399	424	553
Barceloneta	431	282	506	623
Camuy	561	271	540	416
Ciales	366	356	395	653
Hatillo	601	361	658	580
Isabela	627	453	819	671
Manatí	404	366	674	687
Morovis	323	426	482	636
Orocovis	383	470	541	748

(*continued*)

TABLE 5.2

YIELD PER CUERDA IN THE TOBACCO REGIONS, 1910–1940
(IN POUNDS PER CUERDA) (*continued*)

Western Highlands

Quebradillas	461	476	727	589
Utuado	507	360	516	664
Average for Western Highlands	549	376	570	648

Sources: Data for 1910 from *Agricultural Census 1910*, 72–77. Data for 1920 from *Agriculture Census 1920*, 408–415. Data for 1930 from *Census 1930*, 72–77. Data for 1940 from *Agriculture Census 1940*, 226, 237.

yield per cuerda from 1910 to 1940, a remarkable achievement and evidence that IAES programs were effective. Furthermore, the widespread increase in yields suggests that it was not only one or two large farms that adopted scientific methods of cultivation, but that in fact a large number of small-scale farmers—most tobacco farms measured less than 10 cuerdas—must have done so as well.

Funding for the Insular Agricultural Experiment Station had been problematic since its transfer to the insular government in 1914. Until 1917, when the IAES-UPR was placed under the jurisdiction of the Department of Agriculture and Labor, funds for its operation were allocated from the insular treasury. Some experiments, however, were funded by the U.S. Department of Agriculture and its affiliates. To address the lack of a stable operations budget, a fund was created called "Venta de Productos Agrícolas," which would deposit all monies collected from the sale of agricultural products cultivated in IAES's experimental fields into an operation fund for the station. Still, the amount of money collected was too small to make a difference, and in 1919, a law was enacted that taxed sales of chemical fertilizer at 20 cents per ton and mineral fertilizer at 10 cents per ton, with the objective of funding the IAES.[38] With expanded services and a larger staff, this tax was still not enough to cover expenses at the IAES, and another law was approved in 1925 that levied a 20-cent tax for every ton of animal feed sold on the island. The activities of the IAES were so pervasive that funding continued as an issue into the late 1920s, an issue often included in the annual agenda of the Asociación de Agricultores Puertorriqueños and commented upon in the pages of *El agricultor puertorriqueño*.

Relief did not come until 1931, when the Smith-Lever Act of 1914 was extended to Puerto Rico. This federal law allocated funds for the dissemination of agricultural research programs conducted in land-grant colleges and universities to the general community through the Agricultural Extension Service. The law was approved by the Puerto Rican legislature in 1934, at which point the insular Department of Agriculture transferred the jurisdiction of the IAES to the University of Puerto Rico's College of Agriculture in Mayagüez. The change of jurisdiction meant that the IAES could take advantage of funding provided through the Hatch Act of 1887 and the Smith-Lever legislation and that for the first time the station would in fact have an operating budget that was independent from funds raised through taxation.[39] Until 1944, the IAES would be allocated an annual budget of $25,000, at which point it would receive an annual increase of $5,000 according to the law.[40] The name of the IAES was changed to the Agricultural Experiment Station of the College of Agriculture and Mechanical Arts of the University of Puerto Rico (AES-UPR).

Federal funding allowed the AES-UPR, in collaboration with the Agricultural Extension Service, to finally address the expanded mission statement developed in the 1920s and study "the many economic problems affecting the welfare of farmers and the agricultural industry of Puerto Rico."[41] A Division of Agricultural Economics was created to address these problems, and studies began immediately. A comprehensive credit study that examined the mortgage status of 1,731 farms was conducted in 1935.[42] A year later, two separate surveys of small farms were conducted throughout the island.[43] The first project, called "Hatch Project #1," attempted to determine labor efficiency, cash flow, and total receipts of small farms. The other project, "Purnell Project #2 and Bankhead-Jones Project #10," studied 270 tobacco farms to determine the reasons for success or failure.[44] The projects, among many others, contributed to the understanding of the socioeconomic problems affecting not only tobacco farmers, but also the agricultural sector as a whole, and reflected a sincere interest from the scientific community in improving the living conditions of Puerto Ricans in the rural areas.[45]

The Agricultural Extension Service experienced a period of booming activity from 1936 to 1940, when Agricultural Extension Agents who were professional agronomists actively disseminated the new research undertaken by the AES-UPR. Agents were assigned to particular districts made up of several municipalities. Once in their district, agents organized Farmers' Committees that would assist the agent with formulating a scientific education plan appropriate for the particular area. In the tobacco regions, the Extension Service agents assisted farmers with fertilizer application, preparation of seedbeds, dealing with pests and diseases, and marketing advice.[46]

In his first official report as director of the Agricultural Extension Service, Dr. A. Rodríguez Géigel commented, "50% of all farms were visited by

Agricultural Extension Agents ... [as part of] the educational and service programs to improve the social and economic conditions of our rural zones."[47] The agents conducted demonstrations of agricultural techniques and explained the ever-changing legislation to farmers so that they could take advantage of agricultural programs. They also discussed environmental concerns, such as soil conservation, erosion, and water quality. The number of visits carried out by Agricultural Extension agents as well as the number of individual homes and farms more than tripled between 1936 and 1940. (See table 5.3.) Hundreds of thousands of men, women, and children participated in Extension Service programs, not only at field demonstrations, but also by visiting an Agricultural Extension Service office, volunteering as community leaders to implement programs, or joining 4-H Clubs, the program of the Agricultural Extension Service for youth.[48]

The decline of tobacco prices throughout the 1930s and the generalized difficulties faced by rural Puerto Ricans during the Great Depression led to scientific inquiry into the cultivation of subsistence crops. At the same time, funds appropriated for tobacco-specific research began to diminish. Scientific interest, as noted above, had expanded into other socioeconomic areas, and

TABLE 5.3

VISITS AND DEMONSTRATIONS MADE BY AGRICULTURAL
EXTENSION AGENTS AND ATTENDANCE, 1936–1940

	1936	1937	1938	1939	1940
Total number of visits to homes and farms	27,894	36,459	54,993	80,758	88,571
Number of individual home and farms visited[a]	13,233	16,573	26,312	37,886	43,208
Total number of demonstrations	322	2,173	2,812	3,806	4,820
Total number of attendees	n/a	29,144	34,445	39,689	54,590

Source: Rodríguez Géigel, Informe 1939–40, 8–9.

Note: Unfortunately, the data available in the Agricultural Extension Service reports vary from year to year, and so it is not possible to separate which visits were only to homes from those that were to working farms. Since the Agricultural Extension Service argues that the farm is intrinsically tied to the home, the data are useful to note the level of scientific educational activity in the rural zones.

money was diverted to other rural industries such as cattle, poultry, and dairy. The Department of Agriculture and Labor, which had until then worked side by side with the Agricultural Experiment Station to disseminate scientific information to farmers through the Agricultural Extension Service, reassigned that division to the University of Puerto Rico's College of Agriculture to once again take advantage of the availability of federal funds.[49] By 1940, most of the work being done by the Agricultural Experiment Station was limited to socioeconomic studies.[50] The reduction in funding for tobacco research meant that tobacco corporations and farmers had to become advocates for scientific research in tobacco.

The best example of corporate involvement in scientific research is provided by the Porto Rican American Tobacco Company (PRATC), the most important tobacco processor in Puerto Rico.[51] It manufactured and exported cigars in all price ranges and was the principal supplier of cigarettes for local consumption. Although small-scale growers provided most of the tobacco processed by the PRATC, the company became increasingly concerned about the uneven quality of the tobacco produced by Puerto Rican farmers. The PRATC established the subsidiary Porto Rican Leaf Tobacco Company to produce tobacco leaf of uniform quality, and the company became a major investor in tobacco research. With the assistance of the tobacco specialist of the Experiment Station, J.A.B. Nolla, it set up experimental farms where high-quality tobacco seedlings were grown under cloths to protect them from the elements. The farms also included extensive seedbeds with carefully selected seeds of varieties that were resistant to pests and diseases. Since one of the most insidious problems faced by the tobacco economy was the lack of proper curing and fermenting facilities, the company also built barns where tobacco leaf could be cured and warehouses where fermentation could occur. Experimentation with fermentation methods was constant, and included the effect on the leaf of different types and sizes of fermenting tanks, temperatures, and duration of fermentation period.

Facing further reductions in funding for tobacco research, tobacco farmers, with the support of the AAP, lobbied the insular legislature for the protection of the tobacco sector. The Comisión para Proteger el Tabaco de Puerto Rico and the Instituto de Tabaco were established as the result of relentless pressure applied by the farmers through constant lobbying of the insular and federal legislatures, negative press campaigns that portrayed government officials as abusive and indifferent, and the participation of tobacco farmers in agricultural organizations that knew how to pressure and manipulate the colonial bureaucracy.

The Commission for the Protection of Tobacco and the Tobacco Institute

The Comisión para Proteger el Tabaco de Puerto Rico was established on February 18, 1929, by the Puerto Rican legislature. Funding for the commission's operations would come from the personal contributions of each tobacco grower, an amount determined in proportion to production. Almost five months later, on July 8, 1929, a general assembly of the Tobacco Growers of Puerto Rico approved Joint Resolution No. 13 in support of the commission. An executive board was elected at this meeting from members who had been certified as "bona fide tobacco growers" by the assembly. Elected to the executive board were Agustín Fernández as president; Julián Gandía as vice president; Antonio Colón Rivera as secretary; Miguel Meléndez Muñoz, Rafael Arce Rollet, and Cándido Ramírez as members at large; and Francisco M. Zeno as executive director. The treasurer of Puerto Rico and the commissioner of agriculture also served as members of the commission.[52]

The commission's first order of business was to establish local committees in every municipality where tobacco was grown.[53] Tobacco growers fully participated in the establishment of these *juntas locales* (local boards), and only one year after the commission's founding, local committees were operational in all the tobacco districts. The committees assisted the commission in providing information about the condition of the crop during the planting period, acreage under cultivation, and expected yield per cuerda. They also disseminated the commission's reports regarding acreage restrictions due to Agricultural Adjustment Administration programs, market conditions on the island and abroad, and cooperative activities.[54]

The commission was charged with conducting a "survey of the problem of the tobacco market in Puerto Rico, studying cultivation methods and agricultural administration, and [conducting] any other study conducive or needed to protect and improve the agro-industrial conditions of Puerto Rican tobacco."[55] With the help of the tobacco specialist of the Agricultural Experiment Station, the commission set up experimental farms to conduct comparative production tests of tobacco varieties believed to be more resistant to disease and of better overall flavor. Like the AES-UPR, the goals of the commission were wider than scientific discovery and included a study of the development and administration of the tobacco cooperatives that existed in the United States as well as a continuous examination of the worldwide market situation for Puerto Rican tobacco. For example, a bulletin published in 1929 discussed a meeting with representatives from Spain, Austria, and Germany to discuss the possibility of opening up new markets for Puerto Rican tobacco.[56]

An important part of the tobacco survey would be a comprehensive tobacco census that would include names of tobacco growers, acreage planted, fertilizers used and amounts, the number of curing ranches, average yields per cuerda, and the average costs of cultivation. Agustín Fernández, president of the commission, met with Dr. W. A. Orton, president of the Tropical Plant Research Foundation in Washington, to secure an approximate budget of $45,000 to fund the study.

Under the law, the commission would assume the leadership of the Agencia de Garantía del Tabaco de Puerto Rico in New York (Tobacco Guarantee Agency or TGA).[57] The TGA was founded in 1921 to "discover fraud and adulteration of Puerto Rican tobacco, denounced constantly in the island and in the United States, and to that end, to promote the Puerto Rican product to the national market."[58] "Fraud" referred to the tobacco corporations' common practice of not detailing the provenance of the tobacco that they used in the manufacture of cigars. American consumers, as a result, were not aware that the tobacco they enjoyed came from Puerto Rico. "Adulteration" referred to the blending of Puerto Rican tobacco with cheaper cuts of tobacco from other regions in the United States or around the world. As indicated in chapter 1, the quality of Puerto Rican tobacco made it appropriate for blending with higher-priced Cuban tobacco. This allowed the cigar companies to market the cigars as "Cubans," commanding a higher retail price per cigar while paying lower wholesale prices for Puerto Rican, not Cuban, tobacco. The TGA was established as a governmental agency that would protect the interests of tobacco growers through the marketing of Puerto Rican tobacco to American consumers and by ensuring that Puerto Rican tobacco was labeled as such. Unfortunately, the TGA was plagued from its inception by an inadequate budget and frequent staff turnover.[59] Funding for the TGA was supposed to come from the payment of taxes and licensing fees by tobacco corporations, a process that was problematic mostly because corporations would delay or avoid payment.[60] The transfer of jurisdiction to the commission was intended to provide a more stable budget. The commission, now acting as direct supervisor of the TGA, would also be responsible for staffing the office in New York. The commission, however, was overburdened and underfunded, and its work with the TGA was ineffective.

Because the commission's operating budget depended on contributions from tobacco growers, it became an economic burden for them. Returns on the tobacco crop were often just enough to pay day laborers and cover the contrato de refacción. For small growers to give up scarce monetary resources was a hardship. The commission continued lobbying the legislature for increases in appropriations for tobacco research, arguing the unfairness of placing the burden of funding the research on individuals and not on the insular state. The commission continued to exist until 1936, but with such limited funding that its work was curtailed to having weekly briefings on the state of the industry and cooperating with lobbying efforts led by the Asociación de Agricultores Puertorriqueños.

Tobacco growers, disappointed with the outcome of the commission's work, asked once again for the support of the AAP. Growers recognized the importance of continuing scientific investigations into the problems of tobacco and, together with the AAP, pressured the Puerto Rican legislature to establish an institution whose sole purpose would be to sponsor research that would alleviate the economic and agricultural problems of tobacco growers. The Instituto de Tabaco de Puerto Rico was chartered through Joint Resolution #15 of the Puerto Rican legislature on July 22, 1935, as a government agency under the leadership of an executive board made up of the commissioner of agriculture and commerce, two tobacco growers, and two tobacco industrialists appointed by the governor with the consent of the insular Senate.[61] Unlike the commission, which depended on contributions from tobacco growers, the institute would obtain its funds from a line item appropriation from the insular budget. Additional monies would come from a 15-cent tax per hundredweight of tobacco sold on the island.[62]

The institute had both agricultural and industrial objectives. Its agricultural mission was to find the "solution to the problems concerning the cultivation of tobacco" and "the post-harvest manipulation of the crop." To do this, the institute established research branches in agronomy, chemistry, pathology, and genetics. Its industrial mission was to investigate "possible new markets and new uses for tobacco." The institute was also responsible for the promotion of "legislation beneficial to the tobacco industry at large."[63]

The Agricultural Experiment Station of the University of Puerto Rico collaborated with the institute from its inception. In 1935, the University of Puerto Rico ceded 12 cuerdas of land to the institute to establish a physical plant. A newly built structure, funded with monies from the Federal Emergency Relief Administration, housed the director's office, a conference room, and chemistry, genetics, and pathology laboratories.[64] A greenhouse and curing barn were built as well. The institute also set up a substation in Caguas on 16.5 cuerdas with two curing barns and experimental fermentation equipment.[65] Extensive tobacco projects were also established in Cayey, Aibonito, and Morovis. Like the AES-UPR, the institute was committed to publishing scientific findings. In addition, it set up a library with copies of agricultural publications that dealt with tobacco cultivation, such as *Tobacco* magazine and the *Revista de agricultura de*

Puerto Rico, as well as scholarly papers presented at local and international conferences.[66]

The institute became the voice of the industry in the insular legislature. Due to concerns over the authenticity of tobacco being sold in the United States under the "Tobacco from Puerto Rico" label, the institute successfully introduced legislation that regulated labeling. Law #16 was enacted in June 10, 1939, and stated that only tobacco actually grown in Puerto Rico could be labeled as such.[67] Some of the institute's legislative efforts were not successful. For example, it sponsored Bill No. 718 to establish a uniform classification system for filler tobacco used in cigarettes in order to protect farmers against arbitrary classification of crops by dealers and financiers. Although the bill had strong support from the growers, it faced strong opposition from buyers and never made it to the floor for debate.[68]

The institute's ability to effect change was greatly curtailed by the continued decline of the tobacco sector. Carlos Esteva recognized those limitations in 1940, when he wrote that:

> It would be folly, for example, to think that the Tobacco Institute of Puerto Rico or any other Insular Government agency is in a position to counterbalance the unfavorable factors [facing the tobacco industry]. Some of the maladjustments stretch out beyond our Insular geographical boundaries. They are the products of the economical and social evolution of the times, of the elastic interplay of forces in a far-away market where our crop is mainly consumed. Not even the concentrated and cooperative efforts of the people of Puerto Rico, their Insular and their Federal Government agencies, can cope with that broad problem in all its various aspects. Evidently the tobacco industry should readjust itself to the changing rhythm of consumers' preferences.[69]

Although the tobacco industry attempted to "readjust itself," it never recovered and the institute became another casualty of the reallocation of funds from agricultural projects to manufacturing ones during the 1950s.

THE SCIENCE OF THE HOME AND THE HOME DEMONSTRATION PROGRAM

Until 1920, scientific experimentation and education had been focused on maximizing agricultural output. The continued hardships of life in the rural areas of Puerto Rico, however, confronted agricultural scientists on a daily basis and resulted in expanded efforts on the part of the scientific community to conduct research that would shed light on the social and economic issues affecting the standard of living of the rural population. The Agricultural Extension Service argued that the farms (and the farmers who worked them) and the rural homes (and the women who cared for them) were inseparable, and that neither would succeed without the other.[70] The science of tobacco, with the cultivation field as laboratory and farmers as scientists, had succeeded in improving the economic returns of tobacco cultivation. The science of the home would have to do the same in the domestic arena by bringing "to the heart of the rural home the teachings of home economics that will assist the housewife in her household chores and that enable her to carry out a program that includes providing adequate nourishment for the family, the use of farm profits, and the improvement of the home in all its respects."[71]

To accomplish this, the Agricultural Extension Service organized a Home Demonstration program to operate within the jurisdiction of the Agricultural Extension Service, with its own administration and a team of Home Demonstration agents. The Home Demonstration agents, women trained in home economics at the College of Agriculture and Mechanical Arts of the University of Puerto Rico or at colleges and universities on the mainland, visited housewives on a regular basis. When the program began in 1936, there were fifteen agents working in the rural areas. Due to the program's success, the number of agents steadily increased, and by 1940 there were twenty Home Demonstration agents on staff, supported by another twenty-one auxiliary agents, for a total of forty-one agents.[72] Auxiliary agents were paid for by an allocation from the Puerto Rican Reconstruction Administration, an economic and social rehabilitation program established in 1935. Their appointment lasted for less than one year and depended on the needs of particular districts. Each agent, like the Agricultural Extension agents working in the fields, was responsible for a district consisting of two or three municipalities.

The Home Demonstration agent in a district would then organize a Housewives' Committee that would assist the agent in preparing an annual program especially tailored to deal with local problems. Although the agents had the scientific knowledge, the women in the committees were invaluable in creating a program that would be meaningful for local populations and were instrumental in creating excitement and promoting cooperation among those who participated in the programs.[73] The Home Demonstration program was well received by rural housewives, as demonstrated by their participation in sponsored demonstrations. In 1938, Home Demonstration agents visited 11,281 families throughout the rural areas, conducting 1,812 demonstrations that more than 19,000 housewives attended. (See table 5.4.) By 1940, the Home Demonstration Program had expanded dramatically, when agents visited 27,146 families, an increase of over 141 percent from 1938. The number

TABLE 5.4

EXPANSION OF HOME DEMONSTRATION PROGRAM, 1938–1940

	1938	1940	Percentage increase
Families visited by agents	11,281	27,146	140.63%
Number of demonstrations	1,812	2,563	41.45
Housewives who attended demonstrations	19,350	29,963	54.85

Source: A. Rodríguez Géigel, *Informe Anual del Servicio de Extensión Agrícola. Diciembre 1, 1939 a noviembre 30, 1940* (Río Piedras, PR: Universidad de Puerto Rico, 1940), 8–9.

of demonstrations increased by approximately 42 percent to 2,563 and almost 30,000 women were in attendance, an increase of 55 percent from 1938. This expansion is remarkable, especially considering that the number of agents only increased by six, from thirty-five in 1938 to forty-one in 1940.

Like the extension programs operating in the cultivation fields, Home Demonstration programs varied according to district, but they all contained those facets determined as crucial for the success of the rural home. Dr. Rodríguez Géigel noted in his report of 1937 that "the different phases of the Home Demonstration Program, including the production and conservation of food, better nutrition, more efficiency in domestic work, sewing and care of the family's clothes, and the establishment of social relations through recreational activities have no other goal than to raise the living standard for the rural family."[74] Government officials argued that higher standards of living for rural families would foster better social and economic conditions throughout the rural zones.

The nutritional program had two main components. The first was the dissemination of nutritional information so that housewives could learn the different elements of a well-balanced diet. The other was an extensive food production and preservation program. To increase food production for the home, housewives were taught how to plant high-yielding fruits and vegetables and how to raise pigs, rabbits, cows, and chickens, all of which were important sources of protein. To deal with surplus product, housewives were taught canning and preservation techniques that would then allow their families to have nutritious food beyond the harvest season. Some districts had canning centers where housewives could bring their product and work directly with a canning specialist. However, most Home Demonstration agents conducted canning demonstrations in private homes. In 1938, agents conducted 401 demonstrations that were attended by 5,857 women. Just a year later, the number of demonstrations increased to over one thousand and counted more than 6,200 women in attendance.[75]

In addition to home visits, Home Demonstration agents used other techniques to disseminate the science of the home. *El heraldo de extensión*, the magazine of the Agricultural Extension Service, was first published in January 1939. It included, among others, a cooking section with advice on how to prepare nutritious meals and recipes with seasonal products. *El heraldo de extensión* also listed all radio programs for the month, a calendar of community activities sponsored by the Agricultural Extension Service, articles on home economics and farming technologies written by agents, and updates on the latest agricultural legislation. Community-based agricultural fairs served as a showcase for successful projects, and included produce and animal exhibitions, locally processed agricultural products such as cheese or fruit spreads, farm and home equipment demonstrations, and displays of items made for the home by housewives and girls. These fairs also served to "stimulate the community's spirit . . . serving as entertainment and solace" by providing a much-needed distraction from everyday chores, although it is difficult to ascertain from the documents available if women actually experienced these events in this way.[76] Agricultural fairs increased in frequency, from 43 events in 1936 to 123 events in 1939, suggesting that they became more popular as people became more familiar with them.[77] Although the number of events decreased slightly from 1939 to 1940, this may reflect the beginning of the shift in extension activities because of war-related concerns.

Another important piece of the educational Home Demonstration program dealt with "helping the housewife to resolve home administration problems," since agricultural agents believed that a well-managed home supported a well-managed farm.[78] Successful home administration consisted of the efficient completion of household chores, careful care of family clothing, family budgeting (including finding alternative sources of cash income such as needlework) and accounting, food planning, positive child-rearing strategies that included education and games, and the general beautification of the home and its surroundings. Although most programs were active, as is evident from the number of demonstrations occurring throughout the rural areas, the budgeting and accounting piece of the program was not successful. In 1940, for example, out of 201 accounting books given to housewives, only 39 were completed.[79] It is not clear why the program was not well received, although in his 1940 report, the director cites "lack of personnel" as the reason for the discontinuation of the program for the following year. It is possible that housewives needed more assistance with accounting and budgeting than with the other parts of the program and that there just were not enough agents to provide it. It is also possible that the low rates of literacy in the rural areas at the time accounted for the lack of success.

CONCLUSION

Scientific inquiry, experimentation, and the practical application of research findings in the cultivation fields as well as in the homes had a profound impact in the rural areas of Puerto Rico from 1910 to 1940. The diffusion of modern agricultural technology and home management strategies was a collaborative project between the scientific community, farmers and their families, and the insular and federal governments. Puerto Rican legislators, scientists, business owners, and farmers negotiated the colonial relationship with the United States to secure a transfer of technology by accessing scientific research funds, creating institutions, and participating in federal programs that improved living conditions for Puerto Ricans in the rural areas of the island.

In the highland regions of Puerto Rico, scientists demonstrated that selecting more productive varieties of tobacco, maintaining better seedbeds, using appropriate fertilizers, and adopting control methods to check disease and insect damage made growing more profitable. The science of tobacco succeeded in improving the quality of the product and increasing the earning potential for farmers.

Tobacco growers adopted new techniques as a result of these efforts and became involved in a collaborative process of scientific exchange. The station provided new technologies and the growers provided practical application. Their organization and participation were crucial in guaranteeing that tobacco-specific research continued in the face of diminishing appropriations from the insular government. Their constant pressuring of the insular legislature, with the assistance of the Asociación de Agricultores Puertorriqueños, resulted in the creation of the Comisión para Proteger el Tabaco de Puerto Rico and the Instituto de Tabaco. The federal legislature did not escape the political pressure from tobacco growers, who won the extension of federal agricultural laws that guaranteed funding for scientific research in Puerto Rico. Through their participation in the science of tobacco, from the fields to the halls of the insular and federal legislature, tobacco farmers became modern agriculturalists.

Tobacco-processing corporations, like the Porto Rican American Tobacco Leaf Company, bought into the better-product-through-science mentality since it meant that the quality and quantity of the leaf they needed would be improved. Their participation may have been self-serving, but they invested important funds in setting up local experimental fields, maintaining seedbeds, building curing ranches that were technologically sound, and continuing pest and disease research that directly benefited Puerto Rican growers.

The widening of the Agricultural Experiment Station's goals to include home economics, farm administration, and rural infrastructure development shows that there was an interest not only in maximizing crop efficiency but in modernizing the entire rural society, and by effect, Puerto Rico as a whole. The practical application of the science of the home, with its focus on health and nutrition, the importance of a positive home environment, and the successful management of the family's income and expenses, needed the collaboration of the rural housewife. Through their participation in the Home Demonstration programs and the application of home economic techniques such as budgeting, canning, home beautification, and nutrition, the women of the highlands became home managers.

The wider socioeconomic programs of the agricultural scientific establishment did not, however, eliminate hardship across the rural areas of Puerto Rico. The volatile nature of an agricultural sector dependent on international fluctuations of supply and demand, combined with continuous funding reductions for agricultural research and education, contributed to the limited impact of these programs. Nevertheless, the participation of farmers in Agricultural Extension Programs and of rural housewives in Home Demonstration programs suggests that Puerto Ricans understood the role of practical science in the modernization of the island, and willingly and enthusiastically participated in scientific experimentation and its practical application on the fields and in the home. Tobacco growers were interested in the economic solvency of the farm and tobacco housewives were interested in the well-being of the family; science provided a roadmap to both.

Conclusion

The study of tobacco cultivation in the highland regions of Puerto Rico from 1898 to 1940 provides an opportunity to examine the effects of the U.S. occupation and annexation on the island's economy and society from new perspectives. The evidence presented suggests alternatives to the mostly one-dimensional historical narrative constructed by scholars of early twentieth-century Puerto Rico, in which the characteristics of the development of the sugar sector have become the analytical framework used to evaluate all agricultural development on the island. Additionally, the dynamics of economic, social, and political development in the tobacco regions add complexity to the simple dichotomy presented by scholars who have either demonized or idealized the period of U.S. control prior to the Second World War. The colonial system imposed upon Puerto Rico, without consulting Puerto Ricans in any systematic way, had many components and may not be unilaterally analyzed through the perspectives of a single economic sector, political party, social class, or racial or sex group within the population.

More importantly, the economic, social, and political behavior of the tobacco growers demonstrates that the paradigm of victimization in which Puerto Ricans were simply objects of policies effected without their input and largely beyond their control is simplistic and erroneous. Instead of being a victimized population, the tobacco growers took action demonstrating that Puerto Ricans negotiated the colonial structures both in Puerto Rico and in Washington skillfully and often successfully. Puerto Ricans utilized the freedoms of political action and organization guaranteed as part of the new post-1898 colonial system, particularly after 1917, to demand political access, beneficial legislation, and technological know-how in order to provide sustenance for their families by participating in an expanding economic sector.

The first part of this book deals with the intricacies of the tobacco economy in Puerto Rico, which experienced periods of expansion and contraction between 1898 and 1940. The growth of the tobacco sector from 1898 to 1917 both in terms of cuerdas planted and in terms of total production in pounds was steady. After 1917, however, Puerto Rican tobacco growers responded to the widening demand for American tobacco due to the end of World War I by significantly increasing plantings. This second wave of expansion culminated in 1927 with an enormous crop of over 50 million pounds, an excessive amount that the American tobacco market was unable to absorb. The economic consequences of this bumper crop, which led to falling prices for tobacco leaf, were immediately aggravated by the economic depression that began in 1929 and a shift in smoking preferences from larger, heavier, and more expensive cigars to smaller, lighter, and cheaper cigars and cigarettes. Through the 1930s, Puerto Rican tobacco began a calamitous decline, although there was some recovery from 1933 to 1938 due to federal aid programs and wider credit availability. By 1940, the value of the tobacco sector had fallen to levels seen in the early twentieth century, and it would never again recover.

Most of the tobacco in Puerto Rico was cultivated in the eastern and western highland regions. Often referred to as the "poor man's crop," tobacco could be efficiently cultivated on very small parcels of land and had relatively low operating expenses, which made it an economically viable alternative for farmers with limited land and capital resources. Tobacco cultivation in Puerto Rico in the early twentieth century was an owner-operated, small-scale agricultural enterprise, even with heavy private and corporate American investment in the industrial side of the tobacco sector. As the tobacco economy expanded, so did the population in the tobacco regions, both naturally and through migration as people moved into the region to take advantage of economic opportunities. The high rates of population increase among both adult males and females, and in the number of children found in the tobacco districts, suggest that migration was in general a family and not a male-only phenomenon. Although the rural areas of Puerto Rico have historically been discussed as if they were one homogenous unit, it is clear that the arguments made in relation to the development of the sugar sector, such as widespread absentee ownership, the displacement of the small landowner, and high rates of male migration, do not apply to the tobacco regions.

There were some similarities among the tobacco, sugar, and coffee regions, to be sure, such as rapid population growth, the increase in the number of landless families, and the high percentage of family income spent on food products. However, there were important differences in economic organization and patterns of daily life among the three. First, the overall cash earnings of tobacco farmers were much lower than the earnings of sugar and coffee farmers, which limited the material wealth that tobacco farmers could accumulate. Second, because cultivation expenses were the lowest in tobacco regions, tobacco farmers had greater opportunities to participate in a booming agricultural market as independent producers. Third, the tobacco growing season was shorter than those of both sugar and coffee, and farmers were able to use their land to plant secondary agricultural products for both the local market and family consumption. This increased the total benefit that tobacco farmers derived from the cultivation of their land in comparison with the other two major economic zones. It was precisely the importance of the production of secondary agricultural items in addition to the cash-earning potential of tobacco that made tobacco farming such an attractive economic alternative for the thousands of farmers in the eastern and western highland regions of Puerto Rico.

Tobacco cultivation provides a prism through which we can analyze the myriad ways that Puerto Ricans negotiated the American empire, discussed in detail in the second part of this book. Motivated by the unprecedented opportunity to participate in a guaranteed market for their leaf, and what that would mean, of course, in terms of sustenance for their families, tobacco growers became activists, exerting pressure and ultimately negotiating for beneficial legislation and technology. First, however, they had to secure access to the highest political levels of the colonial empire. At the local level, tobacco growers joined local ligas agrícolas, invested in cooperative societies, and demanded legislation to safeguard their economic interests. They attended meetings, drafted proposals and letters, voted in support of or against resolutions, and passionately debated the status of the tobacco industry. Together with many farmers in Puerto Rico, tobacco growers created political pressures on the insular and federal governments by establishing the Asociación de Agricultores Puertorriqueños and contributing to *El agricultor puertorriqueño*. The AAP accepted its self-appointed role as the public voice of the farmers and successfully lobbied for legislation that was not only beneficial to the agricultural economy, but also would foment the development of rural areas and demonstrate the government's commitment to raising the standard of living of all rural residents. Insular and federal officials were regularly visited by the representatives of Puerto Rican tobacco growers, publicly challenged, and criticized.

Once Puerto Ricans had secured political access to the colonial structures in the island and the mainland, they then demanded the agricultural legislation necessary to succeed in their chosen economic endeavor. The extension of agricultural legislation to the island, from federal credit programs to allocations for scientific experimentation and education, demonstrates the extent to which Puerto Ricans were able to effect changes in precisely the one area that is supposedly untouchable in an empire: the laws that govern a colony.

Financing the cultivation of any crop was difficult, and so one of the earliest efforts for the extension of federal legislation to the island had to do with agricultural credit programs. The majority of tobacco farmers obtained credit from noninstitutional sources, such as refaccionistas, lenders who were local landowners, merchants, or leaf traders. Refaccionistas, in addition to being production credit providers, also acted as buyers and marketing agents of the leaf they had financed, thereby exerting a significant level of control over the price paid to farmers. Contratos de refacción, with their high interest rates and additional expenses, were criticized as abusive by farmers, insular administrators, and agricultural representatives. It should not be surprising, therefore, that the federal government, which had enacted agricultural credit legislation to protect American farmers, was constantly pressured to extend such legislation to Puerto Rico. The federal government responded to Puerto Rican demands and extended agricultural credit legislation to the island. Tobacco farmers rapidly took advantage of these programs, requesting credit at higher rates than farmers in other sectors. The result was that by 1940 there was a well-established institutional credit structure in Puerto Rico made up of federal and insular banking institutions and commercial private banks that supplied credit at reasonable rates and for any length of time that a farmer needed.

Puerto Ricans also demanded the transfer of advanced agricultural technology to improve the quality and increase the quantity of their crop. Scientific inquiry and experimentation had a profound impact on the tobacco sector in early twentieth-century Puerto Rico. Tobacco's rise to the second-most-important position in the export trade behind sugar after the U.S. occupation was not haphazard or coincidental. It occurred because scientists, tobacco corporations and growers, and the insular and federal governments cooperated in the development of the tobacco economy, although this was not always accomplished amicably and often took place amid constant criticism, debate, and conflict. Scientists affiliated with the Agricultural Experiment Station of the University of Puerto Rico (AES-UPR), a publicly funded research institution, demonstrated that selecting more productive varieties of tobacco, maintaining better seedbeds, using appropriate fertilizers, and adopting control methods to check disease and insect damage, made growing more profitable.

Tobacco processing corporations such as the Porto Rican American Tobacco Leaf Company collaborated with AES-UPR scientists by investing in local experimental farms. Experiments conducted in fields, such as maintaining seedbeds, building curing ranches that were technologically sound, and continuing pest and disease research, directly benefited Puerto Rican farmers. Tobacco growers adopted the new techniques that resulted from these efforts and became involved in a collaborative process of scientific exchange. The AES-UPR provided new technologies, and the growers provided practical application and real-life experiments. The growers' participation in these projects and continued affiliation with the AAP were crucial in guaranteeing that tobacco-specific research continued in the face of diminishing resources provided by the insular government. Their constant pressuring of the insular and federal legislatures resulted in the creation of the Comisión para Proteger el Tabaco de Puerto Rico and the Instituto de Tabaco as well as the extension of federal funding for scientific research in Puerto Rico.

Unfortunately, none of the efforts by Puerto Rican tobacco growers, the insular and federal governments, or agricultural associations could reverse the demise of tobacco as an important export product after 1940. Economic hardship across all agricultural sectors of the island created the conditions for a major change in the political arena with the rise to power of the Partido Popular Democrático (PPD) under the leadership of Luis Muñoz Marín in the legislative elections of 1940. The PPD's platform of *pan, tierra y libertad* (land, liberty, and bread) resonated with the rural population of the island who had dealt with the cyclical highs and lows of forty years of agricultural development under the American flag. To live up to his promise of a better life for all Puerto Ricans, Muñoz Marín began a comprehensive program of industrialization as a better alternative to agriculture to support the population of Puerto Rico. Although there were attempts at land reform and investment in the promotion of agriculture, these were not successful at reversing the downward trend of the agricultural sector. Insular and federal funds were diverted instead into industrialization programs, and agriculture became a relatively unimportant priority for the PPD-dominated government.

The themes discussed in this book may be useful as a point for departure for the reinterpretation of several themes in Puerto Rican history in the period from the U.S. invasion of 1898 to 1940. First, the agricultural history of Puerto Rico must not be presented as a one-dimensional narrative of colonial abuse based on the development of the sugar sector. The changes in the tobacco regions demonstrate that there were significant variations among the agricultural regions of Puerto Rico in terms of land use, social structure, and income possibilities. Additionally, we have not systematically studied the development of those agricultural products meant for the local market, such as tubers, fruits, and vegetables, cattle and dairy, and poultry and eggs. The debate over the effects of the U.S. occupation on the agricultural sector, and ultimately, on the everyday lives of Puerto Ricans must be reconceptualized to make room for these particularities.

Second, the well-documented efforts of Puerto Rican tobacco farmers to participate in every level of the new American empire demonstrate that they were neither docile nor intimidated. Tobacco growers effectively negotiated the colonial structures to effect changes that had a significant impact on their daily lives. The continued discussion of the effects of American colonialism on the people of Puerto Rico must acknowledge that, even though ultimate authority resided in Washington, Puerto Ricans actively challenged, redefined, and constantly negotiated what colonialism meant in terms of their daily lives.

Finally, and as a continuation of the point above, we must begin to speak of Puerto Rican history as a history of negotiation, not a history of victimization. It is a fact that Puerto Ricans have lived under an imperial flag for over five hundred years, and that the American colonial period that began in 1898 has transformed the island's economy, culture, and society in both positive and negative ways. It is also a fact that the status issue is far from resolved, proven in the latest status referendum that occurred in November 2012, when 54 percent of the people declared that they did not agree with the "present form of territorial status." The status issue, as well as other current concerns, such as drug-related criminality, police brutality and civil rights abuses, high poverty rates, migration and return migration, access to education, and economic development have to be discussed within the colonial context, of course, but not within a victimization paradigm. Puerto Ricans are incredibly successful at effecting change, as demonstrated by the efforts of farmers in the early years of the twentieth century, and a colonial status can no longer be the sine qua non of responses to the current situation on the island. Puerto Ricans—and I include myself, as a Puerto Rican woman and a scholar of the island—must remember the history of negotiation with the American empire. Limited as it may be, it is a position of power. Only one example of that history was presented in this book, the work of the tobacco growers to secure the conditions they needed to participate in the market, but every Puerto Rican that votes, that joins a protest, that visits the halls of the *Capitolio* in San Juan or the aisles of the legislative offices in Washington, is also a participant in that history. We must remember this history and continue to negotiate, which is itself a position of power, in order to effect the positive political, economic, and social changes that are necessary in Puerto Rico today.

Notes

INTRODUCTION

1. "Nuestros Propósitos," *El Agricultor Puertorriqueño* (hereafter cited as *EAP*) 1, no. 1 (Dec. 12, 1925): 1.

2. The paradoxical nature of a colonial relationship is described by Frederick Cooper in his work, *Colonialism in Question: Theory, Knowledge, History* (Berkeley: University of California Press, 2005).

3. Juan José Baldrich, "From Handcrafted Tobacco Rolls to Machine-Made Cigarettes: The Transformation and Americanization of Puerto Rican Tobacco, 1847–1903," *Centro Journal* 17, no. 002 (Fall 2005): 144–169.

4. Harvey S. Perloff's *Puerto Rico's Economic Future* (Chicago: University of Chicago Press, 1950), a study of the economic development of the island, emphasized the expansion of the sugar sector as the defining element of Puerto Rican development during the early twentieth century. See also Earl Parker Hanson, *Transformation: The Story of Modern Puerto Rico* (New York: Simon and Schuster, 1955), 29.

5. Ruth Gruber, *Puerto Rico: Island of Promise* (New York: Hill and Wang, 1960), 32.

6. See César J. Ayala and Laird W. Bergad, "Rural Puerto Rico in the Early 20th Century Reconsidered: Land and Society, 1899–1915," *Latin American Research Review* 37, no. 2 (2001): 65–97. See also Julian H. Steward et al., *The People of Puerto Rico: A Study in Social Anthropology* (Urbana: University of Illinois Press, 1956), for a well-researched study of different agricultural regions in Puerto Rico.

7. For studies of Cuban tobacco, see Fernando Ortiz, *Cuban Counterpoint: Tobacco and Sugar* (New York: Alfred A. Knopf, 1947); and Jean Stubbs, *Tobacco on the Periphery: A Case Study in Cuban Labor History, 1860–1958* (New York: Cambridge University Press, 1985). For studies of tobacco cultivation in the Dominican Republic, see Michiel Baud, *Peasants and Tobacco in the Dominican Republic, 1870–1930* (Knoxville: University of Tennessee Press, 1995); and Pedro San Miguel, *Los campesinos del Cibao: Economía del mercado y transformación agraria en la República Dominicana, 1880–1960* (San Juan, PR: Editorial de la Universidad de Puerto Rico, 1997).

8. For example, see John P. Augelli, "Sugar Cane and Tobacco: A Comparison of Agricultural Types in the Highlands of Eastern Puerto Rico," *Economic Geography* 29,

no. 1 (Jan. 1953): 63–73. Magazines often published technological advice for better cultivation, such as F. H. Bunker, "El tabaco: semilleros, preparación del terreno, abonos y cultivos," *Revista de agricultura de Puerto Rico* 1 (1918): 33; or Roberto Huyke and R. Colón Torres, "Costo de producción de tabaco en Puerto Rico, 1937–38," *Boletín de la Estación Experimental Agrícola* 56 (1940).

9. Studies of tobacco farms can be found in "Division of Agricultural Economics," in Agricultural Experiment Station, College of Agriculture and Mechanic Arts, University of Puerto Rico, *Annual Report of the Agricultural Experiment Station. Fiscal Year 1936–37* (San Juan, PR: Bureau of Supplies, Printing, and Transportation, 1938), 125–130; and in "Special Reports on Projects, Division of Agricultural Economics," in Agricultural Experiment Station, College of Agriculture and Mechanic Arts, University of Puerto Rico, *Annual Report of the Agricultural Experiment Station. Fiscal Year 1938–39* (San Juan, PR: Bureau of Supplies, Printing, and Transportation, 1939), 26.

10. Juan José Baldrich, *Sembraron la no siembra: Los cosecheros de tabaco puertorriqueños frente a las corporaciones tabacaleras, 1920–1934* (Río Piedras, PR: Ediciones Huracán, 1988).

11. Ibid., 165.

12. Ivette M. Rivera-Giusti examines the way women challenged patriarchal structures in "Gender, Labor, and Working-Class Activities in the Puerto Rican Tobacco Industry, 1898–1924" (PhD. diss., State University of New York at Binghamton, 2004). Another example of a study of tobacco workers is Arturo Bird-Carmona, *Parejeros y desafiantes: La comunidad tabaquera de Puerta de Tierra de principio del siglo XX* (San Juan, PR: Ediciones Huracán, 2008).

13. See, for example, Adalberto López, ed., *The Puerto Ricans: Their History, Culture, and Society* (Rochester, VT: Schenkman Books, 1980), in which the colonial relationship is defined as one of imperial convenience.

14. Victor Clark, *Porto Rico and Its Problems* (Washington, DC: Brookings Institution, 1930). The Brookings Report was widely discussed in Puerto Rico. For example, an editorial in the *El agricultor puertorriqueño* took offense that the report accused members of the elite of not supporting the education of the jíbaro. See "Amicus Plato, Sed Magis Amica Veritas," *EAP* 9, no. 11 (June 15, 1930): cover page.

15. Bailey W. Diffie and Justine Whitfield Diffie, *Porto Rico: A Broken Pledge* (New York: Vanguard Press, 1931).

16. José Enamorado-Cuesta, *Porto Rico, Past and Present: The Island after Thirty Years of American Rule* (1929; reprint, New York: Arno Press, 1975).

17. Werner Baer, "Puerto Rico: An Evaluation of a Successful Development Program," *Quarterly Journal of Economics* 73, no. 4 (Nov. 1959): 645. The characterization of the nineteenth-century Puerto Rican economy as "backward" continued into the 1970s in works such as Sol L. Descartes, *Puerto Rico: Trasfondo de su economía, fondo físico, histórico e institucional* (Hato Rey, PR: Inter-American University Press, 1973), 21; and Andrés Sánchez Tarniella, *La economía de Puerto Rico: Etapas en su desarrollo* (Madrid: Afrodisio Aguado, S.A., 1971), 27. The characterization of U.S. capitalism is from Gordon K. Lewis, *Puerto Rico: Freedom and Power in the Caribbean* (New York: Monthly Review Press, 1963), 89.

18. An example is *Puerto Rican Paradox* by Vincenzo Petrullo (Philadelphia: University of Pennsylvania Press, 1947).

19. One example is Earl Parker Hanson's *Transformation: The Story of Modern Puerto Rico* (New York: Simon and Schuster, 1955).

20. Manuel Maldonado-Denis, *Puerto Rico: Mito y realidad* (Madrid: Ediciones Península, 1969), 5, 25.

21. Ibid., 49.

22. Pedreira argued that American colonial policies created an "inferiority complex" in Puerto Ricans that resulted in the self-alienation from political processes that could have effected change. See Antonio S. Pedreira, *Insularismo: Ensayos de interpretación puertorriqueña* (San Juan, PR: Biblioteca de Autores Puertorriqueños, 1957), 133, 217.

23. Manuel Maldonado-Denis, "The Puerto Ricans: Protest or Submission," *Annals of the American Academy of Political and Social Science* 382 (Mar. 1969): 26.

24. Ibid., 30. James Dietz was also critical of the local elite and argued that they "existed, and functioned, primarily to serve foreign interests." See James Dietz, "The Puerto Rican Political Economy," *Latin American Perspectives* 3, no. 3 (Summer 1976): 8.

25. Maldonado-Denis, "Protest," 30.

26. See, for example, David F. Ross, *The Long Uphill Path: A Historical Study of Puerto Rico's Program of Economic Development* (San Juan, PR: Editorial Edil, 1969).

27. For a good discussion of the methodology of the *nueva historia* and examples of scholarly works, see James L. Dietz, "Puerto Rico's New History," *Latin American Research Review* 19, no. 1 (1984): 210–222; and Félix V. Matos Rodríguez, "New Currents in Puerto Rican History: Legacy, Continuity, and Challenges of the 'Nueva Historia,'" *Latin American Research Review* 32, no. 3 (1997): 195, 206.

28. Juan Ángel Silén, *We, the Puerto Rican People: A Story of Oppression and Resistance*, trans. Cedric Belfrage (New York: Monthly Review Press, 1971), 45.

29. Ibid., 22–23.

30. James L. Dietz, *Economic History of Puerto Rico: Institutional Change and Capitalist Development* (Princeton, NJ: Princeton University Press, 1986).

31. Dietz, "Political Economy," 4, 5. See also his later work *Economic History*.

32. Raymond Carr, *Puerto Rico: A Colonial Experiment* (New York: Vintage Books, 1984), 202–203.

33. Ibid., 42. Ronald Fernández later discussed the theme of the ability of Puerto Ricans to participate in the American colonial structure in *The Disenchanted Island: Puerto Rico and the United States in the 20th Century*, 2nd ed. (Westport, CT: Praeger Publishers, 1996). Fernández agreed with Carr and stated that, "for a people with no experience in democratic practices, the Puerto Rican legislators nevertheless manifested an admirable ability to 'talk turkey' with the Americans" (11).

34. Carr, *Colonial Experiment*, 45.

35. Ibid., 238.

36. See, for example, Michael González Cruz, "The United States' Invasion of Puerto Rico: Occupation and Resistance to the Colonial State, 1898 to the Present," *Latin American Perspectives* 25, no. 5 (Sept. 1998): 7–26.

37. See Martin Joseph Collo, "Puerto Rico and the United States: The Effect of the Relationship on Puerto Rican Agrarian Development" (PhD. diss., University of Pennsylvania, 1986).

38. Lillian Guerra, *Popular Expression and National Identity in Puerto Rico: The Struggle for Self-Community and Nation* (Gainesville: University Press of Florida, 1998), 23.

39. See Teresita Martínez-Vergne, *Capitalism in Colonial Puerto Rico: Central San Vicente in the Late Nineteenth Century* (Gainesville: University Press of Florida, 1992), for a study of Puerto Rican participation in the sugar sector. See also César J. Ayala, *American Sugar Kingdom: The Plantation Economy of the Spanish Caribbean, 1898–1934* (Chapel Hill: University of North Carolina Press, 1999).

40. See, for example, Efrén Rivera Ramos, *American Colonialism in Puerto Rico: The Judicial and Social Legacy* (Princeton, NJ: Markus Weiner Publishers, 2007); Christina Duffy Burnett and Burke Marshall, eds., *Foreign in a Domestic Sense: Puerto Rico, American Expansion, and the Constitution* (Durham, NC: Duke University Press, 2001); Héctor R. Marín Román, *El Caldero Quema'o: Contexto social-militar en Puerto Rico y otros lugares del Caribe durante el período entre guerras, 1919–1938* (Río Piedras, PR: Ediciones Gaviota, 2012); and Ramón E. Soto-Crespo, *Mainland Passage: The Cultural Anomaly of Puerto Rico* (Minneapolis: University of Minnesota Press, 2009).

41. For examples of works on women, see Eileen J. Suárez Findlay, *Imposing Decency: The Politics of Sexuality and Race in Puerto Rico, 1870–1920* (Durham, NC: Duke University Press, 2000); Lea E. Osborne, "Bridging the Divide: The Alliances of the Liga Social Sufragista in the Struggle to Enfranchise Puerto Rican Women" (Master's thesis, Sarah Lawrence College, 2004); and Félix V. Matos Rodríguez and Linda C. Delgado, eds., *Puerto Rican Women's History: New Perspectives* (Armonk, NY: M. E. Sharpe, 1998). For works on workers and unionization, see Ivette M. Rivera-Giusti, "Gender, Labor, and Working-Class Activities" (PhD diss., State University of New York at Binghamton, 2004); or Carlos Sanabria, "The Puerto Rican Organized Workers' Movement and the American Federation of Labor, 1901 to 1934" (PhD. diss., City University of New York, 2000).

42. César J. Ayala and Rafael Bernabe, *Puerto Rico in the American Century: A History Since 1898* (Chapel Hill: University of North Carolina Press, 2007).

43. Rosa Carrasquillo, *Our Landless Patria: Marginal Citizenship and Race in Caguas, Puerto Rico, 1880–1910* (Lincoln: University of Nebraska Press, 2006).

44. Ibid., xxi, 5, 118.

45. Dionicio Nodín Valdés, *Organized Agriculture and the Labor Movement before the UFW: Puerto Rico, Hawai'i, California* (Austin: University of Texas Press, 2011).

46. See, among others, Geoffrey Hodgson, *The Myth of American Exceptionalism* (New Haven, CT: Yale University Press, 2010); and Bartholomew Sparrow, *The Insular Cases and the Emergence of American Empire* (Lawrence: University Press of Kansas, 2006).

47. Julian Go, *Patterns of Empire: The British and American Empires, 1868 to the Present* (New York: Cambridge University Press, 2011), Kindle edition.

48. Julian Go, "Chains of Empire, Projects of State: Political Education and U.S. Colonial Rule in Puerto Rico and the Philippines," *Comparative Studies in Society and History* 42, no. 2 (Apr. 2000): 336, 335.

49. Go, *Patterns*, 89, 93.

50. Sparrow, *Insular Cases*, 19.

51. Go, *Patterns*, 7. Emphasis is in the original text.

52. Ibid., 6, 9–10, 61.

53. Rivera Ramos, *American Colonialism*, 13. Also in Go, *Patterns*, 55.

54. Sparrow, *Insular Cases*, 8–9.

55. Go, *Patterns*, 10–11. In fact, the definition of the Commonwealth, the island's current political status vis-à-vis the United States, is a perfected manifestation of informal imperial power, one that was created, lobbied for, and implemented by the local population but with ultimate approval by the U.S. Congress.

56. Rivera Ramos, *American Colonialism*, 220.

57. Go, *Patterns*, 12.

58. The Organic Act of 1917, also known as the Jones Act, was an amendment to the Organic Act of 1900, also known as the Foraker Act. The Jones Act granted U.S. citizenship to all Puerto Ricans and established a locally elected legislature, among other amendments.

59. José A. Cabranes, "Citizenship and the American Empire: Notes on the Legislative History of the United States Citizenship of Puerto Ricans," *University of Pennsylvania Law Review* 127, no. 2 (Dec. 1978): 396. Cabranes mentions that "virtually all prominent Puerto Rican leaders whose views were recorded in the annals of Congress supported the grant of citizenship at one time or another during the period between the Foraker Act of 1900 and the Jones Act of 1917" (443). Cooper also mentions the process of "complicating the relationship of ruler and ruled, of insider and outsider" in his study. See Cooper, *Colonialism*, 52.

60. Cabranes, "Citizenship," 443–444. In her excellent analysis of the meaning of the Insular Cases, the Supreme Court decisions that defined Puerto Rico as "foreign in a domestic sense," Christina Duffy Burnett argued that the significance of these cases is that they allowed for "the creation of a category of domestic territory not bound in permanent union to the rest of the United States." See Christina Duffy Burnett, "United States: American Expansion and Territorial Deannexation," *University of Chicago Law Review* 72, no. 3 (Summer 2005): 804.

61. Lori D. Ginzberg, "Global Goals, Local Acts: Grass-Roots Activism in Imperial Narratives," *Journal of American History* 88, no. 3 (Dec. 2001): 870–871.

62. One cuerda is equivalent to 0.9712 acre and was the standard unit of land area in Puerto Rico. The words "cuerdas" and "acres" were used interchangeably in all documents from 1899 to 1940.

63. Rivera Ramos, *American Colonialism*, 228.

64. Emilio Pantojas-García, "The Puerto Rican Paradox: Colonialism Revisited," *Latin American Research Review* 40, no. 3 (2005): 163–176.

65. Rivera Ramos, *American Colonialism*, 228.

CHAPTER 1 —— THE DEVELOPMENT OF THE TOBACCO
ECONOMY IN PUERTO RICO

1. Rafael Menéndez Ramos, Comisionado de Agricultura y Comercio, *Informe anual del Comisionado de Agricultura y Comercio correspondiente al año fiscal 1933–1934* (San Juan, PR: Negociado de Materiales, Imprenta y Transporte, 1934), 210 (hereafter cited as *Informe 1933–1934*).

2. Bureau of the Census, *Sixteenth Census of the United States: 1940. Reports for Puerto Rico: Census of Agriculture* (Washington, DC, 1942), 181 (hereafter cited as *Agriculture Census 1940*).

3. Carlos Esteva Jr., *Annual Report of the Tobacco Institute of Puerto Rico. Fiscal Years 1939–1940 and 1940–1941* (San Juan, PR: Bureau of Supplies, Printing, and Transportation, 1942), 7.

4. The municipalities were chosen according to census data from 1910 to 1940. These municipalities had the most cuerdas under cultivation and were the largest producers in pounds of tobacco.

5. For a description of how distinct types of tobacco leaf were cultivated in these areas, see Baldrich, "Handcrafted."

6. María Cadilla de Martínez, "El tabaco," *Revista de Agricultura de Puerto Rico* (hereafter cited as *RAPR*) 29 (July 1937): 110.

7. Antonio Rojas, Tobacco Institute of Puerto Rico, *Preliminary Plan to Stabilize the Tobacco Industry Submitted for Consideration to the Planning, Urbanizing, and Zoning Board of Puerto Rico* (San Juan, PR: Bureau of Supplies, Printing, and Transportation, 1944), 3. Also in Cadilla de Martínez, "Tabaco," 112. Currency equivalencies are difficult to pinpoint. The most used currency in Puerto Rico at this time was the Spanish *peso* and the *real*, available in several denominations. One peso was equal to 8 reales. Until 1898, one peso was equivalent to $1. The average price per pound in 1636 was, therefore, 25 cents.

8. Cadilla de Martínez, "Tabaco," 113.

9. Ibid. In 1899 the Porto Rican American Tobacco Company (PRATC) was incorporated in New Jersey. The PRATC purchased two tobacco manufacturing companies in Ponce and San Juan from Luis Toro, and the firm Rucabado y Portela, thereby formally establishing the presence of American capital in the tobacco sector. See José R. Corrales Corrales, "La Cámara de Comercio de Puerto Rico como factor del desarrollo económico nacional, 1913–1933" (PhD. diss., University of Puerto Rico, 1997), 171.

10. Charles E. Gage, *The Tobacco Industry in Puerto Rico*, United States Department of Agriculture, Circular no. 519 (Washington, DC: Government Printing Office, Mar. 1939), 16. Also in Jorge Serrallés Jr. and Martín Vélez Jr., "Precio del tabaco en rama al agricultor en Puerto Rico del 1907–1940," *Boletín de la Estación Experimental Agrícola* 60 (June 1941): 2.

11. Ibid.

12. Gage, *Tobacco Industry*, 16.

13. Ibid., 17.

14. Ibid., 18.

15. Ibid.

16. Bunker, "El tabaco," 33.

17. Gage, *Tobacco Industry*, 18–19. Tobacco farmers could also buy the young plants ready to transplant.

18. Ibid., 22.

19. John Fraser Hart and Eugene Cotton Mather, "The Character of Tobacco Barns and Their Role in the Tobacco Economy of the United States," *Annals of the Association of American Geographers* 51, no. 3 (Sept. 1961): 275.

20. Ibid., 276–277.

21. Gage, *Tobacco Industry*, 23.

22. Hart and Mather, "Tobacco Barns," 290.

23. Gage, *Tobacco Industry*, 22.

24. Chardón Carlos, Commissioner of Agriculture and Labor, *Annual Report of the Commissioner of Agriculture and Labor Submitted to the Governor of Porto Rico, 1924–25*

(San Juan, PR: Bureau of Supplies, Printing, and Transportation, 1926), 21 (hereafter cited as *Report, 1924–25*).

25. R. T. Cotton, "Report on Tobacco and Vegetable Insects," in Board of Commissioners of Agriculture, *Fifth Report of the Board of Commissioners of Agriculture for the Period from July 1, 1915 to July 1, 1916* (San Juan, PR: Bureau of Supplies, Printing, and Transportation, 1917), 86.

26. Ibid., 26.

27. Rojas, *Plan to Stabilize Tobacco*, 4.

28. Data for 1910 from Bureau of the Census, *Thirteenth Census of the United States Taken in the Year 1910. Statistics for Porto Rico: Agriculture* (Washington, DC, 1913), 72–77 (hereafter cited as *Agriculture Census 1910*). Data for 1920 from Bureau of the Census, *Fourteenth Census of the United States Taken in the Year 1920*, Vol. 6, Pt. 3, *Agriculture* (Washington, DC, 1922), 408–415 (hereafter cited as *Agriculture Census 1920*). Data for 1930 from Bureau of the Census, *Fifteenth Census of the United States: 1930. Outlying Territories and Possessions* (Washington, DC, 1932), 232–237 (hereafter cited as *Census 1930*). Data for 1940 from *Sixteenth Census of the United States: 1940. Reports for Puerto Rico: Census of Agriculture* (Washington, DC, 1942), 60 (hereafter cited as *Agriculture Census 1940*).

29. Scientific research was being conducted by the Agricultural Experiment Station out of the experimental farm in the eastern highland municipality of Caguas.

30. Manuel Camuñas, Commissioner of Agriculture and Labor, *Report of the Commissioner of Agriculture and Labor of Porto Rico, 1921. From the Report of the Governor of Porto Rico, 1921, pages 448–503 inclusive* (Washington, DC: Government Printing Office, 1921), 448 (hereafter cited as *Report 1921*). Also in Serrallés and Vélez, "Precio," 37.

31. Corrales Corrales, "Cámara," 173.

32. "300 ranchos de tabaco destruídos," *EAP* 2, no. 4 (July 31, 1926): 5. Also in "Pérdidas," *EAP* 2, no. 5 (Aug. 7, 1926): 3, 7, 17.

33. Farmers in Comerío, for example, reported up to $60,000 in losses and those in Barranquitas, $26,000. See "Pérdidas," 7.

34. "La cosecha de tabaco será grandemente reducida. La caída de los ranchos," *EAP* 2, no. 7 (Aug. 21, 1926): 6.

35. "Tabaco," *EAP* 1, no. 7 (Jan. 23, 1926): 16.

36. "Cotización del Mercado de productos de Puerto Rico en Nueva York," *EAP* 1, no. 1 (Dec. 12, 1925): 17.

37. "El tabaco en Santo Domingo," *EAP* 2, no. 12 (Sept. 25, 1926): 16.

38. "Perspectiva del mercado tabacalero," *EAP* 3, no. 3 (Feb. 15, 1927): 1.

39. "Tabaco," *EAP* 2, no. 22 (Dec. 11, 1926): 13.

40. Serrallés and Vélez, "Precio," 7.

41. Ibid. Carlos Chardón commented on the "fever" that had gripped tobacco farmers in 1927 and the resulting saturation of the tobacco market in Comisionado de Agricultura y Trabajo, *Informe del Comisionado de Agricultura y Trabajo al Honorable Gobernador de Puerto Rico, 1927* (San Juan, PR: Negociado de Materiales, Imprenta y Transporte, 1928), 58.

42. Carlos Chardón, Comisionado de Agricultura y Trabajo, *Informe del Comisionado de Agricultura y Trabajo al Honorable Gobernador de Puerto Rico, 1928*

(San Juan: Negociado de Materiales, Imprenta y Transporte, 1929), 5. Also in "La producción agrícola de la Isla en el año fiscal último," *EAP* 7, no. 9 (May 15, 1929): 28.

43. "Los primeros cálculos de las pérdidas," *EAP* 6, no. 5 (Sept. 15, 1928): 4, 19.

44. "Ante el desastre," *EAP* 12, no. 18 (Oct. 15, 1932): cover page.

45. "Informe preliminar del ciclón de 27 de septiembre de 1932 San Ciprián"; Sección: Secretaría, Subsección: Beneficiencia; Serie: Expedientes y Documentos, Subserie: Huracanes; Años: 1819–1932; Caja #13, Sobre: 1932 B; Archivo Histórico de Caguas.

46. Rafael Menéndez Ramos, Comisionado de Agricultura y Comercio, *Informe Anual del Comisionado de Agricultura y Comercio correspondiente al año fiscal 1932–1933* (San Juan, PR: Negociado de Materiales, Imprenta y Transporte, 1933), 16.

47. Serrallés and Vélez, "Precio," 32–33.

48. Esteva, *Tobacco Institute, 1939–40 and 1940–41*, 5. Also in E. B. Hill and Sol L. Descartes, "An Economic Background for Agricultural Research in Puerto Rico," *Bulletin of the Agricultural Experiment Station* 51 (Dec. 1939): 31.

49. Junta de Salario Mínimo, División de Investigaciones y Estadísticas, Gobierno de Puerto Rico, *La industria del tabaco en rama* (San Juan, PR: Negociado de Materiales, Imprenta y Transporte, 1942), 48.

50. Serrallés and Vélez, "Precio," 5.

51. The agricultural press was well aware that the change from cigars to cigarettes was occurring. *El agricultor puertorriqueño* often published tobacco reports from around the world, noting shifts to the market, consumer preferences, and opinions about Puerto Rican tobacco. Examples of the discussion regarding the increase of cigarette consumption can be found in "La Perspectiva tabacalera," *EAP* 7, no. 4 (Feb. 28, 1929): 8. See also "Notas tabacaleras," *EAP* 7, no. 7 (Apr. 15, 1929): 7. An example of an update on the decline of cigar manufacturing on the island can be found in "Perspectiva agrícola para el 1931," *EAP* 11, no. 6 (Mar. 31, 1931): 23.

52. Gage, *Tobacco Industry*, 45.

53. "La Administración de Créditos Agrícolas y el establecimiento de sus agencias en Puerto Rico," in Menéndez Ramos, *Agricultura 1933–1934*, 164.

54. The Agricultural Adjustment Administration (AAA) was the federal agency responsible for the enforcement of the Agricultural Adjustment Act of May 12, 1933, a New Deal program that would pay farmers to reduce the size of their crop area and leave fields unplanted. The act was extended to Puerto Rico.

CHAPTER 2 — LIFE IN THE TOBACCO REGIONS
OF PUERTO RICO

1. The municipalities chosen for the sugar and coffee regions had the highest number of cuerdas under cultivation and were the largest producers in pounds of sugar cane and coffee. Calculations as to cuerdas and pounds were made using census data from 1910 to 1940.

2. See Julian H. Steward et al., *The People of Puerto Rico: A Study in Social Anthropology* (Urbana: University of Illinois Press, 1956), 116, 162, 467.

3. See Ayala and Bergad, "Rural Puerto Rico."

4. Ramón Colón Torres, "Estudio económico de 270 fincas de tabaco en Puerto Rico, 1936–37," *Boletín de la Estación Experimental Agrícola* 50 (1939): 12.

5. Manuel A. Pérez, *Living Conditions among Small Farmers in Puerto Rico, Research Bulletin on Agriculture and Livestock, Bulletin No. 2* (San Juan, PR: Bureau of Supplies, Printing, and Transportation, 1942); also in Huyke and Colón Torres, "Costo de producción," 3–28. There are no previous studies that offer comparable data, so it is impossible to make comparisons between these data collected from 1936 to 1938 and data from the 1920s, when tobacco prices were highest.

6. The farms classified as sugar farms for the Pérez study cited here were independent farms that cultivated and sold sugar cane. It does not appear from the description of the farms presented by Pérez that any of them dealt in the sale of refined sugar.

7. Pérez, *Living Conditions,* 4.

8. Colón Torres, "270 fincas," 24.

9. John Lounsbury, "Farmsteads in Puerto Rico and Their Interpretative Value," *Geographical Review* 45, no. 3 (July 1955): 352.

10. Data for 1910 from *Agriculture Census 1910,* 72–77. Data for 1920 from *Agriculture Census 1920,* 392–399. Data for 1930 from *Census 1930,* 212–215, 232–237. Data for 1940 from *Agriculture Census 1940,* 36–37.

11. Rafael Picó, "Land Tenure in the Leading Types of Farming of Puerto Rico," *Economic Geography* 15, no. 2 (Apr. 1939): 143.

12. *Colonos* were independent farmers that contracted the sale of their sugar cane to a sugar refinery for a predetermined price. For more details on the development of the *colonato* in the Spanish Caribbean, see Ayala, *American Sugar Kingdom.*

13. Colón Torres, "270 Fincas," 3, 10.

14. Sol L. Descartes, "Land Reform in Puerto Rico," *Journal of Land and Public Utilities* 19, no. 4 (Nov. 1943): 405.

15. Ibid.

16. Pérez, *Living Conditions,* 11.

17. For 1930, there are no data dividing agricultural workers by crop. There is a category of "Agricultural Laborer," which also existed for 1910, 1920, and 1940. To calculate the number of agricultural laborers per crop for 1930, the percentage of laborers employed in each crop for 1920 was calculated. That percentage was then used to calculate the agricultural laborers per crop from the total number of agricultural laborers. Data on agricultural laborers for 1930 from *Census 1930,* 186–189.

18. For details on the expansion of the sugar market, see Ayala, *Sugar Kingdom.*

19. The percentage of landless families from 1910 to 1930 was calculated using the number of rural inhabitants and the number of rural families. For the 1940 Census, there was no "Number of Families" category. Instead, there was a "Number of Heads of Private Households" category. As described in the introduction to the section, "the number of heads of private households is the same as the number of private households. This number is roughly comparable with the number of families shown in the census reports of 1935, 1930, and 1920" (3). In addition, the 1940 figures were not published by municipality, but by region. The average number of families was also omitted. The average number of family members per region was calculated by dividing the total population by the number of heads of private households. Then the average number of family members per region was assigned to each municipality in that region. The number of rural families in each municipality was calculated by dividing the total rural population by the average number of family members. The number of

landless families was then calculated by subtracting the number of rural families from the number of farms.

CHAPTER 3 — POLITICS: TOBACCO GROWERS AND
AGRICULTURAL ORGANIZATIONS

1. Manuel Camuñas, Commissioner of Agriculture and Labor, *Report of the Commissioner of Agriculture and Labor of Porto Rico, 1917. From the Report of the Governor of Porto Rico, 1917, pages 545–562 inclusive* (Washington, DC: Government Printing Office, 1917), 545.

2. Details of Marcelino and Modesto Solá's economic activities can be found in José Ramón Abad, *La exposición agrícola e industrial de tabaco realizada en Puerto Rico, diciembre 1883. Memorias de la Junta Directiva* (Ponce, PR: Establecimiento Tipográfico EL VAPOR, 1884), 49.

3. Baldrich, *Sembraron la no siembra*, 23–27.

4. Bureau of Insular Affairs, *Report of the Governor of Porto Rico, 1920, pages 503–566 inclusive* (Washington, DC: Government Printing Office, 1920), 517 (hereafter cited as *Governor 1920*). Camuñas, *Report 1921*, 462.

5. Manuel Camuñas, Commissioner of Agriculture and Labor, *Report of the Commissioner of Agriculture and Labor of Porto Rico, 1919. From the Report of the Governor of Porto Rico, 1919, pages 685–713 inclusive* (Washington, DC: Government Printing Office, 1919), 687.

6. Serrallés and Vélez, "Precio del tabaco," 5.

7. Ibid.

8. Silvia Álvarez Curbelo, "La patria agrícola: la ideología de los agricultores de Puerto Rico, 1924–1928" (Master's thesis, University of Puerto Rico, 1986), n.p.

9. Cooperative societies were legally approved in the Extraordinary Legislative Session of the Puerto Rican legislature of 1920 as "Act No. 3, For the Incorporation and Regulation of Cooperative Associations of Production and Consumption." Described in the Insular Experiment Station of Puerto Rico, Department of Agriculture and Labor of Puerto Rico, *Tenth Annual Report of the Insular Experimental Station of the Department of Agriculture and Labor of Puerto Rico. Fiscal Year 1919–20* (San Juan, PR: Bureau of Supplies, Printing, and Transportation, 1920), 5 (hereafter cited as *IES 1919–20*).

10. *Governor 1920*, 523.

11. Camuñas, *Report 1921*, 449.

12. "La dirección de la Agencia de Garantía del Tabaco de Puerto Rico en Nueva York," *EAP* 3, no. 3 (Feb. 15, 1927): 18–19.

13. "Los Bancos Tabacaleros siguen prosperando," *EAP* 2, no. 3 (July 24, 1926): 18.

14. "Organizaciones agrícolas," *EAP* 1, no. 25 (May 29, 1926): 4.

15. Tabacaleros de San Lorenzo was established on June 14, 1925. The Banco Tabacalero de Naranjito was established in June 1926. See "Naranjito organiza su Banco Tabacalero," *EAP* 1, no. 28 (June 19, 1926): 10.

16. "Tabacaleros de Aibonito, Inc.," *EAP* 1, no. 30 (July 3, 1926): 6; and "Tabacaleros de Aibonito, Inc. construyen su almacén," *EAP* 2, no. 6 (Aug. 14, 1926): 9.

17. Established July 16, 1925. "Tabacaleros de Cayey, Inc.," *EAP* 2, no. 1 (July 10, 1926): 9; and "Tabacaleros de Cayey, Inc. progresa," *EAP* 2, no. 6 (Aug. 14, 1926): 9.

18. The decision to establish the bank was made in 1926, but it was not until February 27, 1927, that it was actually operational. "La unión hace la fuerza," *EAP* 1, no. 30 (July 3, 1926): 6; and "Se organiza el Banco Tabacalero de Utuado," *EAP* 3, no. 5 (Mar. 15, 1927): 17.

19. "Nuestra asociación en la isla," *EAP* 2, no. 7 (Aug. 21, 1926): 3.

20. "Prestigiando al país," *EAP* 3, no. 7 (Apr. 15, 1927): 21.

21. The establishment of Tabacaleros de Manatí, Morovis y Barceloneta, Inc. was reported in "Importante reunión de Tabacaleros de Manatí," *EAP* 3, no. 11 (June 15, 1927): 30.

22. See Minutes of the Asociación de Agricultores Puertorriqueños, July 19, 1927; Colección: Asociación de Agricultores de PR; Serie: Actas de la Junta Directiva; Microficha: 1924–1937; Centro de Investigaciones Históricas, University of Puerto Rico, Río Piedras, Puerto Rico (hereafter cited as Minutes, AAP). Resolution also reported in "Resoluciones de la Asamblea General de la Asociación de Agricultores," *EAP* 4, no. 2 (July 31, 1927): 26–32. The first meeting of the cooperative is detailed in "Pormenores de la primera reunión para constituir la Cooperativa Insular de Tabacaleros," *EAP* 5, no. 2 (Jan. 31, 1928): 25–31.

23. "La Cooperativa Insular Tabacalera celebró una importante reunión en Cayey," *EAP* 5, no. 3 (Feb. 15, 1928): 19.

24. "Texto del discurso leído por el Sr. E. Landrón ante la Asamblea de Agricultores que se llevó a efectos en la Estación Experimental de Río Piedras," *EAP* 11, no. 3 (Feb. 15, 1931): 4–7, 35.

25. *La Marketing: un logro del tabacal. Organización y vida de la Puerto Rico Tobacco Marketing Association* (Santurce, PR: Publicaciones Yocauna, 1956), 1.

26. Ibid., 8.

27. Ibid., 10.

28. Ibid., 13–16, 18.

29. Ibid., 17. The exception was the crop of 1936–1937, when prices were lower than those paid by outside buyers.

30. "Asamblea Organizadora de la Asociación de Agricultores de PR," Minutes, AAP (June 27, 1924).

31. Ibid.

32. Ibid.

33. "Nuestros propósitos," *EAP* 1, no. 1 (Dec. 12, 1925): 2.

34. Minutes, AAP (Mar. 27, 1925).

35. "Resumen de los acuerdos tomados por la Asamblea General de la AAPR en el teatro Broadway de Ponce, el día 20 de diciembre de 1925," *EAP* 1, no. 4 (Jan. 2, 1926): 11 (hereafter cited as "Resumen 1925").

36. Ibid., 11–12; and "La Asamblea," *EAP* 1, no. 2 (Dec. 19, 1925): 3.

37. Minutes, AAP (Apr. 5, 1926).

38. "La Asamblea," 3. Also in Minutes, AAP (July 19, 1926).

39. The Curtis-Aswell project was eventually enacted as Senate Bill No. 2844. See John D. Black, "The Role of Public Agencies in the Internal Readjustments of the Farm," *Journal of Farm Economics* 7, no. 2 (Apr. 1925): 153–175.

40. The 500-acre law, enacted in 1900 and included in the Jones Act of 1917, stipulated that no corporation could own more than 500 acres of land. There had been no enforcement of the law.

41. Minutes, AAP (Feb. 26, 1926).

42. "Resumen 1925," 11.

43. Minutes, AAP (Apr. 5, 1926).

44. "Nuestra comisión en Washington," *EAP* 1, no. 22 (May 8, 1926): 5. Also reported in "La comisión de la Asociación de Agricultores," *EAP* 2, no. 3 (July 24, 1926): 6–7.

45. "Comisión en Washington," 6.

46. Ibid., 7. Also in Minutes, AAP (Jan. 21, 1926 and Feb. 26, 1926).

47. Minutes, AAP (Feb. 26, 1926 and Apr. 5, 1926).

48. José L. Pesquera was one of the founding members of the AAP. He was later elected president of the AAP and in 1932 became the resident commissioner of Puerto Rico in Washington, DC. The report of his meeting can be found in Minutes, AAP (June 6, 1927).

49. See for example, Ayala and Bernabe, *Puerto Rico in the American Century.*

50. Minutes, AAP (Sept. 21, 1928).

51. Minutes, AAP (Nov. 20, 1928).

52. "Resoluciones aprobadas por la Asamblea General de Agricultores, celebrada el día 28 de diciembre de 1930 en la ciudad de Ponce, Puerto Rico," *EAP* 11, no. 1 (Jan. 15, 1931): 15–21.

53. M. González Quiñones, "Pasando balance, parte II," *EAP* 11, no. 24 (Dec. 31, 1931): 1–2.

54. "Memorial presentado por la directiva de la Asociación de Agricultores a la Legislatura de Puerto Rico, y en su nombre a los presidentes de ambas cámaras Hon. Antonio R. Barceló y Hon. José Tous Soto," *EAP* 3, no. 1 (Jan. 15, 1927): 11.

55. Ibid.

56. Minutes, AAP (Nov. 15, 1926).

57. "Memorial," 11–14.

58. "Resoluciones aprobadas por la Asamblea," *EAP* 5, no. 7 (Apr. 15, 1928): 26–27.

59. Ibid., 28. For a detailed explanation of the AAP political platform, see "El programa legislativo de la Asociación de Agricultores," *EAP* 6, no. 12 (Dec. 31, 1928): 12–15.

60. For an example see "Editorial," *EAP* 1, no. 3 (Dec. 26, 1925): 1, where the editors criticize the government's lack of care about landowners losing their farms because they can't afford taxes. See also "Sección Editorial: La valoración de nuestra propiedad," *EAP* 1, no. 21 (May 1, 1926): 1. Governor Towner had recently submitted his 1926 report where he cited the low valuation of the land (and the low taxes paid by owners) as a budgetary problem.

61. "La crisis del tabaco y el gobernador de Puerto Rico," *EAP* 4, no. 6 (Sept. 30, 1927): 12.

62. "Texto íntegro del Proyecto de Ley aprobado por la Legislatura sobre el tabaco," *EAP* 5, no. 8 (Apr. 30, 1928): 30–34 (hereafter cited as "Texto íntegro"). The details of the tobacco growers' assembly where the members of the commission were elected can be found in "La Magna Asamblea de Tabacaleros celebrada en San Juan," *EAP* 8, no. 3 (Aug. 15, 1929): 18–20.

63. "Texto íntegro," 34.

64. "El Gobernador veda el proyecto del tabaco: Un nuevo aspecto de la acción destructora del Gobernador," *EAP* 7, no. 9 (May 15, 1929): 26.

65. "Demanda contra la Comisión Protectora del Tabaco declarada sin lugar," *EAP* 14, no. 6 (June 1934): 15.

66. Carlos Esteva Jr., *Third Annual Report of the Tobacco Institute of Puerto Rico (1938–1939)* (San Juan, PR: Bureau of Supplies, Printing, and Transportation, 1940), 5.

67. Minutes, AAP (Sept. 7, 1937).

68. For an example of a publication in the local press, see M. A. Manzano, "Apuntes sobre la química de los tabacos claros para cigarillos," *Revista de Agricultura, Industria y Comercio de Puerto Rico* 31 (1939): 209–211. In the American press, see F. H. Bunker, "Many Economic and Field Problems Facing Puerto Rican Leaf Planters," *Tobacco* 107, no. 26 (1938): 8–11.

69. "10,000 miembros en la AAPR," *EAP* 9, no. 4 (Feb. 28, 1930): 8. Also in "Al país," *EAP* 12, no. 7 (Apr. 15, 1932): 5, 12.

70. "Fomentemos las Cooperativas," *EAP* 4, no. 5 (Sept. 15, 1927): 1.

71. For example, "Mensaje del Presidente de la AAPR a la Asamblea General Ordinaria del día 11 de julio de 1926," *EAP* 2, no. 2 (July 17, 1926): 4, is full of praise for farmers who joined credit cooperatives (also called "banks"). The editorial in *EAP* 2, no. 24 (Dec. 25, 1926): 2, describes the benefits of joining cooperative societies. The editors also described their visits to tobacco regions to speak of credit cooperatives in "La Asociación de Agricultores aconseja a los cosecheros no forzar las ventas hasta que hayan precio remuneradores," *EAP* 3, no. 8 (Apr. 30, 1927): 24.

72. "Sección agrícola," *EAP* 2, no. 17 (Oct. 30, 1926): 12.

73. For examples, see "Pesquera y la política nacional," *EAP* 12, no. 20 (Nov. 15, 1932): 1; "El ausentismo," *EAP* 2, no. 16 (Oct. 23, 1926): 1; or Pedro González Iglesias, "Una de las causas de nuestra pobreza," *EAP* 10, no. 4 (Aug. 31, 1930): 20. For a running commentary on the status of the Puerto Rican infrastructure, see the magazine section titled "Cómo andan los servicios públicos en Puerto Rico," which first appeared in *EAP* 11, no. 5 (Mar. 15, 1931).

74. For examples of tobacco-specific articles, see J. D. Stubbes, "La selección de la semilla del tabaco en Puerto Rico," *EAP* 1, no. 6 (Jan. 16, 1926): 13; M. Meléndez Muñoz, "El presente y el porvenir del tabaco en Puerto Rico," parts 1 and 2, *EAP* 1, no. 8 (Jan. 30, 1926): 15–17, and 1, no. 9 (Feb. 6, 1926): 7–9; or Agustín Fernández, "El cultivo de tabaco en Puerto Rico," *EAP* 11, no. 15 (Aug. 15, 1931): 12, 21–22. Rafael Arce Rollet, tobacco grower from Caguas, wrote a two-part article on the contratos de refacción, or agricultural contracts, arguing the disadvantages of borrowing money from speculators or merchants. and instead promoted the use of banks for agricultural loans. See "Los contratos de refacción," parts 1 and 2, *EAP* 1, no. 3 (Dec. 26, 1925): 7, and no. 6 (Jan. 16, 1926): 9–10. For other articles on banking and credit, see "Lo que significa el crédito intermedio para Puerto Rico," *EAP* 1, no. 13 (Mar. 6, 1926): 9; or "Las ventajas del Banco Federal de Crédito Intermedio," *EAP* 1, no. 15 (Mar. 20, 1926): 10. Ramón Gandía Córdova wrote a fascinating five-part article on the Federal Farm Loan Act. See "Comentarios a la Ley Federal de Préstamos Agrícolas," parts 1–5, *EAP* 5, no. 9 (May 15, 1928): 19–20; no. 10 (May 31, 1928): 24–25; no. 11 (June 15, 1928): 23–24; 6, no. 4 (Aug. 31, 1928): 15–17; and no. 10 (Nov. 30, 1928): 20–21.

75. See "Plan completo para hacer la tasación de fincas rústicas," *EAP* 1, no. 7 (Jan. 23, 1926): 10–14; or "Modo de hacer la tasación de las fincas agrícolas," *EAP* 1, no. 2 (Dec. 19, 1925): 7.

76. For comments on nutrition, see M. Meléndez Muñoz, "La habitación campesina en sus relaciones con la higiene y la moral. Alimentación del campesino," *EAP* 1, no. 11 (Feb. 20, 1926): 7. For general economic and living conditions, see Ignacio Lizardi

Flores, "Problemas rurales," parts 1–4, *EAP* 11, no. 19 (Oct. 15, 1931): 16–17; no. 21 (Nov. 15, 1931): 8, 22; no. 22 (Nov. 30, 1931): 3, 19; and no. 24 (Dec. 31, 1931): 14. For issues of general interest, see Sandalio Torres Monge, "Las corporaciones y las tierras," *EAP* 8, no. 9 (Nov. 15, 1929): 29–30.

77. Read the eyewitness report by a member of the editorial board of the 1926 tobacco crop in "Tabaco," *EAP* 2, no. 22 (Dec. 11, 1926): 13. See "Los engaños en el abono para tabaco," *EAP* 10, no. 8 (Oct. 31, 1930): 16, for a report of refunds being given for tainted fertilizer and instructions on how to apply.

78. The minutes of the meeting can be found at Minutes, AAP (Dec. 20, 1925). For an explanation of the process by which the second picking affects the market, see "Por qué no debe cogerse el segundo cosecho del tabaco," *EAP* 3, no. 2 (Jan. 31, 1927): 38.

79. "Resumen 1925," 11.

80. In the farmers' words: "Let's not pick the seconds and the crop will be smaller and of better quality, and we'll see what story they will invent to lower the prices." The report of the meetings can be found in "Los cosecheros de tabaco," *EAP* 1, no. 7 (Jan. 23, 1926): 7, 18.

81. "Importante reunión de cooperativas tabacaleras. Existe absoluta unión entre todas," *EAP* 1, no. 11 (Feb. 20, 1926): 9; and "Importante mensaje de D. Modesto Cobián Rivera, Presidente de 'Tabacaleros de Comerío Inc.,' a la reunión de Cooperativas Tabacaleras," *EAP* 1, no. 11 (Feb. 20, 1926): n.p.

82. Minutes, AAP (July 19, 1927). The full report can be found in "Tabaco: Se discute la necesidad de reducir las siembras," *EAP* 3, no. 13 (July 15, 1927): 10. Proceedings of the tobacco assembly were described in "Importante asamblea de tabacaleros: Se ha acordado restringir las siembras para la próxima cosecha," *EAP* 4, no. 3 (Aug. 15, 1927): 4–5.

83. "Se reducen las siembras de tabaco," *EAP* 4, no. 7 (Oct. 15, 1927): cover page.

84. "Resoluciones aprobadas por la Asamblea General de Agricultores de Ponce," *EAP* 6, no. 2 (July 31, 1928): 29.

85. M. Meléndez Muñoz, "La situación tabacalera en la Isla: Opiniones y comentos," *EAP* 8, no. 8 (Oct. 31, 1929): 7–9.

86. "¿Resuelve la limitación de la cosecha el problema tabacalero?," *EAP* 9, no. 10 (May 31, 1930): 1.

87. Rafael Arroyo Zeppenfeldt, "Su Majestad el 'Esmayao,'" *EAP* 11, no. 14 (July 31, 1931): 1–2.

88. "Sección del Secretario," *EAP* 11, no. 17 (Sept. 15, 1931): 2.

89. For examples, see "Notas varias," *EAP* 11, no. 17 (Sept. 15, 1931): 10, 27; "El obrero y la huelga contra la siembra de tabaco," *EAP* 11, no. 18 (Sept. 30, 1931): 1–2; or "Notas editoriales: La hora de los débiles," *EAP* 11, no. 19 (Oct. 15, 1931): 1.

90. "Notas varias," 10.

91. José L. Pesquera, "Cumplirán su deber," *EAP* 11, no. 19 (Oct. 15, 1931): 9, 19.

92. José L. Pesquera, "Rectificaciones que honran," *EAP* 11, no. 20 (Oct. 31, 1931): 4.

93. For a detailed discussion of the workings of the Puerto Rican Leaf Tobacco Company and how its participation in the 1932 planting affected the no siembra campaign, see Baldrich, *No siembra*, 40–42, and for the resulting fires, 91–103.

94. Ibid., 125–136.

CHAPTER 4 — LAW: THE EXTENSION OF FEDERAL
AGRICULTURAL CREDIT LEGISLATION TO PUERTO RICO

1. From 1910 through 1940, small farmers planting less than 10 cuerdas of land culti-vated the greatest share of the Puerto Rican tobacco crop.

2. Joseph S. Tulchin classifies agricultural credit systems as formal/institutional or informal/noninstitutional in his article "El crédito agrario en Argentina, 1910–1926," *Desarrollo Económico* 18, no. 71 (Oct. 1978): 381–408.

3. Colón Torres, "Financing Low-Income Farmers," 944.

4. Among the founding goals of the AAP was to "solicit the extension [to the island] of the Intermediary Credit Act under the Federal banking system."

5. Pérez, *Living Conditions*, 43. According to statistical data contained in this report, tobacco farms used 16.8 percent of available credit. However, the report also mentions farms that produce tobacco in combination with another minor crop. Those "tobacco-minor" farms used 28.9 percent of credit. To arrive at the 45.7 percent figure, I added the percentage of available credit used by the tobacco farms and the tobacco-minor farms. The percentage of credit in sugar cane farms was also calculated by adding the credit used by sugar farms (38.6 percent) and "sugar-minor" farms (3 per-cent). These figures refer to production credit, and not to mortgage loans.

6. Gage, *Tobacco Industry*, 28.

7. Because an individual is acting as a lender, this type of credit is classified as noninstitutional for the purpose of this study.

8. Gage, *Tobacco Industry*, 28.

9. Ibid., 29.

10. Ibid., 30.

11. Maurice Perkins et al., *Credit and Related Problems in the Agriculture of Puerto Rico*, Report prepared for the Department of Agriculture, Economic Development Administration, the Government Development Bank for Puerto Rico, the Land Authority for Puerto Rico, the Puerto Rico Industrial Development Co., and the Autoridad de Energía Eléctrica, Dec. 1956, 37–38.

12. "Contrato de refacción agrícola," Andrés Mena Latorre, vol. 3, no. 597 (Dec. 2, 1927), 1662, Oficina de Protocolos Notariales, Caguas, Puerto Rico (hereafter cited as AML 3).

13. For a fascinating and detailed history of the tobacco industry in Caguas, see Juan David Hernández, "El tabaco de Caguas" (Archivo Histórico de Caguas, photocopy).

14. "Contrato de refacción agrícola," AML 3, no. 598 (Dec. 2, 1927), 1668.

15. "Contrato de refacción agrícola," AML 3, no. 618 (Dec. 14, 1927), 1732.

16. "Dación en pago, arrendamiento y contrato de refacción agrícola," AML 3, no. 626 (Dec. 19, 1927), 1756.

17. Some contracts included the designation *"venta y retroventa"* or *"venta con pacto de retroventa."* Ocasio and Cruz's contract did not include this designation, although it is clear that a *retroventa* was agreed upon.

18. Average farm price per pound, average export price per pound, and average yield per cuerda from Serrallés and Vélez, "Precio del tabaco," 5, 7. Labor expense fig-ure from Jorge J. Serrallés Jr., Ramón Colón Torres, and Frank J. Juliá, "Analysis of the Organization and Factors Influencing the Returns on 194 Small Tobacco Farms in Puerto Rico, 1935–1936," *Bulletin of the Agricultural Experiment Station* 46 (Mar. 1938): 20.

19. Chardón, *Annual Report 1924–25*, 62. Average food expense was based on the typical farmer's diet of rice, beans, cod, corn flour, sugar, coffee, tubers, and lard.

20. Rafael Arce Rollet, "Los contratos de refacción," part 1, 7 and part 2, 10.

21. Chardón, *Report 1924–25*, 21.

22. The literature on the development and effects of agricultural legislation in the United States is long-standing and extensive. For good background articles, see G. C. Henderson, "The Agricultural Credits Act of 1923," *Quarterly Journal of Economics* 37, no. 3 (May 1923): 518–522; Howard H. Preston and Victor W. Bennett, "Agricultural Credit Legislation of 1933," *Journal of Political Economy* 42, no. 1 (Feb. 1934): 6–33; and Harold W. Torgerson, "Agricultural Finance in the United States," *Journal of Land and Public Utility Economics* 16, no. 2 (May 1940): 196–206. For an interesting legal explanation of the Rural Rehabilitation Loan Program, see Monroe Oppenheimer's article "The Development of the Rural Rehabilitation Loan Program," in *Law and Contemporary Problems* 4, no. 4 (Oct. 1937): 473–488. Most of these programs were designed for ranchers, cotton producers, and tobacco farmers, although they benefited agriculture across the United States. For a discussion of how agricultural programs affected the tobacco sector, see B. U. Ratchford, "Federal Agricultural Policy in Relation to Tobacco," *Journal of Politics* 11, no. 4 (Nov. 1949): 655–677.

23. Federal Farm Land Banks were established in Springfield, Massachusetts; Baltimore, Maryland; Columbia, South Carolina; Louisville, Kentucky; New Orleans, Louisiana; St. Louis, Missouri; St. Paul, Minnesota; Omaha, Nebraska; Wichita, Kansas; Houston, Texas; Berkeley, California; and Spokane, Washington. The land bank in Baltimore served Puerto Rico.

24. William G. Murray, "Farm Mortgages and the Government," *Journal of Farm Economics* 17, no. 4 (Nov. 1935): 615.

25. Camuñas, *Report 1919*, 689.

26. Chardón, *Report 1924–25*, 32–33.

27. Data for 1922–1925 from Chardón, *Report 1924–25*, 33. Data for 1926 from Carlos Chardón, Comisionado de Agricultura y Trabajo, *Informe del Comisionado de Agricultura y Trabajo al Honorable Gobernador de Puerto Rico, 1925–1926* (San Juan, PR: Negociado de Materiales, Imprenta y Transporte, 1927), 20.

28. V. P. Lee, "The Intermediate Credit Banks," *Journal of Farm Economics* 7, no. 4 (Oct. 1925): 425.

29. Henderson, "Act of 1923," 518–519.

30. Lee, "Intermediate," 431.

31. Preston and Bennett, "Legislation of 1933," 30.

32. Henderson, "Act of 1923," 521.

33. "Lo que significa el crédito intermedio para Puerto Rico," *EAP* 1, no. 13 (Mar. 6, 1926): 9. This article explains the basic tenets of the FICB legislation. More details of the FICB program were published in M. González Quiñones, "Las ventajas del Banco Federal de Crédito Intermedio," parts 1 and 2, *EAP* 1, no. 15 (Mar. 20, 1926): 10; no. 18 (Apr. 10, 1926): 10. As an example, the article mentions that Tabacaleros de Aibonito, Inc. bought their fertilizer from only one supplier and paid $10 less per ton than unaffiliated farmers.

34. Chardón, *Report 1924–25*, 21.

35. Minutes, AAP (July 19, 1927).

36. In fact, articles were published on a regular basis discussing, criticizing, and advocating for federal credit programs. For example, Ramón Gandía Córdova, who explained the intricacies of the latest Federal Farm Loan Act in a series of articles published in 1928, was a civil engineer who served as subcommissioner of the Department of Agriculture and Labor from 1916 to 1922. He founded the *Revista de Agricultura* in 1917 and continued his involvement in agricultural projects in Puerto Rico throughout the remainder of his life.

37. "Visita con Mr. E. B. Thomas, Director del Federal Land Bank," *EAP* 1, no. 6 (Jan. 16, 1926): 10.

38. "Sección editorial: El crédito," *EAP* 2, no. 8 (Aug. 28, 1926): 1.

39. "Hipoteca," AML 3, no. 511 (Oct. 7, 1927), 1424.

40. "Los préstamos agrícolas hechos en Puerto Rico," *EAP* 7, no 8 (Apr. 30, 1929): 16.

41. "Reglas que deben seguir los agricultores que han de gestionar Préstamos Federales autorizados por la Comisión Rehabilitadora," *EAP* 7, no 8 (Apr. 30, 1929): 20–22.

42. "Texto íntegro de la ley que crea la Junta Federal y Agrícola y cuyos beneficios se han extendido a Puerto Rico," parts 1 and 2, *EAP* 10, no. 7 (Oct. 15, 1930): 26; no. 8 (Oct. 31, 1930): 25–27. Additional information and updates on the FFB activities were published in "Comentarios a la Ley de Compraventa Agrícola: Reglas de interpretación acordadas por la Junta Agrícola Federal," *EAP* 10, no. 9 (Nov. 15, 1930): 23–26.

43. "La atención de préstamos de la Junta Federal Agrícola de Estados Unidos se considera posible por los fruteros de Puerto Rico," *EAP* 9, no. 1 (Jan. 15, 1930): 20.

44. The resident commissioner is the only elected representative of Puerto Rico in the U.S. Congress. The resident commissioner has a voice and can address Congress like other members, as well as vote in committee deliberations. The resident commissioner, however, does not have a vote on the floor, where legislation is enacted.

45. "Una comisión de la Asociación de Agricultores visita al Gobernador Roosevelt," *EAP* 8, No. 7 (Oct. 15, 1929): 11.

46. For an example of the debate between Puerto Rican and American officials, see "Interesante correspondencia cruzada entre el Juez Williams y el Comisionado Residente," *EAP* 9, no. 5 (Mar. 15, 1930): 15. For an example of correspondence from the AAP to insular legislators, see "La importante legislación que está propulsando la Asociación de Agricultores," *EAP* 9, no. 7 (Apr. 15, 1930): 9–10.

47. "Texto íntegro" part 1, 26; and "Texto íntegro" part 2," 25–27.

48. "Gestiones que a solicitud de la AA llevará a cabo en Washington el Gobernador Roosevelt y el Comisionado Residente," *EAP* 10, no. 10 (Nov. 30, 1930): 9, 11.

49. "Resoluciones aprobadas por la Asamblea de Agricultores," *EAP* 9, no. 1 (Jan. 15, 1930): 31, 36.

50. The visit was published in "El Banco Federal y los agricultores," *EAP* 11, no. 16 (Aug. 31, 1931): cover page. The letter from the directors of the bank and response from the AAP were published in the same issue, "Carta de los Directores del Banco Federal al Presidente de la AA," 2, 31; and "Acuerdos de la Junta Directiva de la AA, en relación con la carta de los Sres. Directores del Banco Federal de Baltimore," 3. Additional details of the visit were published in "Notas sobre la visita de los Directores del Banco Federal de Baltimore," *EAP* 11, no. 17 (Sept. 15, 1931): 3–4, 29–30.

51. "La corporación de crédito agrícola," *EAP* 12, no. 19 (Oct. 30, 1932): cover page.

52. "La Administración de Créditos Agrícolas y el establecimiento de sus agencias en Puerto Rico," in Menéndez Ramos, *Informe 1933–1934*, 156.

53. Torgerson, "Agricultural Finance," 199.

54. Preston and Bennet, "Legislation of 1933," 12–13.

55. "Administración," 154–166.

56. Ibid., 155.

57. Ibid., 159.

58. Ibid., 160. The details of the Farm Credit Act programs and the Production Credit Corporations were also discussed in the local agricultural press in "Organización de la Administración de Créditos Agrícolas," *EAP* 14, no. 1 (Jan. 1934): 4.

59. Menéndez Ramos, *Informe 1933–1934*, 161.

60. F. B. Garver and Harry Trelogan, "The Agricultural Adjustment Act and The Reports of the Brookings Institution," *Quarterly Journal of Economics* 50, no. 4 (Aug. 1936): 600. The Agricultural Adjustment Act was recorded as Public Law 73-10, and was enacted on May 12, 1933.

61. Ratchford, "Federal Policy," 660.

62. Such taxing was allowed under the Kerr-Smith Tobacco Control Act passed in June 1934 to penalize tobacco growers who did not sign Agricultural Adjustment Administration contracts for reduction in acreage. This act was ruled unconstitutional by the U.S. Supreme Court in April 1935. Amendments to the Agricultural Adjustment Act in 1938 once again allowed for penalties of 5 to 10 cents per pound for tobacco sold in excess of quotas.

63. Menéndez Ramos, *Informe 1933–1934*, 165.

64. Gage, *Tobacco Industry in Puerto Rico*, 14.

65. United States Department of Labor, Age and Hour Division, Research and Statistics Branch, *Puerto Rico: The Leaf Tobacco Industry* (Washington, DC: Government Printing Office, 1941), 59.

66. A detailed discussion of the PRRA is beyond the scope of this study. For a detailed explanation of the land reform program of the PRRA, see Sol L. Descartes, "Land Reform in Puerto Rico," *Journal of Land and Public Utility Economics* 19, no. 4 (Nov. 1943): 397–417. For an evaluation of the reforms, see Keith S. Rosenn, "Puerto Rican Land Reform: The History of an Instructive Experiment," *Yale Law Journal* 73, no. 2 (Dec. 1963): 334–356.

67. Details about the Bankhead-Jones Act can be found in Oppenheimer, "Rehabilitation," 473–488, and in Torgerson, "Agricultural Finance," 201. Emergency crop loans were made available to Puerto Rican farmers as of 1939. See "Préstamos para pequeños agricultores (Nota Oficial)," *EAP* 19, no. 8 (Aug. 1939): 12. See also "Farm Security Administration. La Administración de Protección Agrícola hace los primeros préstamos en Puerto Rico: arrendatarios y medianeros serán dueños de fincas," *El heraldo de extensión* 1, no. 1 (Jan. 1939), 1.

68. Perkins et al., *Credit*, vii, 10.

69. Pérez, *Living Conditions*, 44.

70. Ibid., 12.

71. "Contrato de refacción agrícola," AML 3, no. 551 (Oct. 27, 1927), 1532.

72. See Jesse E. Pope, "Agricultural Credit in the United States," *Quarterly Journal of Economics* 28, no. 4 (Aug. 1914): 722.

CHAPTER 5 — TECHNOLOGY: MODERN AGRICULTURE,
HOME MANAGEMENT, AND RURAL PROGRESS

1. The idea of a science-led model of agricultural modernization is eloquently presented by Stuart McCook in "Promoting the 'Practical': Science and Agricultural Modernization in Puerto Rico and Colombia, 1920–1940," *Agricultural History 75*, no. 1 (2001): 52–82.

2. Clark, *Porto Rico and Its Problems*, 34.

3. Ibid.

4. Isabel Becerra de Weierich, "Las primeras estaciones agronómicas en Puerto Rico" (Master's thesis, University of Puerto Rico, 1969), 29.

5. Becerra de Weierich, "Las primeras estaciones agronómicas," 35, 40, 41.

6. Ibid., 47, 102.

7. Ibid., 161–167. Also in McCook, "Promoting the 'Practical,'" 54.

8. McCook, "Promoting the 'Practical,'" 55.

9. Nilsa Díaz de Acín, "La participación de la Estación Experimental de Agricultura de la Universidad de Puerto Rico en el desarrollo agrícola de Puerto Rico" (Master's thesis, University of Puerto Rico, 1967), 4.

10. J. T. Crowley, "Organization of the Station and Cultivation of Sugar Cane in Porto Rico," *Boletín de la Estación Experimental Agrícola* 1 (1911): 6.

11. Caguas cultivated 1,974,900 pounds of tobacco, over a million pounds more than Cayey, the next largest tobacco-growing municipality. In *Census 1910*, 72–77.

12. Mention of the experiment is made in Board of Commissioners of Agriculture, *Third Report of the Board of Commissioners of Agriculture for the period from July 1, 1913 to July 1, 1914* (San Juan, PR: Bureau of Supplies, Printing, and Transportation, 1915), 24. Merrill's full report was included as "Report of the Tobacco Insect Investigation," in Board of Commissioners of Agriculture, *Fourth Report of the Board of Commissioners of Agriculture for the period from July 1, 1914 to July 1, 1915* (San Juan, PR: Bureau of Supplies, Printing, and Transportation, 1916), 50 (hereafter cited as *BCA 1914–15*).

13. *BCA 1914–15*, 9.

14. John A. Stevenson, "Report of the Pathologist," in *BCA 1914–15*, 41.

15. R. T. Cotton, "Report on Tobacco and Vegetable Insects," in Board of Commissioners of Agriculture, *Fifth Report of the Board of Commissioners of Agriculture for the Period from July 1, 1915 to June 30, 1916* (San Juan, PR: Bureau of Supplies, Printing, and Transportation, 1917), 86.

16. R. T. Cotton, "Report of the Assistant Entomologist," in Insular Experiment Station of Puerto Rico, *Annual Report of the Insular Experiment Station of Puerto Rico for the Period from July 1, 1916 to July 1, 1917* (San Juan, PR: Bureau of Supplies, Printing, and Transportation, 1917), 107.

17. Insular Experiment Station of Puerto Rico, Department of Agriculture and Labor of Puerto Rico, *Eighth Annual Report of the Insular Experiment Station of the Department of Agriculture and Labor of Puerto Rico for the Period from July 1, 1917 to June 30, 1918* (San Juan, PR: Bureau of Supplies, Printing, and Transportation, 1919), 50, 128.

18. Michael Camuñas, Commissioner of Agriculture and Labor, *Report of the Commissioner of Agriculture and Labor of Porto Rico, 1917*. From the *Report of the Governor of Porto Rico, 1917, pages 545–562 inclusive* (Washington, DC: Government Printing Office, 1917), 545.

19. Ibid., 545.

20. Díaz de Acín, "La participación de la Estación Experimental de Agricultura," 8.

21. Insular Experiment Station of Puerto Rico, Department of Agriculture and Labor of Puerto Rico, *Tenth Annual Report of the Insular Experiment Station of the Department of Agriculture and Labor of Puerto Rico. Fiscal Year 1919–20* (San Juan, PR: Bureau of Supplies, Printing, and Transportation, 1920), 25 (hereafter cited as *IES Report 1919–20*).

22. Insular Experiment Station of Puerto Rico, Department of Agriculture and Labor of Puerto Rico, *Eleventh Annual Report of the Insular Experimental Station of the Department of Agriculture and Labor of Puerto Rico. Fiscal Year 1919–21* (San Juan, PR: Bureau of Supplies, Printing, and Transportation, 1921), 32 (hereafter cited as *IES Report 1919–21*).

23. Insular Experiment Station of Puerto Rico, Department of Agriculture and Labor of Puerto Rico, *Thirteenth Annual Report of the Insular Experimental Station of the Department of Agriculture and Labor of Puerto Rico. Fiscal Year 1922–23* (San Juan, PR: Bureau of Supplies, Printing, and Transportation, 1924), 24.

24. Francisco A. López Domínguez, *Seventeenth Annual Report of Director of the Insular Experimental Station of the Department of Agriculture and Labor of Puerto Rico. Fiscal Year 1926–27* (San Juan, PR: Bureau of Supplies, Printing, and Transportation, 1929), 30. Nolla later served as the director of the Tobacco Institute.

25. Carlos Chardón was educated at the University of Mayagüez and at Cornell University. He returned to Puerto Rico in 1921 and worked at the IAES. He was appointed commissioner of agriculture in 1923 and later rector of the University of Puerto Rico in 1930. He was also appointed as executive director of the Puerto Rico Land Authority in 1941.

26. Camuñas, *Report 1919*, 687.

27. Ramón Gandía Córdova, Acting Commissioner of Agriculture and Labor, *Report of the Commissioner of Agriculture and Labor of Porto Rico, 1920. From the Report of the Governor of Porto Rico, 1920, pages 503–566 inclusive* (Washington DC: Government Printing Office, 1920), 518–519.

28. *IES Report 1919–20*, 25.

29. Ibid., 57.

30. *IES Report 1920–21*, 14. Also in Insular Experiment Station of the Department of Agriculture and Labor of Puerto Rico, *Twelfth Annual Report of the Insular Experimental Station of the Department of Agriculture and Labor of Puerto Rico. Fiscal Year 1921–22* (San Juan, PR: Bureau of Supplies, Printing, and Transportation, 1922), 13.

31. The new and expanded mission for the IAES is outlined in "Opportunities for Service," in *IES Report 1919–20*, 58.

32. In 1920, over 70 percent of men aged forty-five and older were illiterate, but the rate of illiteracy fell to about 50 percent for those under nineteen. The illiteracy rates for women were similar, with 80 percent of women over forty-five being illiterate, and about 50 percent of those under nineteen. It is clear that education programs were having an impact on the younger generations at the time.

33. Insular Experimental Station, Department of Agriculture and Labor of Puerto Rico, *Annual Report of the Insular Experimental Station of the Department of Agriculture and Labor of Puerto Rico. Fiscal Year 1929–30* (San Juan, PR: Bureau of Supplies, Printing, and Transportation, 1931), 5 (hereafter cited as *IES Report 1929–30*).

34. Cotton, "Entomologist," 107.

35. Agricultural Experiment Station, College of Agriculture and Mechanic Arts, University of Puerto Rico, *Annual Report of the Agricultural Experiment Station. Fiscal Year 1937–38* (San Juan, PR: Bureau of Supplies, Printing, and Transportation, 1939), 100.

36. Ibid., 46.

37. Insular Experiment Station of the Department of Agriculture and Labor of Puerto Rico, *Fourteenth Annual Report of the Insular Experimental Station of the Department of Agriculture and Labor of Puerto Rico. Fiscal Year 1923–24* (San Juan, PR: Bureau of Supplies, Printing, and Transportation, 1924), 18.

38. Díaz de Acín, "La participación de la Estación Experimental de Agricultura," 9, 12–13.

39. Ibid., 13. The Hatch Act of 1887 authorized federal funds for the establishment of agricultural experiment stations in connection with a college. The writings of New York reporter Samuel Hopkins Adams sparked the enactment of the Pure Food and Drug Act of 1906. Under this act, funds were available to the Bureau of Chemistry of the Department of Agriculture to conduct experiments to determine the purity of any food product. "Insular territories" were included in these acts.

40. Agricultural Experiment Station, College of Agriculture and Mechanic Arts, University of Puerto Rico, *Annual Report of the Director for the Year 1933–34* (San Juan, PR: Bureau of Supplies, Printing, and Transportation, 1935), 6.

41. Melville T. Cook and José I. Otero, "History of the First Quarter of a Century of the Agricultural Experiment Station at Río Piedras, Puerto Rico," *Boletín de la Estación Experimental Agrícola* 44 (1937): 77.

42. Results of the study are detailed in "A Preliminary Study of the Credit Situation," in Agricultural Experiment Station, College of Agriculture and Mechanic Arts, University of Puerto Rico, *Annual Report of the Agricultural Experiment Station. Fiscal Year 1935–36* (San Juan, PR: Bureau of Supplies, Printing, and Transportation, 1937), 68–69.

43. Results of the studies are detailed in "Division of Agricultural Economics," in Agricultural Experiment Station, College of Agriculture and Mechanic Arts, University of Puerto Rico, *Annual Report of the Agricultural Experiment Station. Fiscal Year 1936–37* (San Juan, PR: Bureau of Supplies, Printing, and Transportation, 1938), 125–130. An additional report on the tobacco farm study can be found in "Special Reports on Projects, Division of Agricultural Economics," in Agricultural Experiment Station, College of Agriculture and Mechanic Arts, University of Puerto Rico, *Annual Report of the Agricultural Experiment Station. Fiscal Year 1938–39* (San Juan, PR: Bureau of Supplies, Printing, and Transportation, 1939), 26.

44. These projects were so named because of the federal grants that funded them. The Bankhead-Jones Act of 1935 provided additional funding for colleges and universities in Puerto Rico and other locations. The Purnell Act of 1925 provided funds to agricultural experiment stations for agricultural, economic, and sociological research.

45. Many of these programs were part of the New Deal projects on the island. See Manuel R. Rodríguez, *A New Deal for the Tropics: Puerto Rico during the Depression Era, 1932–1935* (Princeton, NJ: Markus Wiener, 2010).

46. Servicio de Extensión Agrícola. Colegio de Agricultura y Artes Mecánicas de la Universidad de Puerto Rico. *Sirviendo al Agro. Informe de las actividades del Servicio de Extensión Agrícola de la Universidad de Puerto Rico. Diciembre 1, 1937 a noviembre 30,*

1938 (Río Piedras, PR: University of Puerto Rico, 1938), 7–8 (hereafter cited as *Sirviendo 1937–1938*).

47. Ibid., 5.

48. The *Sirviendo al Agro* reports estimate approximately 400,000 people in the rural communities of Puerto Rico were served annually by the Agricultural Extension Service for the years 1936 to 1940.

49. The Smith-Lever Act provided funds for the establishment of agricultural educational services as part of a college or university.

50. Agricultural Experiment Station, College of Agriculture and Mechanic Arts, University of Puerto Rico, *Annual Report of the Agricultural Experiment Station. Fiscal year 1940–41* (Lancaster, PA: Lancaster Press, 1941), 8.

51. There is evidence that Porto Rican Leaf Tobacco Company was involved in formal scientific study as early as 1926. That year, the corporation appropriated $1,000 to the IAES to conduct research in tobacco diseases, provided the land for and furnished a field laboratory, and appointed a dedicated field manager, Dr. G. H. Chapman, to manage the project. The IAES appointed J.A.B. Nolla to collaborate. The details can be found in López Domínguez, *IES 1926–27*, 5, 30. Several years later, the IAES report notes that "Large corporations have cooperated by establishing experimental plots all over the island and have aided us in the soil survey." See *IES 1929–30*, 5.

52. Details are in the Comisión Para Proteger el Tabaco de Puerto Rico, *Informe Anual de la Comisión para Proteger el Tabaco de Puerto Rico (1929–1930)* (San Juan, PR: Negociado de Materiales, Imprenta y Transporte, 1930), 3 (hereafter cited as *Comisión 1929–30*).

53. For a complete list of the thirty-four municipalities, see *Comisión 1929–30*, 13.

54. *Circulares* were commission bulletins that included press releases, report updates, the latest tobacco cultivation news, and price reports. *Circular #3*, for example, argued that the plantings had to be dramatically restricted for 1931 in order to avoid another year of low prices (30–32). *Circular #10* reported that Philip Shorin from the American Leaf Tobacco Co. visited the offices of the commission to inquire about purchasing tobacco (40–41). *Circular #17* announced that the commission would act as a selling agent for any grower who needed help negotiating with buyers. In return, the commission would keep a 1 percent commission to be deposited into the operating fund (50).

55. *Comisión 1929–30*, 16–18.

56. *Circular #8*, 37–38.

57. F. M. Zeno, *Informe sobre la investigación y el estudio practicados por el Jefe Ejecutivo de la Comisión para Proteger el Tabaco de Puerto Rico* (San Juan, PR: Negociado de Materiales, Imprenta y Transporte, 1931), 3.

58. Ibid., 5–6. See also Rojas, *Preliminary Plan*, 5.

59. Zeno, *Comisión*, 4.

60. See Truman Clark, *Puerto Rico and the Unites States, 1917–1933* (Pittsburgh: University of Pittsburgh Press, 1975), 113.

61. J.A.B. Nolla, *First Report of the Tobacco Institute of Puerto Rico. Fiscal Year 1936–37* (San Juan, PR: Bureau of Supplies, Printing, and Transportation, 1937), 7 (hereafter cited as *Tobacco Institute 1936–37*).

62. Carlos Esteva Jr., *Third Annual Report of the Tobacco Institute of Puerto Rico (1938–1939)* (San Juan, PR: Bureau of Supplies, Printing, and Transportation, 1940), 5 (hereafter cited as *Tobacco Institute 1938–39*).

63. Ibid.

64. Nolla, *Tobacco Institute 1936–37*, 36. The Federal Emergency Relief Administration (1933–1935) provided assistance to unemployed workers through the funding of public works projects. Because the University of Puerto Rico and the Tobacco Institute were public institutions on public land, FERA funds could be used to build facilities like laboratories, greenhouses, or other buildings.

65. Esteva, *Tobacco Institute 1938–39*, 12–14.

66. Ibid., 26–27.

67. Ibid., 28.

68. Ibid.

69. Carlos Esteva Jr., *Annual Reports of the Tobacco Institute of Puerto Rico. Fiscal Years 1939–1940 and 1940–1941* (San Juan, PR: Bureau of Supplies, Printing, and Transportation, 1942), 6.

70. Edward V. Pope, "Extension Service Programs Affecting American Families," *Marriage and Family Living* 20, no. 3 (Aug. 1958): 271.

71. A. Rodríguez Géigel, Servicio de Extensión Agrícola. Colegio de Agricultura y Artes Mecánicas de la Universidad de Puerto Rico, *Informe Anual del Servicio de Extensión Agrícola. Diciembre 1, 1939 a noviembre 30, 1940* (Río Piedras, PR: Universidad de Puerto Rico, 1940), 6 (hereafter cited as *Informe 1939–40*).

72. Ibid., 8–9.

73. *Sirviendo 1937–38*, 28.

74. A. Rodríguez Géigel, Servicio de Extensión Agrícola, Colegio de Agricultura y Artes Mecánicas de la Universidad de Puerto Rico, *Informe Anual del Servicio de Extensión Agrícola. Diciembre 1, 1938 a noviembre 30, 1939* (Río Piedras, PR: Universidad de Puerto Rico, 1939), 17 (hereafter cited as *Informe 1938–39*).

75. *Sirviendo 1937–38*, 30–31; and Rodríguez Géigel, *Informe 1938–39*, 18. The 1937 and 1940 reports do not have the statistics for food conservation programs apart from general demonstrations and attendance, although it is clear from the reports that the programs were active and among the housewives' favorite ones.

76. *Sirviendo 1937–38*, 29.

77. Rodríguez Géigel, *Informe 1939–40*, 8–9.

78. *Sirviendo 1937–38*, 33.

79. Rodríguez Géigel, *Informe 1939–40*, 31.

Selected Bibliography

ARCHIVAL COLLECTIONS

Archivo Histórico de Caguas, Caguas, Puerto Rico

Sección: Secretaría; Subsección: Beneficiencia y Salud Pública; Serie: Expedientes y Documentos; Subserie: Huracanes; Años: 1819–1932; Caja #13, Sobre: 1932 B.

Centro de Investigaciones Históricas, University of Puerto Rico,
Río Piedras, Puerto Rico

Colección: Asociación de Agricultores de PR; Serie: Actas de la Junta Directiva; Microficha: 1924–1937.

Oficina de Protocolos Notariales, Caguas, Puerto Rico

Mena Latorre, Andrés, 1912–1960, Tomo 3.

PRIMARY SOURCES

Agricultural Experiment Station, College of Agriculture and Mechanic Arts, University of Puerto Rico. *Annual Report of the Director for the Year 1933–34.* San Juan, PR: Bureau of Supplies, Printing, and Transportation, 1935.

———. *Annual Report of the Agricultural Experiment Station. Fiscal Year 1935–36.* San Juan, PR: Bureau of Supplies, Printing, and Transportation, 1937.

———. *Annual Report of the Agricultural Experiment Station. Fiscal Year 1936–37.* San Juan, PR: Bureau of Supplies, Printing, and Transportation, 1938.

———. *Annual Report of the Agricultural Experiment Station. Fiscal Year 1937–38.* San Juan, PR: Bureau of Supplies, Printing, and Transportation, 1939.

———. *Annual Report of the Agricultural Experiment Station. Fiscal Year 1938–39.* San Juan, PR: Bureau of Supplies, Printing, and Transportation, 1939.

———. *Annual Report of the Agricultural Experiment Station. Fiscal Year 1940–41.* Lancaster, PA: Lancaster Press, 1941.

Board of Commissioners of Agriculture. *Second Report of the Board of Commissioners of Agriculture for the Period from January 1, 1912 to June 30, 1913. Issued June 30, 1913.* San Juan, PR: Bureau of Supplies, Printing, and Transportation, 1913.

———. *Third Report of the Board of Commissioners of Agriculture for the Period from July 1, 1913 to July 1, 1914*. San Juan, PR: Bureau of Supplies, Printing, and Transportation, 1915.

———. *Fourth Report of the Board of Commissioners of Agriculture for the Period from July 1, 1914 to July 1, 1915*. San Juan, PR: Bureau of Supplies, Printing, and Transportation, 1916.

———. *Fifth Report of the Board of Commissioners of Agriculture for the Period from July 1, 1915 to June 30, 1916*. Issued June 30, 1916. San Juan: Bureau of Supplies, Printing, and Transportation, 1917.

Bureau of Insular Affairs. *Report of the Governor of Porto Rico, 1920, pages 503–566 inclusive*. Washington, DC: Government Printing Office, 1920.

Bureau of the Census. *Thirteenth Census of the United States Taken in the Year 1910. Statistics for Porto Rico; Agriculture; and Volume 4, Population 1910, Occupation Statistics*. Washington, DC, 1913.

———. *Fourteenth Census of the United States Taken in the Year 1920*. Volume 3, *Population;* Volume 4, *Occupations;* and Volume 6, Part 3, *Agriculture*. Washington, DC, 1922.

———. *Fifteenth Census of the United States: 1930. Outlying Territories and Possessions*. Washington, DC, 1932.

———. *Sixteenth Census of the United States: 1940*. Bulletin No. 2: *Characteristics of the Population;* Bulletin No. 3: *Occupations and Other Characteristics by Age;* and *Reports for Puerto Rico: Census of Agriculture*. Washington, DC, 1942.

Camuñas, Manuel. Commissioner of Agriculture and Labor. *Report of the Commissioner of Agriculture and Labor of Porto Rico, 1917. From the Report of the Governor of Porto Rico, 1917, pages 545–562 inclusive*. Washington, DC: Government Printing Office, 1917.

———. *Report of the Commissioner of Agriculture and Labor of Porto Rico, 1918. From the Report of the Governor of Porto Rico, 1918, pages 621–649 inclusive*. Washington, DC: Government Printing Office, 1918.

———. *Report of the Commissioner of Agriculture and Labor of Porto Rico, 1919. From the Report of the Governor of Porto Rico, 1919, pages 685–713 inclusive*. Washington, DC: Government Printing Office, 1919.

———. *Report of the Commissioner of Agriculture and Labor of Porto Rico, 1921. From the Report of the Governor of Porto Rico, 1921, pages 448–503 inclusive*. Washington, DC: Government Printing Office, 1921.

Chardón, Carlos. Commissioner of Agriculture and Labor. *Annual Report of the Commissioner of Agriculture and Labor Submitted to the Governor of Porto Rico, 1924–25*. San Juan, PR: Bureau of Supplies, Printing, and Transportation, 1926.

———. *Informe del Comisionado de Agricultura y Trabajo al Honorable Gobernador de Puerto Rico, 1925–1926*. San Juan, PR: Negociado de Materiales, Imprenta y Transporte, 1927.

———. *Informe del Comisionado de Agricultura y Trabajo al Honorable Gobernador de Puerto Rico, 1927*. San Juan, PR: Negociado de Materiales, Imprenta y Transporte, 1928.

———. *Informe del Comisionado de Agricultura y Trabajo al Honorable Gobernador de Puerto Rico, 1928*. San Juan, PR: Negociado de Materiales, Imprenta y Transporte, 1929.

Comisión Para Proteger el Tabaco de Puerto Rico. *Informe Anual de la Comisión para Proteger el Tabaco de Puerto Rico (1929–1930)*. San Juan, PR: Negociado de Materiales, Imprenta y Transporte, 1930.

Division of Agricultural Economics, Agricultural Extension Service. *Annual Report of the Division of Agricultural Economics of the Agricultural Extension Service, 1934–1935*. San Juan, PR: Bureau of Supplies, Printing, and Transportation, 1935.

Esteva, Carlos Jr. *Third Annual Report of the Tobacco Institute of Puerto Rico (1938–1939)*. San Juan, PR: Bureau of Supplies, Printing, and Transportation, 1940.

———. *Annual Reports of the Tobacco Institute of Puerto Rico. Fiscal Years 1939–1940 and 1940–1941*. San Juan, PR: Bureau of Supplies, Printing, and Transportation, 1942.

Gage, Charles E. *The Tobacco Industry in Puerto Rico*. United States Department of Agriculture, Circular No. 519. Washington, DC: Government Printing Office, 1939.

Gandía Córdova, Ramón, Acting Commissioner of Agriculture and Labor. *Report of the Commissioner of Agriculture and Labor of Porto Rico, 1920. From the Report of the Governor of Porto Rico, 1920, pages 503–566 inclusive*. Washington, DC: Government Printing Office, 1920.

Insular Experiment Station of Puerto Rico. *Annual Report of the Insular Experiment Station of Puerto Rico for the Period from July 1, 1916 to July 1, 1917*. San Juan, PR: Bureau of Supplies, Printing, and Transportation, 1917.

Insular Experiment Station of Puerto Rico, Department of Agriculture and Labor of Puerto Rico. *Eighth Annual Report of the Insular Experiment Station of the Department of Agriculture and Labor of Puerto Rico for the Period from July 1, 1917 to June 30, 1918*. San Juan, PR: Bureau of Supplies, Printing, and Transportation, 1919.

———. *Tenth Annual Report of the Insular Experimental Station of the Department of Agriculture and Labor of Puerto Rico. Fiscal Year 1919–20*. San Juan, PR: Bureau of Supplies, Printing, and Transportation, 1920.

———. *Eleventh Annual Report of the Insular Experimental Station of the Department of Agriculture and Labor of Puerto Rico. Fiscal Year 1920–21*. San Juan, PR: Bureau of Supplies, Printing, and Transportation, 1921.

———. *Twelfth Annual Report of the Insular Experimental Station of the Department of Agriculture and Labor of Puerto Rico. Fiscal Year 1921–22*. San Juan, PR: Bureau of Supplies, Printing, and Transportation, 1922.

———. *Thirteenth Annual Report of the Insular Experimental Station of the Department of Agriculture and Labor of Puerto Rico. Fiscal Year 1922–23*. San Juan, PR: Bureau of Supplies, Printing, and Transportation, 1924.

———. *Fourteenth Annual Report of the Insular Experimental Station of the Department of Agriculture and Labor of Puerto Rico. Fiscal Year 1923–24*. San Juan, PR: Bureau of Supplies, Printing, and Transportation, 1924.

———. *Annual Report of the Insular Experimental Station of the Department of Agriculture and Labor of Puerto Rico. Fiscal Year 1929–30*. San Juan, PR: Bureau of Supplies, Printing, and Transportation, 1931.

Junta de Salario Mínimo, División de Investigaciones y Estadísticas, Gobierno de Puerto Rico. *La industria del tabaco en rama*. San Juan, PR: Negociado de Materiales, Imprenta y Transporte, 1942.

López Domínguez, Francisco A. *Seventeenth Annual Report of Director of the Insular Experimental Station of the Department of Agriculture and Labor of Puerto Rico. Fiscal Year 1926–27*. San Juan, PR: Bureau of Supplies, Printing, and Transportation, 1929.

La Marketing: un logro del tabacal. Organización y vida de la Puerto Rico Tobacco Marketing Association. Santurce, PR: Publicaciones Yocauna, 1956.

Menéndez Ramos, Rafael. Comisionado de Agricultura y Comercio. *Informe Anual del Comisionado de Agricultura y Comercio correspondiente al año fiscal 1932–1933.* San Juan, PR: Departamento de Materiales, Imprenta y Transporte, 1933.

———. *Informe Anual del Comisionado de Agricultura y Comercio correspondiente al año fiscal 1933–1934.* San Juan, PR: Negociado de Materiales, Imprenta y Transporte, 1934.

Nolla, J.A.B. *First Report of the Tobacco Institute of Puerto Rico. Fiscal Year 1936–37.* San Juan, PR: Bureau of Supplies, Printing, and Transportation, 1937.

———. *Second Annual Report of the Tobacco Institute of Puerto Rico.* San Juan, PR: Bureau of Supplies, Printing, and Transportation, 1939.

Pérez, Manuel A. *Living Conditions among Small Farmers in Puerto Rico.* Research Bulletin on Agriculture and Livestock, Bulletin No. 2. San Juan, PR: Bureau of Supplies, Printing, and Transportation, 1942.

Perkins, Maurice, Pierre Courbois Perkins, Antonio A. Llorens, Carlos M. Matos, Luis A. Nazario, and Jorge J. Serrallés Jr. *Credit and Related Problems in the Agriculture of Puerto Rico.* Report prepared for the Department of Agriculture, Economic Development Administration, the Government Development Bank for Puerto Rico, the Land Authority for Puerto Rico, the Puerto Rico Industrial Development Co., and the Autoridad de Energía Eléctrica. Dec. 1956.

Rodríguez Géigel, A. Servicio de Extensión Agrícola. Colegio de Agricultura y Artes Mecánicas de la Universidad de Puerto Rico. *Informe Anual del Servicio de Extensión Agrícola. Diciembre 1, 1938 a noviembre 30, 1939.* Río Piedras, PR: Universidad de Puerto Rico, 1939.

———. *Informe Anual del Servicio de Extensión Agrícola. Diciembre 1, 1939 a noviembre 30, 1940.* Río Piedras, PR: Universidad de Puerto Rico, 1940.

———. *Informe Anual del Servicio de Extensión Agrícola. Diciembre 1, 1940 a noviembre 30, 1941.* Río Piedras, PR: Universidad de Puerto Rico, 1941.

Rojas, Antonio. Tobacco Institute of Puerto Rico. *Preliminary Plan to Stabilize the Tobacco Industry Submitted for Consideration to the Planning, Urbanizing, and Zoning Board of Puerto Rico.* San Juan, PR: Bureau of Supplies, Printing, and Transportation, 1944.

Servicio de Extensión Agrícola. Colegio de Agricultura y Artes Mecánicas de la Universidad de Puerto Rico. *Sirviendo al Agro. Informe de las actividades del Servicio de Extensión Agrícola de la Universidad de Puerto Rico. December 1, 1937 to November 30, 1938.* Río Piedras, PR: Universidad de Puerto Rico, 1938.

Tobacco Institute of Puerto Rico. *The Tobacco Industry in Puerto Rico and the Fair Labor Standards Act.* Report of the Subcommittee Appointed by the Governor's Committee to Study General Aspects of the Fair Labor Standards Act. San Juan, PR: Bureau of Supplies, Printing, and Transportation, 1937.

———. *Tobacco Institute Report. Fiscal Years 1941–42, 1942–43.* San Juan, PR: Real Hermanos, Inc. S.J., 1945.

United States Department of Labor. Wage and Hour Division. Research and Statistics Branch. *Puerto Rico: The Leaf Tobacco Industry.* Washington, DC: Government Printing Office, 1941.

War Department. Office of the Director of the Census of Porto Rico. *Report on the Census of Porto Rico, 1899*. Washington, DC: Government Printing Office, 1900.

Zeno, F. M. *Informe sobre la investigación y el estudio practicados por el Jefe Ejecutivo de la Comisión para Proteger el Tabaco de Puerto Rico*. San Juan, PR: Negociado de Materiales, Imprenta y Transporte, 1931.

SECONDARY SOURCES

"300 ranchos de tabaco destruídos." *El agricultor puertorriqueño* 2, no. 4 (July 31, 1926): 5.

"10,000 miembros en la AAPR." *El agricultor puertorriqueño* 9, no. 4 (Feb. 28, 1930): 8.

Abad, José Ramón. *La exposición agrícola e industrial de tabaco realizada en Puerto Rico, diciembre 1883. Memorias de la Junta Directiva*. Ponce, PR: Establecimiento Tipográfico EL VAPOR, 1884.

"Acuerdos de la Junta Directiva de la AA, en relación con la carta de los Sres. Directores del Banco Federal de Baltimore." *El agricultor puertorriqueño* 11, no. 16 (Aug. 31, 1931): 3.

"Al país." *El agricultor puertorriqueño* 12, no. 7 (Apr. 15, 1932): 5, 12.

Álvarez Curbelo, Silvia. "La patria agrícola: la ideología de los agricultores de Puerto Rico, 1924–1928." Master's thesis, University of Puerto Rico, 1986.

"Amicus Plato, Sed Magis Amica Veritas." *El agricultor puertorriqueño* 9, no. 11 (June 15, 1930): cover page.

"Ante el desastre." *El agricultor puertorriqueño* 12, no. 18 (Oct. 15, 1932): cover page.

Arce Rollet, Rafael. "Los contratos de refacción," parts 1 and 2. *El agricultor puertorriqueño* 1, no. 3 (Dec. 26, 1925): 7, and no. 6 (Jan. 16, 1926): 9–10.

Arroyo Zeppenfeldt, Rafael. "Su Majestad el 'Esmayao.'" *El agricultor puertorriqueño* 11, no. 14 (July 31, 1931): 1–2.

"La Asamblea." *El agricultor puertorriqueño* 1, no. 2 (Dec. 19, 1925): 3.

"La Asamblea de Ponce." *El agricultor puertorriqueño* 1, no. 4 (Jan. 2, 1926): 11–12.

"La Asociación de Agricultores aconseja a los cosecheros no forzar las ventas hasta que hayan precio remuneradores." *El agricultor puertorriqueño* 3, no. 8 (Apr. 30, 1927): 24.

"La atención de préstamos de la Junta Federal Agrícola de Estados Unidos se considera posible por los fruteros de Puerto Rico." *El agricultor puertorriqueño* 9, no. 1 (Jan. 15, 1930): 20.

Augelli, John P. "Sugar Cane and Tobacco: A Comparison of Agricultural Types in the Highlands of Eastern Puerto Rico." *Economic Geography* 29, no. 1 (Jan. 1953): 63–73.

"El ausentismo." *El agricultor puertorriqueño* 2, no. 16 (Oct. 23, 1926): 1.

Ayala, César J. *American Sugar Kingdom: The Plantation Economy of the Spanish Caribbean, 1898–1934*. Chapel Hill: University of North Carolina Press, 1999.

Ayala, César J., and Laird W. Bergad. "Rural Puerto Rico in the Early 20th Century Reconsidered: Land and Society, 1899–1915." *Latin American Research Review* 37, no. 2 (2001): 65–97.

Ayala, César J., and Rafael Bernabe. *Puerto Rico in the American Century: A History Since 1898*. Chapel Hill: University of North Carolina Press, 2007.

Baer, Werner. "Puerto Rico: An Evaluation of a Successful Development Program." *Quarterly Journal of Economics* 73, no. 4 (Nov. 1959): 645–671.

Baldrich, Juan José. "From Handcrafted Tobacco Rolls to Machine-Made Cigarettes: The Transformation and Americanization of Puerto Rican Tobacco, 1847–1903." *Centro Journal* 17, no. 002 (Fall 2005): 144–169.

————. *Sembraron la no siembra: Los cosecheros de tabaco puertorriqueños frente a las corporaciones tabacaleras, 1920–1934*. Río Piedras, PR: Ediciones Huracán, 1988.

"El Banco Federal y los agricultores." *El agricultor puertorriqueño* 11, no. 16 (August 31, 1931): cover page.

"Los Bancos Tabacaleros siguen prosperando." *El agricultor puertorriqueño* 2, no. 3 (July 24, 1926): 18.

Baud, Michiel. *Peasants and Tobacco in the Dominican Republic, 1870–1930*. Knoxville: University of Tennessee Press, 1995.

Baud, Michiel, and Kees Kooning. "*A lovoura dos pobres*: Tobacco Farming and the Development of Commercial Agriculture in Bahia, 1870–1930." *Journal of Latin American Studies* 31 (1999): 287–329.

Baver, Sherrie. "Puerto Rico: Colonialism Revisited." *Latin American Research Review* 22, no. 2 (1987): 227–234.

Becerra de Weierich, Isabel. "Las primeras estaciones agronómicas en Puerto Rico." Master's thesis, University of Puerto Rico, 1969.

Bird-Carmona, Arturo. *Parejeros y desafiantes: La comunidad tabaquera de Puerta de Tierra de principio del siglo XX*. San Juan, PR: Ediciones Huracán, 2008.

Black, John D. "The Role of Public Agencies in the Internal Readjustments of the Farm." *Journal of Farm Economics* 7, no. 2 (Apr. 1925): 153–175.

Bunker, F. H. "Many Economic and Field Problems Facing Puerto Rican Leaf Planters." *Tobacco* 107, no. 26 (1938): 8–11.

————. "El tabaco: semilleros, preparación del terreno, abonos y cultivos." *Revista de agricultura de Puerto Rico* 1 (1918): 33.

Cabranes, José A. "Citizenship and the American Empire: Notes on the Legislative History of the United States Citizenship of Puerto Ricans." *University of Pennsylvania Law Review* 127, no. 2 (Dec. 1978): 391–492.

Cadilla de Martinez, María. "El tabaco." *Revista de agricultura de Puerto Rico* 29 (July 1937): 110–113.

Carr, Raymond. *Puerto Rico: A Colonial Experiment*. New York: Vintage Books, 1984.

Carrasquillo, Rosa. *Our Landless Patria: Marginal Citizenship and Race in Caguas, Puerto Rico, 1880–1910*. Lincoln: University of Nebraska Press, 2006.

"Carta de los Directores del Banco Federal al Presidente de la AA." *El agricultor puertorriqueño* 11, no. 16 (Aug. 31, 1931): 2, 31.

Clark, Truman R. *Puerto Rico and the United States, 1917–1933*. Pittsburgh: University of Pittsburgh Press, 1975.

Clark, Victor. *Porto Rico and Its Problems*. Washington, DC: Brookings Institution, 1930.

Coates, Glenn. "Agricultural Profit-Sharing in Puerto Rico." *Land Economics* 24, no. 3 (Aug. 1948): 309–311.

Collo, Martin Joseph. "Puerto Rico and the United States: The Effect of the Relationship on Puerto Rican Agrarian Development." PhD. diss., University of Pennsylvania, 1986.

Colón Torres, Ramón. "Estudio económico de 270 fincas de tabaco en Puerto Rico, 1936–37." *Boletín de la Estación Experimental Agrícola* 50 (1939).

————. "Financing Low-Income Farmers in Puerto Rico." *Journal of Farm Economics* 34, no. 5 (Dec. 1952): 944–948.

"Comentarios a la Ley de Compraventa Agrícola: Reglas de interpretación acordadas por la Junta Agrícola Federal." *El agricultor puertorriqueño* 10, no. 9 (Nov. 15, 1930): 23–26.

"La comisión de la Asociación de Agricultores." *El agricultor puertorriqueño* 2, no. 3 (July 24, 1926): 6–7.

"Una comisión de la Asociación de Agricultores visita al Gobernador Roosevelt." *El agricultor puertorriqueño* 8, no. 7 (Oct. 15, 1929): 11.

"Cómo andan los servicios públicos en Puerto Rico." *El agricultor puertorriqueño* 11, no. 5 (Mar. 15, 1931): n.p.

Cook, Melville T., and José I. Otero. "History of the First Quarter of a Century of the Agricultural Experiment Station at Río Piedras, Puerto Rico." *Boletín de la Estación Experimental Agrícola* 44 (1937).

Cooper, Frederick. *Colonialism in Question: Theory, Knowledge, History*. Berkeley: University of California Press, 2005.

"La cooperativa Insular Tabacalera celebró una importante reunión en Cayey." *El agricultor puertorriqueño* 5, no. 3 (Feb. 15, 1928): 19.

"La corporación de crédito agrícola." *El agricultor puertorriqueño* 12, no. 19 (Oct. 30, 1932): cover page.

Corrales Corrales, José R. "La Cámara de Comercio de Puerto Rico como factor del desarrollo económico nacional, 1913–1933." PhD. diss., University of Puerto Rico, 1997.

"La cosecha de tabaco será grandemente reducida. La caída de los ranchos." *El agricultor puertorriqueño* 2, no. 7 (Aug. 21, 1926): 6.

"Los cosecheros de tabaco." *El agricultor puertorriqueño* 1, no. 7 (Jan. 23, 1926): 7, 18.

"Cotización del Mercado de productos de Puerto Rico en Nueva York." *El agricultor puertorriqueño* 1, no. 1 (Dec. 12, 1925): 17.

"La crisis del tabaco y el gobernador de Puerto Rico." *El agricultor puertorriqueño* 4, no. 6 (Sept. 30, 1927): 12.

Crowley, J. T. "Organization of the Station and Cultivation of Sugar Cane in Porto Rico." *Boletín de la Estación Experimental Agrícola* 1 (1911): 6.

Cruz, Michael González. "The United States' Invasion of Puerto Rico: Occupation and Resistance to the Colonial State, 1898 to the Present." *Latin American Perspectives* 25, no. 5 (Sept. 1998): 7–26.

"Demanda contra la Comisión Protectora del Tabaco declarada sin lugar." *El agricultor puertorriqueño* 14, no. 6 (June 1934): 15.

Descartes, Sol L. "Land Reform in Puerto Rico." *Journal of Land and Public Utility* 19, no. 4 (Nov. 1943): 397–417.

———. *Puerto Rico: trasfondo de su economía, fondo físico, histórico e institucional.* Hato Rey, PR: Inter-American University Press, 1973.

Díaz de Acín, Nilsa. "La participación de la Estación Experimental de Agricultura de la Universidad de Puerto Rico en el desarrollo agrícola de Puerto Rico." Master's thesis, University of Puerto Rico, 1967.

Dietz, James L. *Economic History of Puerto Rico: Institutional Change and Capitalist Development.* Princeton, NJ: Princeton University Press, 1986.

———. "The Puerto Rican Political Economy." *Latin American Perspectives* 3, no. 3 (Summer 1976): 3–16.

————. "Puerto Rico's New History." *Latin American Research Review* 19, no. 1 (1984): 210–222.

Diffie, Bailey W., and Justine Whitfield Diffie. *Porto Rico: A Broken Pledge*. New York: Vanguard Press, 1931.

"La dirección de la Agencia de Garantía del Tabaco de Puerto Rico en Nueva York." *El agricultor puertorriqueño* 3, no. 3 (Feb. 15, 1927): 18–19.

Duffy Burnett, Christina. "United States: American Expansion and Territorial Deannexation." *University of Chicago Law Review* 72, no. 3 (Summer 2005): 797–879.

Duffy Burnett, Christina, and Burke Marshall, eds. *Foreign in a Domestic Sense: Puerto Rico, American Expansion, and the Constitution*. Durham, NC: Duke University Press, 2001.

"Editorial." *El agricultor puertorriqueño* 1, no. 3 (Dec. 26, 1925): 1.

"Editorial." *El agricultor puertorriqueño* 2, no. 24 (Dec. 25, 1926): 2.

Enamorado Cuesta, José. *Porto Rico, Past and Present: The Island after Thirty Years of American Rule*. 1929. Reprint, New York: Arno Press, 1975.

"Los engaños en el abono para tabaco." *El agricultor puertorriqueño* 10, no. 8 (Oct. 31, 1930): 16.

"Estimados preliminares de las pérdidas sufridas por motivo del temporal." *El agricultor puertorriqueño* 6, no. 6 (Sept. 30, 1928): 13–15.

"Farm Security Administration. La Administración de Protección Agrícola hace los primeros préstamos en Puerto Rico: arrendatarios y medianeros serán dueños de fincas." *El heraldo de extensión* 1, no. 1 (Jan. 1939): 1.

Fernández, Agustín. "El cultivo de tabaco en Puerto Rico." *El agricultor puertorriqueño* 11, no. 15 (Aug. 15, 1931): 12, 21–22.

Fernández, Ronald. *The Disenchanted Island: Puerto Rico and the United States in the 20th Century*. 2nd ed. Westport, CT: Praeger Publishers, 1996.

"Fomentemos las Cooperativas." *El agricultor puertorriqueño* 4, no. 5 (Sept. 15, 1927): 1.

Gandía Córdova, Ramón. "Comentarios a la Ley Federal de Préstamos Agrícolas," parts 1–5. *El agricultor puertorriqueño* 5, no. 9 (May 15, 1928): 19–20; no. 10 (May 31, 1928): 24–25; no. 11 (June 15, 1928): 23–24; 6, no. 4 (Aug. 31, 1928): 15–17; no. 10 (Nov. 30, 1928): 20–21.

Garver, F. B., and Harry Trelogan. "The Agricultural Adjustment Act and the Reports of the Brookings Institution." *Quarterly Journal of Economics* 50, no. 4 (Aug. 1936): 594–621.

"Gestiones que a solicitud de la AA llevará a cabo en Washington el Gobernador Roosevelt y el Comisionado Residente." *El agricultor puertorriqueño* 10, no. 10 (Nov. 30, 1930): 9, 11.

Ginzberg, Lori D. "Global Goals, Local Acts: Grass-Roots Activism in Imperial Narratives." *Journal of American History* 88, no. 3 (Dec. 2001): 870–873.

Go, Julian. "Chains of Empire, Projects of State: Political Education and U.S. Colonial Rule in Puerto Rico and the Philippines." *Comparative Studies in Society and History* 42, no. 2 (Apr. 2000): 333–362.

————. *Patterns of Empire: The British and American Empires, 1868 to the Present*. Kindle ed. New York: Cambridge University Press, 2011.

"El Gobernador veda el proyecto del tabaco: Un nuevo aspecto de la acción destructora del Gobernador." *El agricultor puertorriqueño* 7, no. 9 (May 15, 1929): 26.

González Cruz, Michael. "The U.S. Invasion of Puerto Rico: Occupation and Resistance to the Colonial State, 1898 to the Present." *Latin American Perspectives* 25, no. 5 (Sept. 1998): 7–26.

González Iglesias, Pedro. "Una de las causas de nuestra pobreza." *El agricultor puertorriqueño* 10, no. 4 (Aug. 31, 1930): 20.

González Quiñones, M. "Pasando balance, parte II." *El agricultor puertorriqueño* 11, no. 24 (Dec. 31, 1931): 1–2.

———. "Las ventajas del Banco Federal de Crédito Intermedio," parts 1 and 2. *El agricultor puertorriqueño* 1, no. 15 (Mar. 20, 1926): 10; and no. 18 (Apr. 10, 1926): 10.

Gruber, Ruth. *Puerto Rico: Island of Promise.* New York: Hill and Wang, 1960.

Guerra, Lillian. *Popular Expression and National Identity in Puerto Rico: The Struggle for Self-Community and Nation.* Gainesville: University Press of Florida, 1998.

Hanson, Earl Parker. *Transformation: The Story of Modern Puerto Rico.* New York: Simon and Schuster, 1955.

Hart, John Fraser, and Eugene Cotton Mather. "The Character of Tobacco Barns and Their Role in the Tobacco Economy of the United States." *Annals of the Association of American Geographers* 51, no. 3 (Sept. 1961): 274–293.

Henderson, G. C. "The Agricultural Credits Act of 1923." *Quarterly Journal of Economics* 37, no. 3 (May 1923): 518–522.

Hernández, Juan David. "El tabaco de Caguas." Photocopy, Archivo Histórico de Caguas, Caguas, PR.

Hill, E. B., and Sol L. Descartes. "An Economic Background for Agricultural Research in Puerto Rico." *Bulletin of the Agricultural Experiment Station* 51 (1939).

Hodgson, Geoffrey. *The Myth of American Exceptionalism.* New Haven, CT: Yale University Press, 2010.

Huyke, Roberto, and R. Colón Torres. "Costo de producción de tabaco en Puerto Rico, 1937–38." *Boletín de la Estación Experimental Agrícola* 56 (1940).

"Importante asamblea de tabacaleros: Se ha acordado restringir las siembras para la próxima cosecha." *El agricultor puertorriqueño* 4, no. 3 (Aug. 15, 1927): 4–5.

"La importante legislación que está propulsando la Asociación de Agricultores." *El agricultor puertorriqueño* 9, no. 7 (Apr. 15, 1930): 9–10.

"Importante mensaje de D. Modesto Cobián Rivera, Presidente de 'Tabacaleros de Comerío Inc.,' a la reunión de Cooperativas Tabacaleras." *El agricultor puertor-riqueño* 1, no. 11 (Feb. 20, 1926): n.p.

"Importante reunión de cooperativas tabacaleras. Existe absoluta unión entre todas." *El agricultor puertorriqueño* 1, no. 11 (Feb. 20, 1926): 9

"Importante reunión de Tabacaleros de Manatí." *El agricultor puertorriqueño* 3, no. 11 (June 15, 1927): 30.

"Interesante correspondencia cruzada entre el Juez Williams y el Comisionado Residente." *El agricultor puertorriqueño* 9, no. 5 (Mar. 15, 1930): 15.

Johnson, Dale. "Class Formation and Struggle in Latin America." *Latin American Perspectives* 10, nos. 2 and 3 (Spring–Summer 1983): 2–18.

Lee, V. P. "The Intermediate Credit Banks." *Journal of Farm Economics* 7, no. 4 (Oct. 1925): 425–434.

Lewis, Gordon K. *Puerto Rico: Freedom and Power in the Caribbean.* New York: Monthly Review Press, 1963.

Lizardi Flores, Ignacio. "Problemas rurales," parts 1–4. *El agricultor puertorriqueño* 11, no. 19 (Oct. 15, 1931): 16–17; no. 21 (Nov. 15, 1931): 8, 22; no. 22 (Nov. 30, 1931): 3, 19; and no. 24 (Dec. 31, 1931): 14.

"Lo que significa el crédito intermedio para Puerto Rico." *El agricultor puertorriqueño* 1, no. 13 (Mar. 6, 1926): 9.

López, Adalberto, ed. *The Puerto Ricans: Their History, Culture, and Society*. Rochester, VT: Schenkman Books, 1980.

Lounsbury, John. "Farmsteads in Puerto Rico and Their Interpretative Value." *Geographical Review* 45, no. 3 (July 1955): 337–358.

"La Magna Asamblea de Tabacaleros celebrada en San Juan." *El agricultor puertorriqueño* 8, no. 3 (Aug. 15, 1929): 18–20.

Maldonado-Denis, Manuel. "The Puerto Ricans: Protest or Submission." *Annals of the American Academy of Political and Social Science* 382 (Mar. 1969): 26–31.

———. *Puerto Rico: Mito y realidad*. Madrid: Ediciones Península, 1969.

Manzano, M. A. "Apuntes sobre la química de los tabacos claros para cigarillos." *Revista de agricultura, industria y comercio de Puerto Rico* 31 (1939): 209–211.

Marín Román, Héctor R. *El Caldero Quema'o: contexto social-militar en Puerto Rico y otros lugares del Caribe durante el período entre guerras, 1919–1938*. Río Piedras, PR: Ediciones Gaviota, 2012.

Martínez-Vergne, Teresita. *Capitalism in Colonial Puerto Rico: Central San Vicente in the Late Nineteenth Century*. Gainesville: University Press of Florida, 1992.

Matos Rodríguez, Félix V. "New Currents in Puerto Rican History: Legacy, Continuity, and Challenges of the 'Nueva Historia.'" *Latin American Research Review* 32, no. 3 (1997): 193–208.

Matos Rodríguez, Félix V., and Linda C. Delgado, eds. *Puerto Rican Women's History: New Perspectives*. Armonk, NY: M. E. Sharpe, 1998.

McCook, Stuart. "Promoting the 'Practical': Science and Agricultural Modernization in Puerto Rico and Colombia, 1920–1940." *Agricultural History* 75, no. 1 (2001): 52–82.

Meléndez Muñoz, M. "La habitación campesina en sus relaciones con la higiene y la moral. Alimentación del campesino." *El agricultor puertorriqueño* 1, no. 11 (Feb. 20, 1926): 7.

———. "El presente y el porvenir del tabaco en Puerto Rico," parts 1 and 2. *El agricultor puertorriqueño* 1, no. 8 (Jan. 30, 1926): 15–17, and no. 9 (Feb. 6, 1926): 7–9.

———. "La situación tabacalera en la Isla: Opiniones y comentos." *El agricultor puertorriqueño* 8, no. 8 (Oct. 31, 1929): 7–9.

"Memorial presentado por la directiva de la Asociación de Agricultores a la Legislatura de Puerto Rico, y en su nombre a los presidentes de ambas cámaras Hon. Antonio R. Barceló y Hon. José Tous Soto." *El agricultor puertorriqueño* 3, no. 1 (Jan. 15, 1927): 11.

"Mensaje del Presidente de la AAPR a la Asamblea General Ordinaria del día 11 de julio de 1926." *El agricultor puertorriqueño* 2, no. 2 (July 17, 1926): 4.

"Modo de hacer la tasación de las fincas agrícolas." *El agricultor puertorriqueño* 1, no. 2 (Dec. 19, 1925): 7.

Murray, William G. "Farm Mortgages and the Government." *Journal of Farm Economics* 17, no. 4 (Nov. 1935): 613–624.

"Naranjito organiza su Banco Tabacalero." *El agricultor puertorriqueño* 1, no. 28 (June 19, 1926): 10.

Nodín Valdés, Dionicio. *Organized Agriculture and the Labor Movement before the UFW: Puerto Rico, Hawai'i, California.* Austin: University of Texas Press, 2011.

"Notas editoriales: La hora de los débiles." *El agricultor puertorriqueño* 11, no. 19 (Oct. 15, 1931): 1.

"Notas sobre la visita de los Directores del Banco Federal de Baltimore." *El agricultor puertorriqueño* 11, no. 17 (Sept. 15, 1931): 3–4, 29–30.

"Notas tabacaleras." *El agricultor puertorriqueño* 7, no. 7 (Apr. 15, 1929): 7.

"Notas varias." *El agricultor puertorriqueño* 11, no. 17 (Sept. 15, 1931): 10, 27.

"Nuestra asociación en la isla." *El agricultor puertorriqueño* 2, no. 7 (Aug. 21, 1926): 3.

"Nuestra comisión en Washington." *El agricultor puertorriqueño* 1, no. 22 (May 8, 1926): 5.

"Nuestros propósitos." *El agricultor puertorriqueño* 1, no. 1 (Dec. 12, 1925): 1

"El obrero y la huelga contra la siembra de tabaco." *El agricultor puertorriqueño* 11, no. 18 (Sept. 30, 1931): 1–2.

Oppenheimer, Monroe. "The Development of the Rural Rehabilitation Loan Program." *Law and Contemporary Problems* 4, no. 4 (Oct. 1937): 473–488.

"Organización de la Administración de Créditos Agrícolas." *El agricultor puertorriqueño* 14, no. 1 (Jan. 1934): 4.

"Organizaciones agrícolas." *El agricultor puertorriqueño* 1, no. 25 (May 29, 1926): 4.

Ortiz, Fernando. *Cuban Counterpoint: Tobacco and Sugar.* New York: Alfred A. Knopf, 1947.

Osborne, Lea E. "Bridging the Divide: The Alliances of the Liga Social Sufragista in the Struggle to Enfranchise Puerto Rican Women." Master's thesis, Sarah Lawrence College, 2004.

Pantojas-García, Emilio. "The Puerto Rican Paradox: Colonialism Revisited." *Latin American Research Review* 40, no. 3 (2005): 163–176.

Pedreira, Antonio S. *Insularismo: Ensayos de interpretación puertorriqueña.* 1957 ed. San Juan, PR: Biblioteca de Autores Puertorriqueños.

"Pérdidas." *El agricultor puertorriqueño* 2, no. 5 (Aug. 7, 1926): 3, 7, 17.

Perloff, Harvey S. *Puerto Rico's Economic Future.* Chicago: University of Chicago Press, 1950.

"Perspectiva agrícola para el 1931." *El agricultor puertorriqueño* 11, no. 6 (Mar. 31, 1931): 23.

"Perspectiva del mercado tabacalero." *El agricultor puertorriqueño* 3, no. 3 (Feb. 15, 1927): 1–6.

"La perspectiva tabacalera." *El agricultor puertorriqueño* 7, no. 4 (Feb. 28, 1929): 8.

Pesquera, José L. "Cumplirán su deber." *El agricultor puertorriqueño* 11, no. 19 (Oct. 15, 1931): 9, 19.

———. "Rectificaciones que honran." *El agricultor puertorriqueño* 11, no. 20 (Oct. 31, 1931): 4.

"Pesquera y la política nacional." *El agricultor puertorriqueño* 12, no. 20 (Nov. 15, 1932): 1.

Petrullo, Vincenzo. *Puerto Rican Paradox.* Philadelphia: University of Pennsylvania Press, 1947.

Picó, Rafael. "Land Tenure in the Leading Types of Farming of Puerto Rico." *Economic Geography* 15, no. 2 (Apr. 1939): 135–145.

"Plan completo para hacer la tasación de fincas rústicas." *El agricultor puertorriqueño* 1, no. 7 (Jan. 23, 1926): 10–14.

Pope, Edward V. "Extension Service Programs Affecting American Families." *Marriage and Family Living* 20, no. 3 (Aug. 1958): 270–277.

Pope, Jesse E. "Agricultural Credit in the United States." *Quarterly Journal of Economics* 28, no. 4 (Aug. 1914): 701–746.

"Pormenores de la primera reunión para constituir la Cooperativa Insular de Tabacaleros." *El agricultor puertorriqueño* 5, no. 2 (Jan. 31, 1928): 25–31.

"Por qué no debe cogerse el segundo cosecho del tabaco." *El agricultor puertorriqueño* 3, no. 2 (Jan. 31, 1927): 38.

"Los préstamos agrícolas hechos en Puerto Rico." *El agricultor puertorriqueño* 7, no. 8 (Apr. 30, 1929): 16.

"Préstamos para pequeños agricultores (Nota Oficial)." *El agricultor puertorriqueño* 19, no. 8 (Aug. 1939): 12.

"Prestigiando al país." *El agricultor puertorriqueño* 3, no. 7 (Apr. 15, 1927): 21.

Preston, Howard H., and Victor W. Bennett. "Agricultural Credit Legislation of 1933." *Journal of Political Economy* 42, no. 1 (Feb. 1934): 6–33.

"Los primeros cálculos de las pérdidas." *El agricultor puertorriqueño* 6, no. 5 (Sept. 15, 1928): 4, 19.

"La producción agrícola de la Isla en el año fiscal último." *El agricultor puertorriqueño* 7, no. 9 (May 15, 1929): 28.

"El programa legislativo de la Asociación de Agricultores." *El agricultor puertorriqueño* 6, no. 12 (Dec. 31, 1928): 12–15.

Putnam, George E. "The Federal Farm Loan System." *American Economic Review* 9, no. 1 (Mar. 1919): 57–78.

Ratchford, B. U. "Federal Agricultural Policy in Relation to Tobacco." *Journal of Politics* 11, no. 4 (Nov. 1949): 655–677.

"Reglas que deben seguir los agricultores que han de gestionar Préstamos Federales autorizados por la Comisión Rehabilitadora." *El agricultor puertorriqueño* 7, no. 8 (Apr. 30, 1929): 20–22.

"Resoluciones aprobadas por la Asamblea." *El agricultor puertorriqueño* 5, no. 7 (Apr. 15, 1928): 26–27.

"Resoluciones aprobadas por la Asamblea de Agricultores." *El agricultor puertorriqueño* 9, no. 1 (Jan. 15, 1930): 31, 36.

"Resoluciones aprobadas por la Asamblea General de Agricultores, celebrada el día 28 de diciembre de 1930 en la ciudad de Ponce, Puerto Rico." *El agricultor puertorriqueño* 11, no. 1 (Jan. 15, 1931): 15–21.

"Resoluciones aprobadas por la Asamblea General de Agricultores de Ponce." *El agricultor puertorriqueño* 6, no. 2 (July 31, 1928): 29.

"Resoluciones de la Asamblea General de la Asociación de Agricultores." *El agricultor puertorriqueño* 4, no. 2 (July 31, 1927): 26–32.

"¿Resuelve la limitación de la cosecha el problema tabacalero?" *El agricultor puertorriqueño* 9, no. 10 (May 31, 1930): 1.

"Resumen de los acuerdos tomados por la Asamblea General de la AAPR en el Teatro Broadway de Ponce, el día 20 de diciembre de 1925." *El agricultor puertorriqueño* 1, no. 4 (Jan. 2, 1926): 11.

Rivera-Giusti, Ivette M. "Gender, Labor, and Working-Class Activities in the Puerto Rican Tobacco Industry, 1898–1924." PhD. diss., State University of New York at Binghamton, 2004.

Rivera Ramos, Efrén. *American Colonialism in Puerto Rico: The Judicial and Social Legacy*. Princeton, NJ: Markus Weiner Publishers, 2007.

Rodríguez, Manuel R. *A New Deal for the Tropics: Puerto Rico during the Depression Era, 1932–1935*. Princeton, NJ: Markus Wiener, 2010.

Rosenn, Keith S. "Puerto Rican Land Reform: The History of an Instructive Experiment." *Yale Law Journal* 73, no. 2 (Dec. 1963): 334–356.

Ross, David F. *The Long Uphill Path: A Historical Study of Puerto Rico's Program of Economic Development*. San Juan, PR: Editorial Edil, 1969.

Sanabria, Carlos. "The Puerto Rican Organized Workers' Movement and the American Federation of Labor, 1901 to 1934." PhD. diss., City University of New York, 2000.

Sánchez Tarniella, Andrés. *La economía de Puerto Rico: Etapas en su desarrollo*. Madrid: Afrodisio Aguado, S.A., 1971.

San Miguel, Pedro. *Los campesinos del Cibao: Economía del mercado y transformación agraria en la República Dominicana, 1880–1960*. San Juan, PR: Editorial de la Universidad de Puerto Rico, 1997.

"Sección agrícola." *El agricultor puertorriqueño* 2, no. 17 (Oct. 30, 1926): 12.

"Sección del Secretario." *El agricultor puertorriqueño* 11, no. 17 (Sept. 15, 1931): 2.

"Sección editorial: El crédito." *El agricultor puertorriqueño* 2, no. 8 (Aug. 28, 1926): 1.

"Sección editorial: La valoración de nuestra propiedad." *El agricultor puertorriqueño* 1, no. 21 (May 1, 1926): 1.

"Se organiza el Banco Tabacalero de Utuado." *El agricultor puertorriqueño* 3, no. 5 (Mar. 15, 1927): 17.

"Se reducen las siembras de tabaco." *El agricultor puertorriqueño* 4, no. 7 (Oct. 15, 1927): cover page.

Serrallés, Jorge Jr., Ramón Colón Torres, and Frank J. Juliá. "Analysis of the Organization and Factors Influencing the Returns on 194 Small Tobacco Farms in Puerto Rico, 1935–1936." *Bulletin of the Agricultural Experiment Station* 46 (Mar. 1938).

Serrallés, Jorge Jr., and Martín Vélez Jr. "Precio del Tabaco en Rama al Agricultor en Puerto Rico del 1907 al 1940." *Boletín de la Estación Experimental Agrícola* 60 (June 1941).

Silén, Juan Ángel. *We, the Puerto Rican People: A Story of Oppression and Resistance*. Trans. Cedric Belfrage. New York: Monthly Review Press, 1971.

Soto-Crespo, Ramón E. *Mainland Passage: The Cultural Anomaly of Puerto Rico*. Minneapolis: University of Minnesota Press, 2009.

Sparrow, Bartholomew. *The Insular Cases and the Emergence of American Empire*. Lawrence: University Press of Kansas, 2006.

"Speech of Charles Curtis accepting the Nomination for the Vice Presidency" given in Topeka, Kansas, on Aug. 18, 1928. http://www.vpcharlescurtis.net/ksstudies/speech.htm.

Steward, Julian H., Robert A. Manners, Eric R. Wolf, Elena Padilla Seda, Sidney W. Mintz, and Raymond L. Scheele. *The People of Puerto Rico: A Study in Social Anthropology*. Urbana: University of Illinois Press, 1956.

Stubbes, J. D. "La selección de la semilla del tabaco en Puerto Rico." *El agricultor puertorriqueño* 1, no. 6 (Jan. 16, 1926): 13.

Stubbs, Jean. *Tobacco on the Periphery: A Case Study in Cuban Labor History, 1860–1958*. New York: Cambridge University Press, 1985.

Suárez Findlay, Eileen J. *Imposing Decency: The Politics of Sexuality and Race in Puerto Rico, 1870–1920*. Durham, NC: Duke University Press, 2000.

"Tabacaleros de Aibonito, Inc." *El agricultor puertorriqueño* 1, no. 30 (July 3, 1926): 6.

"Tabacaleros de Aibonito, Inc. construyen su almacén." *El agricultor puertorriqueño* 2, no. 6 (Aug. 14, 1926): 9.

"Tabacaleros de Cayey, Inc." *El agricultor puertorriqueño* 2, no. 1 (July 10, 1926): 9.

"Tabacaleros de Cayey, Inc. progresa." *El agricultor puertorriqueño* 2, no. 6 (Aug. 14, 1926): 9.

"Tabaco." *El agricultor puertorriqueño* 1, no. 7 (Jan. 23, 1926): 16.

"Tabaco." *El agricultor puertorriqueño* 2, no. 22 (Dec. 11, 1926): 13.

"El tabaco en Santo Domingo." *El agricultor puertorriqueño* 2, no. 12 (Sept. 25, 1926): 16.

"Tabaco: Se discute la necesidad de reducir las siembras." *El agricultor puertorriqueño* 3, no. 13 (July 15, 1927): 10.

"Texto del discurso leído por el Sr. E. Landrón ante la Asamblea de Agricultores que se llevó a efectos en la Estación Experimental de Río Piedras." *El agricultor puertorriqueño* 11, no. 3 (Feb. 15, 1931): 4–7, 35.

"Texto íntegro de la ley que crea la Junta Federal y Agrícola y cuyos beneficios se han extendido a Puerto Rico," parts 1 and 2. *El agricultor puertorriqueño* 10, no. 7 (Oct. 15, 1930): 26; no. 8 (Oct. 31, 1930): 25–27.

"Texto íntegro del Proyecto de Ley aprobado por la Legislatura sobre el tabaco." *El agricultor puertorriqueño* 5, no. 8 (Apr. 30, 1928): 30–34.

Torgerson, Harold W. "Agricultural Finance in the United States." *Journal of Land and Public Utility Economics* 16, no. 2 (May 1940): 196–206.

Torres Grillo, Herminio. *Historia de la Ciudad de Caguas*. Barcelona, Spain: Ediciones Rumbos, 1965.

Torres Monge, Sandalio. "Las corporaciones y las tierras." *El agricultor puertorriqueño* 8, no. 9 (Nov. 15, 1929): 29–30.

Trías Monge, José. *Puerto Rico: The Trials of the Oldest Colony in the World*. New Haven, CT: Yale University Press, 1997.

Tulchin, Joseph S. "El crédito agrario en Argentina, 1910–1926." Trans. Sibila Seibert. *Desarrollo Económico* 18, no. 71 (Oct. 1978): 381–408.

"La unión hace la fuerza." *El agricultor puertorriqueño* 1, no. 30 (July 3, 1926): 6.

"Las ventajas del Banco Federal de Crédito Intermedio." *El agricultor puertorriqueño* 1, no. 15 (Mar. 20, 1926): 10.

"Visita con Mr. E. B. Thomas, Director del Federal Land Bank." *El agricultor puertorriqueño* 1, no. 6 (Jan. 16, 1926): 10.

Index

Page numbers in *italics* refer to tables and figures.

About the Author

Teresita A. Levy (Ph.D., History, The Graduate Center, CUNY, 2007) was born in Puerto Rico and has lived in New York since 1996. She is an assistant professor in the Department of Latin American, Latino, and Puerto Rican Studies at Lehman College of the City University of New York and the associate director of the Center for Latin American, Caribbean, and Latino Studies at the Graduate Center of the City University of New York.

CPSIA information can be obtained
at www.ICGtesting.com
Printed in the USA
LVHW03s0747210818
587556LV00001B/3/P